PEARL S. BUCK'S ORIENTAL COOKBOOK

Illustrations by
JEANYEE WONG

SIMON AND SCHUSTER
NEW YORK

First printing

SBN 671–21366–0
Library of Congress Catalog Card Number: 72-83913
Designed by Eve Metz
Manufactured in the United States of America
Printed by The Murray Printing Co., Forge Village, Mass.
Bound by The Book Press, Brattleboro, Vt.

PRODUCED BY LYLE KENYON ENGEL

Grateful acknowledgment is made to the following
for their help in preparing the manuscript: Marla Ray,
Ella Elvin, Valerie Moolman, May Wong Trent,
Gertrude Engel, George Engel

CONTENTS

PEARL S. BUCK'S ORIENTAL COOKBOOK

NOTE

Because of customs and styles of eating and since the quantities consumed by the individual vary so much from country to country, we have prepared most of the recipes in this book to serve two to four people if only one course is served and from six to eight when four or five courses are served.

INTRODUCTION

Let me say at once that many hands contributed to this book of Asian cookery. It is not a compendium of Asian recipes nor was it designed to be. My idea was rather to give samples of the infinite variety of Asian foods, these samples first to be representative of what Asians themselves like to eat, and second, recipes that can be prepared easily in American kitchens. I am grateful to all those persons who helped to make this book what I wanted it to be.

Next let me say bluntly that I consider Asian cookery the best in the world. This means only that I enjoy Asian dishes more than I do those of the West and this was true even during my childhood in China, when I preferred to share the meals our Chinese servants prepared for themselves in their own quarters rather than to eat at our own family table, where we ate American food. My mother habitually worried over my small appetite but I never enlightened her, naughty child I, that I was already well fed. If she suspected it she never said so and the loyal servants, always on the side of the child, never betrayed me.

It would, of course, be impossible to put between the covers of one book a complete collection of recipes for Asian dishes. Asian countries differ very much from one another—more, in fact, than do the countries of the Western world. Nothing could be more different, for example, than China and Japan, geographically and demographically, or in their cuisines. Moreover there are differences within the countries themselves. Food and cookery in South China are different indeed from those of the North, rice being the staple in the South and wheat in the North. North and South share a common virtue, however, which is that the food is delicious, whether it is food for a feast or food at a wayside inn. I have many times eaten a meal at the best restaurants of Peking but I have even more often eaten breakfast or lunch or dinner at a small inn somewhere beside a cobbled country road. The dishes were different indeed but the twisted feather—the light cruller of the North—was as toothsome as the famous Peking duck. The Asian peoples have a long history, many thousands of years, and perhaps it takes that long to develop the finest taste in cookery.

9

Taste differs, of course, in Asian and Western cuisine. If one must speak generally, it is obvious even from this highly selective book of recipes that Asians like their dishes much more highly spiced than we do. When a people likes pepper-hot dishes, as, for example, in Mexico, it is because of Asian origins, however early. It is perhaps natural that Asians should use more spices than we of the West do, for spices are grown in Asia. Moreover it seems true that people in hot climates enjoy highly spiced food, perhaps to tempt their appetites. In the cool climate of North China, for example, and in the sea-cooled islands of Japan, food is more blandly prepared than in South China or in more southerly island countries or in India. But reducing or increasing the hot elements in recipes does not change their essential flavor.

At this point I pause to reflect upon the eating habits of the people who have produced the foods described in this book. Japanese dishes, for example, reflect faithfully the nature of the Japanese people. Artistic to the point of spareness, their recipes produce the effect of the people who created them. Japanese dishes consider texture as well as taste. Taste is emphasized in the singular. It is pure and undiluted and not changed by much seasoning. The simplicity of soy sauce, the auxiliary of decorations and arrangement for the eye rather than for the enrich- ment of blending or contrasting flavors follow the Japanese emphasis upon the same elements in art, house decoration and architecture— simplicity, purity and exquisite arrangement.

Chinese dishes, on the other hand, exhibit the fullness, the richness, the variety of Chinese culture. A great continental people, individualistic and complete, their cookery reflects all of these traits. Each locality, each province, has its own specialities. The gustatory traveler goes to Szech- uan or Hunan provinces for red-pepper dishes. For the finest hams my own area in the province of Kiangsu must be visited. For mutton dishes one seeks a Muslim inn. Duck is a specialty in Peking, to which one must devote an entire evening many hours long, for the duck is brought in freshly killed and plucked and exhibited to host and guests. If approved, it is then submitted to a hot-coal fire and the skin is roasted to crispness. This is the first dish. The skin is cut into small pieces and served with thin pancakes and haw jam. The skillful gourmand must, with his chopsticks, roll the skin and jam into the pancake. The result is delicious and worth the effort. A succession of dishes then appears from the rest of the duck, ending with the head cracked open so that the most honored guest can be offered the final tidbit, which is the brains.

Ceremony has its part in every important Asian meal. Each dish is discussed, criticized and praised. The chef is called in and receives either praise or blame and perhaps some of both. To this neither host nor chef can object, for a perfectly cooked dish is a work of art, and an artist desires no consideration of his feelings. His only concern is the perfection of his art.

Contrast is an important element in Asian cookery—contrast in color, texture and flavor. The red-hot dishes of India, for example, are alleviated by the bland white coolness of milk curds. Japanese dishes are decorated with flowerlike arrangements of herbs, small radishes, slices of cucumber and so forth. One must always pause to admire before one eats. Only in family cooking is a dish served in plain bowls. Rice, of course, is the Asian mainstay and staple. Even at the end of a Peking duck dinner a substantial course of rice and four vegetable-and-meat dishes is served. Sometimes millet is substituted for rice, and in that case it is a gruel that may be supped from the bowl.

Desserts are not important in the Asian menu. However, the North Chinese enjoy one called "Eight Precious Pudding." It is made of glutinous rice with eight sweet dried fruits in it, and it is served in the middle of the meal. Indians serve an almond cream mixture, well sweetened. But for the most part fruit is the dessert, sections of peeled tangerine, for example, each with a toothpick for easy handling, or slices of crisp sweet pear similarly treated, or perhaps melon in season. Sweets are normally, however, considered between-meal enjoyments.

But it would take many books to describe Asian cookery. Asians enjoy eating. Asians value food not only as a necessity but as a pleasure and as a means of communication as well as an artistic occupation. With this brief introduction, let us proceed to the matter in hand, which is to share with Asia her finest food.

INDONESIA

If there was ever a land that could truly be called an island paradise, Indonesia must surely be that place. It is not just one island; it is three thousand islands, lying languorously along the equator between Asia and Australia south of the Philippines. It is musical, exotic Bali; it is sultry, exciting Java; it is Sumatra, Borneo, Sulawesi (Celebes) and West Iran, the western half of still near-savage New Guinea. It is all these and very much more, adding up to the world's largest archipelago and one of its most heterogeneous nations. Many races are represented in this scattered land; there are Bataks and Sasaks, Javanese and Balinese, Dayaks and Papuans and more. Indonesians are essentially a Malayo-Polynesian people; but in addition to the many native strains, other influences are felt . . . Chinese, Dutch, Indian, some Portuguese . . . so that there is in Indonesia a fascinatingly spicy mixture of peoples and cultures and a cuisine that is just as complex and fascinatingly spicy.

In fact, Indonesian food is very spicy indeed. But, rather than being merely hot, the Indonesian cuisine is varied and sophisticated, running the gamut from very simple native foods to subtly complicated Javanese-European dishes and from the mildly spicy to the ferociously hot. (Some of the recipes in the following pages have been slightly tamed for the benefit of those unused to hot foods.) The islands are fabulously rich in natural resources, including agricultural products, and no resource is wasted. Bananas and coconuts grow in profusion; so do soybeans and peanuts, coffee, rice and cassava, tea and sugar, pepper and spices and herbs of all kinds. The lush green land is also lavishly supplied with succulent vege-

13

tables and fresh fruits—mangoes, mangosteens, papayas, pineapples and oranges—and meats of every kind.

In spite of its availability, milk—cow's milk—is rarely used in Indonesian recipes. However, coconut milk is widely used, in accordance with the custom of centuries. In fact, the coconut is extremely basic to Indonesian cooking. Not only does it substitute for the needed milk, but also it takes the place of butter and other fats. It is not difficult to prepare your own coconut milk if you wish to go native or cook Indonesian-style. When fresh coconut is available, just grate 4 cups of the coconut meat, soak it in 2 cups of boiling water for about a half hour, then squeeze the liquid out through a cheesecloth. If shredded dried coconut is what you have on hand, soak it in water for half an hour (two cups of water to one cup of coconut) and then squeeze the liquid through the cloth.

For rice there is no substitute. Rice in one form or another, either steamed and served plain or cooked into some other dish, is eaten three times a day—for breakfast, lunch and dinner. The Indonesian breakfast consists of rice with a boiled or fried egg or rice with fried fish or meat seasoned with soy sauce and hot pepper. Lunches and dinners consist of rice and several other dishes. These dishes are designed so that all together they form a harmonious whole; each contrasts with and supplements the others. There is likely to be a vegetable soup, fried fish or an egg dish, a chicken curry, a meat dish and some sliced raw cucumbers and carrots. With the meat dish there is almost certain to be a hot pepper sauce, one that is seldom missing from the Indonesian meal. The soup, usually brought to the table with the rest of the food, may be eaten before, after or *with* the rice from a separate bowl, or if the diner elects to have it from the same plate as the other dishes, he will pour his soup over his rice and eat it rather than sip it. Desserts in Indonesia, as in so many other Oriental lands, nearly always consists of fresh fruit. There are, however, a number of sweet snacks that are served at various times throughout the day; these are quite similar to American desserts and may easily be served as desserts for an American-Indonesian meal.

At first exposure to Indonesian food, most people take fairly readily to *soto ajam,* a chicken and bean sprout soup; to the various rice dishes going under names such as *nasi goreng, nasi rames, nasi gudek* and *nasi opor;* to *gado-gado,* a mixture of vegetables with garlic-peanut sauce; to the Balinese specialty *babi guling,* or succulent roast pig; to the baked meat-filled pancakes called *rissoles*

(a Dutch item absorbed into the Indonesian diet); but probably the
dish—or multi-course meal—that spells Indonesia more typically
than anything else is *rijsttafel.*

Although the word *"rijsttafel"* (rice table) is Dutch, the meal is
truly Indonesian in origin. The classic *rijsttafel* consists of rice and
some twenty or thirty different dishes brought one by one to the
table in an aromatic, eye-catching parade. The guest who is not sure
just what he feels like *or* what the different offerings taste like usually takes one spoonful of each, testing and tasting until he decides
what he likes best. Then he requests more of his favorites, confining
himself to them to his heart's delight. Some people take a little of
everything (or even a lot), find that most of it is extremely hot on
the tongue, and then mix everything together with the rice in an
attempt to take the cutting edge off the heat. But this is not the Indonesian way to do it; each dish of the *rijsttafel* is supposed to be
eaten separately. The thoughtful hostess supplies plenty of ice
water, cold beer and sliced papaya and banana to keep the tongue
from burning.

This is the way a *rijsttafel* is served: First, as a rule, comes the
sajur, the thick, hot and spicy vegetable soup that is the Indonesian
favorite. Immediately after this comes the rice, in case you want to
sample it drenched in soup. Then, perhaps, a dish of *rissoles,* to
take the place of an appetizer. Now begins the parade of main dishes
and their tantalizing accompaniments: some *satés,* bite-size chunks
of meat broiled on a skewer; *oppor daging,* thin slices of beef fried
in coconut cream; *goreng ati,* fried beef liver. Now usually pork:
daging ketchap, fried pork with the flavor of soybean sauce and garlic, or pork croquettes; a chicken dish: *ajam abon-abon,* shredded
chicken, or *por ajam,* chicken and pineapple, and perhaps *nasi
goreng,* curried fried rice with chicken; and some fish dishes:
oedang masak, cooked shrimp, and *smoor djawa,* spicy fried Java-
nese-style fish, and perhaps *iekan bandang panggang,* spiced baked
fish with lemon juice and butter.

Now comes a surprise to the non-Indonesian guest: either *telor
besengkek* or *telor asin. Telor besengkek* proves to be spiced eggs of
distinctive taste, and *telor asin,* we find, is a dish of salted duck eggs
that have been buried in mud and aged for weeks.

Here we draw breath and observe the approach of the *sambals,*
of which there are several varieties. Basically, a *sambal* is a side
dish, savory, strongly flavored with red peppers. Most *sambals* are
very hot. One will probably be a shrimp *sambal,* or *sambal oedang,*

and another, liver, or *sambal ati*. Then we are likely to see *sambal tomat*, featuring tomatoes, and *sambal boontjies*, a *sambal* of green beans. In contrast, now, come the feather-light and delicate shrimp-flavored wafers known as *krupuk*, or *kroepoek*, side dishes of fried onions and roasted peanuts, and the banana fritters called *pisang goreng*. Somewhere along the line you will be served a condiment called *seroendeng*, or fried coconut paste, to enhance the flavor of any of your chosen main dishes; and *atjar*, or pickled vegetables; and *ketchap*, a soybean sauce that is roughly the equivalent of our ketchup.

Now we sample, spoonful by spoonful until we find something in keeping with our mood and appetite. It is a sumptuous meal; and in it Indonesia has given us an enormously varied menu, a striking gustatory experience and a feast fit for the gods.

RICE

BOILED RICE

2 *cups rice*   3 *cups water*

Place the rice and water in a heavy aluminum pan. Bring to a quick boil. When all the water has been absorbed by the rice, turn the heat very low. In about 20 minutes the rice should be tender.

STEAMED RICE

1 *pound rice*   2 *cups water*

Boil the rice in the water until all the water has been absorbed. Transfer the rice to a colander and set it in a pan of boiling water, cover and let steam until tender (about 20 minutes).

The preparation of steamed rice is not as simple as that of boiled rice, but there is no risk of the rice burning in the pan. Steaming is also used for reheating the rice before serving.

NASI WUDUK
Rice Boiled or Steamed in Coconut Milk

Use the same procedure as for boiling or steaming rice, but instead of water, use coconut milk (*see Glossary*) and add ½ teaspoon of salt and 1 bay leaf.

NASI KUNING
Yellow Rice

Same as Nasi Wuduk but add 1 teaspoon of powdered turmeric. Nasi Wuduk and Nasi Kuning are often served on birthdays and for special parties.

17

SOUPS

SAJUR BENING
Vegetable Soup

2 ears corn, husked
2 tablespoons chopped onions
1 teaspoon chopped garlic
   (optional)
2 tablespoons sugar

1 teaspoon salt
3 cups water
2 bouillon cubes (optional)
4 ounces spinach

Slice the corn from the cob. Cook it with the other ingredients except the spinach until done. Add the spinach, mix and continue cooking for 2 minutes. Remove from heat. Serve hot.

SAJUR TJAMPUR
Mixed Soup

1 teaspoon chopped garlic
1 tablespoon dried onion flakes,
   fried in 2 teaspoons oil
2 tablespoons butter or
   margarine
½ cup diced raw beef or chicken
1 bay leaf
   Dash of ground ginger
   Pepper and salt to taste

4 cups chicken broth
½ cup cooked noodles
½ cup shredded cabbage
½ cup cut green beans
1 tablespoon chopped celery
¼ cup bean curd, cubed (see
   Glossary)
½ cup sliced carrots
1 tablespoon chopped tomatoes

In a saucepan sauté the garlic and onion flakes in the butter. Add the meat and the spices. Cover and cook until the meat is tender. Add the broth; bring to a boil. Add the remaining ingredients. Continue cooking until the vegetables are just tender. Remove from heat. Serve hot.

SAJUR BOBOR
Milk Soup

2 tablespoons chopped onions
1 teaspoon chopped garlic
2 tablespoons butter or margarine
1 bay leaf
   Dash of ground coriander
   Salt to taste

2 cups chicken bouillon
1 small stalk Chinese cabbage,
   chopped
1 cup coconut milk

In a saucepan sauté the onions and garlic in the butter. Add the remaining spices and the bouillon. Bring to a boil. Add the cabbage and cook over medium heat until just tender. Add the milk and bring to a boil, stirring occasionally. Remove from heat. Serve hot.

LODEH TERONG
Eggplant Soup

1 *medium-size eggplant*
2 *tablespoons butter or margarine*
1 *tablespoon chopped onions*
1 *teaspoon chopped garlic*
2 *tablespoons chopped raw shrimp*
    or chicken

1 *tablespoon chopped green*
    peppers
1 *tablespoon chopped tomatoes*
½ *teaspoon sugar*
1 *bay leaf*
1 *cup chicken broth*
1 *cup coconut milk*

Peel and cut the eggplant into small pieces; cover with water and set aside. In a saucepan melt the butter. Add and sauté the onions, garlic, shrimp and green peppers. Add the tomatoes, sugar, bay leaf and broth. Bring to a boil. Add the eggplant. When just tender add the milk. Bring to a boil, stirring occasionally. Remove from heat. Serve hot.

SAJUR KARE
Curry Soup

1 *teaspoon ground chestnuts or*
    cashews, or peanut butter
½ *cup meat or chicken, cut into*
    cubes
2 *tablespoons butter or*
    margarine
¼ *teaspoon curry powder*
1 *cup vegetable bouillon (made*
    from a bouillon cube)

½ *cup diced peeled potatoes*
½ *cup sliced green beans*
½ *cup diced carrots*
1 *bay leaf*
1 *cup coconut milk*
  Salt to taste
1 *tablespoon dried onion flakes,*
    sautéed in 2 teaspoons oil

In a saucepan sauté the nuts and the meat in the butter with the curry powder. Add the bouillon and bring to a boil. Add the vegetables and the bay leaf. Cover the pan and cook over medium heat until the vegetables are just tender. Add the milk, stirring occasionally. Taste and add salt if necessary. Bring to a boil. Remove from heat. Serve hot topped with the onion flakes.

SAJUR LODEH
Thick Vegetable Soup

½ cup raw chopped beef or
    chicken (optional)
1 bay leaf (optional)
1½ cups chicken broth
4 cups chopped vegetables
    (cabbage, green beans,
    cauliflower, carrots, and
    lima beans)

1 tablespoon chopped green
    pepper
1 tablespoon chopped onions
    Salt to taste
1½ cups coconut milk

Cook the meat with the bay leaf in the broth. Add the vegetables and salt to taste and cook until done. Add the milk, stirring occasionally. Heat, taking care not to boil. Cook for 2 minutes. Remove from heat. Serve hot.

SIDE DISH

KRUPUK UDANG
Fried Shrimp Crispies

Uncooked shrimp crispies can be bought at Chinese markets and specialty food stores.

Directions for frying: Heat 2 cups of oil in a large frying pan. Lower the heat. Add large shrimp crispies one by one. With smaller crispies a few may be dropped in at the same time. Turn crispies to prevent burning or curling. Remove from the oil and drain on paper towels.

MAIN DISHES

BAKMI GORENG
Dry Noodle Dish

½ teaspoon garlic powder or
   1 teaspoon chopped garlic
   Dash of ground ginger
½ teaspoon salt
¼ teaspoon pepper
1 cup chicken
1 cup chopped raw shrimp
¼ pound butter or margarine

4 cabbage leaves, cut fine
2 carrots, thinly sliced
1 tablespoon chopped celery
1 tablespoon chopped tomato
½ pound thin egg noodles, cooked
2 cups bouillon
2 tablespoons dried onion flakes,
   sautéed in 1 tablespoon oil

Combine the spices with the meat and the shrimp. In a saucepan sauté the meat and shrimp in the butter; cover the pan. Stir occasionally until done. Add the fresh vegetables and mix. Add the noodles and the bouillon and mix. Lower the heat. Cover and cook until the carrots are tender. Remove from heat. Serve hot topped with the onion flakes. This dish may be served as a one-meal dish with pickles and chili sauce.

BREGEDEL DJAGUNG
Corn Patties

3 ears corn, husked
2 eggs
1 tablespoon flour
4 tablespoons chopped chicken or
   shrimp
2 tablespoons chopped onions
½ tablespoon chopped garlic

1 tablespoon chopped celery
1 tablespoon chopped green
   pepper (optional)
¼ teaspoon ground coriander
   Salt to taste
   Oil for frying

Slice the corn from the cob. Combine all the ingredients except the oil in a bowl and mix. Form into patties with a tablespoon and fry in the hot oil in a frying pan until golden brown on both sides. Remove from pan and drain on paper towels. Serve hot.

TAHU GORENG
Fried Bean Curd with Sauce

6 squares bean curd, cut into cubes
  Oil for deep frying
1 cup cooked soybean sprouts
½ cup shredded raw cabbage

1 tablespoon dried onion flakes,
  sautéed in 2 teaspoons oil
1 teaspoon chopped celery leaves

Deep fry the bean curd cubes in the hot oil. Drain them on a paper towel and place them on a platter and cover with the bean sprouts and cabbage. Top with the onion flakes and celery leaves. Cover with the sauce or serve the sauce in a separate bowl.

Sauce
½ teaspoon chopped garlic
1 tablespoon peanut butter
3 tablespoons sugar
¼ teaspoon ground red pepper

¼ cup soy sauce
½ cup water
  Salt to taste

Sauté the garlic in the peanut butter in a saucepan. Add the sugar, red pepper and soy sauce. Add the water gradually, stirring constantly. Cook over medium heat until thickened. Taste and add salt if needed.

NASI GORENG
Fried Rice

2 onions, chopped
1 clove garlic, chopped
2 tablespoons chopped fresh raw
  shrimp
½ teaspoon ground red pepper or
  ¼ teaspoon black pepper
  (**optional**)

1 tablespoon tomato ketchup
4 tablespoons butter or margarine
4 cups cooked rice
1 chicken bouillon cube dissolved
  in ½ cup boiling water
  Dadar Iris (see next recipe)

In a saucepan sauté the onions, garlic, shrimp, pepper and ketchup in the butter over low heat. Add the rice and bouillon and mix thoroughly for 3 to 5 minutes. Remove from heat. Serve hot, garnished with Dadar Iris (Shredded Omelet), fried peanuts and pickles. May also be served with any other dry dish, but no sauces.

DADAR IRIS
Shredded Omelet

3 *eggs*
½ *teaspoon salt*
   Dash of pepper

Butter or margarine
¼ *cup chopped onion*

Beat the eggs in a bowl. Add the salt and pepper. Melt the butter in a frying pan. Sauté onions for 2 minutes. Pour the eggs into the pan, spreading them to cover the bottom of the pan. Turn. Remove from the pan and slice very thin before serving.

SAMBAL GORENG TELOR
Egg in Red-Pepper Sauce

1 *tablespoon chopped onions*
1 *teaspoon chopped garlic*
2 *tablespoons oil or margarine*
1 *tablespoon chopped tomatoes*
1 *bay leaf*
1 *teaspoon crushed or ground red
    pepper*

1 *cup vegetable bouillon*
1 *cup milk*
  Salt to taste
4 *hard-cooked eggs, halved*
½ *cup fried potatoes*

In a saucepan sauté the onions and garlic in the oil. Add the remaining ingredients except the eggs and potatoes. Bring to a boil, stirring occasionally. Add the eggs and potatoes. Continue cooking until heated through. Remove from heat. Serve hot.

IKAN GORENG
Fried Fish

1 *1-pound whole fish (mackerel,
   red snapper or other sea fish)*
1 *tablespoon lemon juice*
  Pepper and salt to taste

1 *egg*
2 *tablespoons flour*
  Salt to taste
  Oil for deep frying

Score the fish slightly on both sides. Wipe with a clean cloth to remove moisture. Combine the lemon juice, pepper and salt in a bowl. Brush it on both sides of the fish. In another bowl combine the egg, flour and salt. Dip the fish into this mixture. Deep fry in the hot oil until cooked. Serve hot with slices of tomato and parsley.

UDANG BUMBU DENDENG
Spiced Fried Shrimp

1 teaspoon ground coriander
¼ teaspoon garlic powder
1 teaspoon vinegar
  Dash of ground ginger
1 teaspoon sugar
  Salt to taste

¼ teaspoon laos powder (see
  Glossary)
1 cup peeled deveined raw
  shrimp
  Oil for deep frying

In a bowl mix thoroughly all the ingredients except the shrimp and oil. Add the shrimp and set aside for 2 hours. (In the summer spread it on a strainer and dry it in the sun.) Deep fry in the hot oil.

LAPIS DAGING
Beef Slices

3 tablespoons chopped onions
2 tablespoons chopped tomatoes
2 whole peppercorns
  Dash of ground nutmeg
½ inch cinnamon stick

1 tablespoon soy sauce
2 eggs
1 tablespoon butter or margarine
1 pound beef round, sliced

Combine the onions, tomatoes, spices and soy sauce in a bowl. Beat the eggs separately and mix with the vegetables. Melt the butter in a frying pan. Spread the beef slices in the pan. Cover and cook over medium heat. Turn the meat when browned. When both sides are browned, lower the heat and add the vegetables and a bit of water to prevent burning. Sauté until done. Remove from heat and discard the cinnamon stick and peppercorns. Serve hot.

ATI BUMBU BALI
Balinese Calves' Liver

1 teaspoon dried onion flakes
½ teaspoon garlic powder or
  1 tablespoon chopped garlic
2 tablespoons butter or margarine
¼ teaspoon ground turmeric
1 bay leaf
1 teaspoon crushed or ground red
  pepper
  Dash of black pepper

½ teaspoon sugar
1 tablespoon soy sauce
  Salt to taste
1 tablespoon ground peanuts,
  cashews or chestnuts
1 tablespoon chopped tomatoes
1 pound calves' liver, sliced
  very thin
1 cup milk

In a saucepan sauté the onion flakes and garlic in the butter. Add the remaining ingredients except the liver and milk and mix. Add the liver and cook briefly. Reduce heat and add the milk. Continue cooking, stirring constantly, until thickened. Remove from heat. Serve hot.

JAVANESE FRIED CHICKEN

1 frying chicken	¼ teaspoon pepper
1 teaspoon vinegar	1 cup water
1 teaspoon garlic salt	Oil or other fat for deep frying

Cut the chicken into pieces and place in a bowl. In another bowl mix the vinegar, garlic salt and pepper in the water and pour over the chicken. Marinate the chicken in this liquid for 2 hours. Deep fry in the hot oil. Remove from oil and drain on paper toweling. Serve hot.

SATE AJAM
Chicken Kabobs

3 cups raw chicken, cut into cubes approximately 1½ inches	½ teaspoon vinegar
	2 cloves garlic, crushed
	½ cup water
20 to 25 small skewers	

Put 5 cubes of chicken on each skewer. Mix the remaining ingredients in a bowl and marinate chicken in it for 1 hour. Thread chicken on skewers and barbecue over hot coals or bake in preheated 400° F. oven for 15 minutes or until done. Serve hot with the following sauce.

Sauce
4 tablespoons peanut butter	1 teaspoon soy sauce
½ teaspoon chopped garlic	1 teaspoon sugar
½ cup milk	1 bay leaf
½ cup chicken bouillon or broth	Salt to taste
1 teaspoon ground red pepper	

Combine all the ingredients in a saucepan. Cook over low heat, stirring constantly, until sauce is thick. Remove from heat. Pour over chicken.

25

GADO-GADO
Cooked Salad

½ cup cooked shredded cabbage
½ cup cooked sliced carrots
½ cup cooked cut green beans
1 medium tomato, sliced
A few lettuce leaves
1 medium cucumber, sliced

1 cup sliced soybean cake fried in peanut oil until crisp (optional)
½ cup fried potatoes
2 hard-cooked eggs, sliced

Arrange the vegetables and soybean slices on a platter. Garnish with the fried potatoes and sliced hard-cooked eggs. Serve with the following sauce.

Sauce

2 cloves garlic, mashed
6 tablespoons chunk-style peanut butter
1 teaspoon sugar
1 teaspoon crushed red pepper (or less to taste)

1 bay leaf
1 small slice lemon peel
1 cup water
½ cup coconut milk (see Glossary)
Salt to taste

In a saucepan sauté the garlic in the peanut butter with the sugar, pepper, bay leaf and lemon peel. Add the water and milk gradually. Add salt if desired. Cook over low heat, stirring constantly, until thickened. Remove from heat. Serve hot.

26

SAUCES

SAMBAL KETJAP
Hot Soy Sauce

½ cup soy sauce
¼ teaspoon chopped garlic

1 tablespoon red pepper
1 teaspoon molasses (optional)

Combine the ingredients in a bowl and serve with Javanese Fried Chicken or Fried Fish.

SAMBAL TOMAT
Hot Sauce of Fresh Tomatoes

2 tablespoons crushed red peppers
1 tablespoon water
2 tablespoons chopped fresh
    tomatoes

1 teaspoon shrimp or anchovy
    paste
½ teaspoon salt

Soak the red peppers in the water in a bowl for 10 minutes. Add the other ingredients and mix and mash them together, preferably in a mortar. Serve cold over fried fish, shrimp or chicken.

SAMBAL DJELANTAH
Fried Garlic Hot Sauce

¼ teaspoon chopped garlic
1 tablespoon crushed red peppers
½ teaspoon salt

1 teaspoon shrimp or anchovy
    paste
1 tablespoon oil

Combine the garlic, peppers, salt and shrimp sauce and sauté in the hot oil in a frying pan. Remove from heat.

SAMBAL BADJAG
Fried Hot Pepper Sauce

2 tablespoons chopped onions
2 tablespoons oil or butter
1 tablespoon chopped garlic
2 tablespoons crushed red peppers
3 tablespoons chopped tomatoes
1 teaspoon salt

2 teaspoons sugar
1 teaspoon shrimp or anchovy
   paste
½ teaspoon monosodium
   glutamate

In a frying pan sauté the onions in the oil over low heat. Add the garlic and sauté until golden brown. Add the remaining ingredients. Stir and mix until done, about 10 minutes. Remove from heat. Chopped fried shrimp may be added if desired.

SAMBAL EBI
Hot Sauce with Dried Shrimp

2 tablespoons crushed red peppers
1 tablespoon water
2 tablespoons dried shrimp (see
   Glossary)
1 tablespoon oil

2 tablespoons chopped tomatoes
1 teaspoon shrimp or anchovy
   paste
½ teaspoon salt

Soak the red peppers in the water in a bowl for 10 minutes. Sauté the dried shrimp in the oil. Add the shrimp and the remaining ingredients to the peppers. Mix, preferably in a mortar.

SAMBAL KELAPA
Hot Sauce with Shredded Coconut

1 tablespoon crushed red peppers
1 teaspoon shrimp or anchovy
   paste

½ teaspoon salt
2 tablespoons shredded
   unsweetened coconut

Combine the ingredients and mix, preferably in a mortar.

SWEETS

PILUS
Sweet-Potato Balls

2 cups mashed cooked sweet
    potatoes
1 tablespoon flour
1½ tablespoons sugar

1 egg
Oil for deep frying
Confectioners' sugar, if desired

In a bowl mix the potatoes, flour, sugar and egg thoroughly. Form into small balls (1-inch diameter). Deep fry in the hot oil until golden brown and drain on a paper towel. Serve hot or cold. Sprinkle with confectioners' sugar if desired.

BUBUR DELIMA
Pudding of Pearl Tapioca

½ pound pearl tapioca
½ cup sugar
3 cups water

1 teaspoon vanilla extract
A few drops of red food coloring
Dash of salt

Soak the tapioca in water to cover overnight. Drain and combine with the remaining ingredients in a saucepan. Cook over medium heat until done. Remove from heat. Serve cold with milk.

RUDJAK TEGAL
Fruit Salad

2 cups honey
2 tablespoons peanut butter
1 teaspoon vinegar
1 teaspoon salt

1 teaspoon red pepper
4 cups shredded carrots, apples
    (sour and sweet), pears,
    cucumbers

In a bowl combine all the ingredients except the vegetables and fruit. Stir in the vegetables and fruit. Put in the refrigerator for a couple of hours. Serve cold.

SERIKAJA
Steamed Banana Pudding

3 eggs
1 cup sugar
1 cup coconut milk (see
    Glossary)

1 teaspoon vanilla extract
3 bananas, sliced

Beat the eggs in a bowl. Add the sugar, milk and vanilla extract and mix thoroughly. Stir in the bananas. Put the mixture in a deep dish and steam for about 30 minutes until thickened. Serve hot.

KOLAK UBI
Sweet Potatoes in Sauce

2 cups diced raw sweet potatoes
3 cups coconut milk (see
    Glossary
½ cup sugar

1 inch cinnamon stick
1 whole clove
Dash of salt

Combine all the ingredients in a saucepan and cook over low heat, stirring occasionally, for 20 minutes. The potatoes should remain in cubes. Serve hot or cold.

PISANG GORENG
Banana Fritters

4 ripe bananas, mashed
¾ cup flour
½ teaspoon salt

3 tablespoons sugar
Oil
Cinnamon sugar (1 teaspoon
    cinnamon to ⅓ cup
    sugar)

Combine bananas, flour, salt and sugar in a bowl. Mix thoroughly and beat slightly. Take one full tablespoon of this mixture for each fritter. Heat oil in frying pan and fry fritters, a few at a time, turning, until golden brown on both sides. Drain on paper towels. Sprinkle with cinnamon sugar.

NANAS GORENG
Fried Pineapple

2 *tablespoons flour*
1 *egg*
   Dash of salt
6 *to 8 slices of pineapple, ½ inch*
   thick

Oil
Cinnamon sugar
Cinnamon sugar (1 teaspoon
   cinnamon to ⅓ cup sugar)

Mix the flour, egg and salt in a bowl. Dip the pineapple slices in this mixture and fry in the hot oil, turning, until golden brown on both sides. Drain on paper towels. Serve with cinnamon sugar.

31

THAILAND

"Come and eat rice!" is a literal translation of the Thai invitation to dinner. Rice *is* dinner. All dishes served with it, spicy and distinctive though they may be, are merely side dishes; they "come with the rice," as the Thais put it. And it is true that many gourmets consider Thai rice to be the best in the world, worthy of the place of honor at any table.

But Thai food isn't only rice. Little Thailand (not quite the size of Texas) has many food resources. There is livestock in the pasturelands; there are fish in the rivers and seas. Sea carp and other fish, mussels, oysters, crabs, lobsters and crayfish are major items on the Thai menu. Stalls at the canalside market places astound the visitor's eye with an extravagance of mangoes, mangosteens, guavas, rose apples, bananas in twenty varieties, pineapples, papayas, litchis, oranges, pomelos, rambutans, durians and others so exotic that their very names defy translation. And there are fresh young coconuts, too, still green and juicy; peanuts, for chopping into salads and meat dishes; cassava, for the tapioca flour used in soups and sweet dishes; young plant shoots and other crisp green vegetables; pepper, soybeans, sesame; tongue-biting red and green chilies and spices for the curries that complement the rice.

The curries . . . ! Curry and warm weather seem to go together; Thailand's climate is hot, and so is the food. Most of the favorite Thai dishes are spicy-hot and peppery, sometimes too hot for Western tastes. The mildest of curries packs a jolt and the little chili pepper has the kick of a miniature mule; they must be approached with care. Yet there are many Thai foods that can be enjoyed by Westerners, even those who firmly believe they will never learn to like curry. "Season to taste" is the clue to Thai cooking for the American housewife.

To be invited to "come and eat rice" in a Thai home is to taste a new experience. The Thai cook—"mother of the kitchen," as she is called in Thailand—uses her skills to produce a meal that will tempt and stimulate the appetites of her guests, appetites that tend to become dulled by the hot and humid climate of the country. She provides a little of this and a little of that; a bowl of rice and a bowl of crisp fish balls; a delicate flavor here and a sharp sauce there; a biting curry of meat and a taste of sweet-and-sour dishes; a smooth or tangy soup, a custardlike dessert, a cool and juicy fruit. Her plan is one of contrasts, in texture and flavor, color and shape, against the backdrop of the main dish—rice.

As a guest in a typical Thai home you could expect to be treated to a meal consisting of the rice centerpiece; four or five "side dishes" including fish, meat, vegetables and a salad; two or three sauces; a clear or thick soup; and finally some small sweetmeats and three or four varieties of fruit in season.

You would be shown to one of a series of cushions arranged around a low table, and before you would be a soup plate, a spoon and fork and a china soupspoon. There would be no knife because all food is cut into bite-sized portions during its preparation. All dishes except dessert and fruit are brought to the table at the same time. Dessert and fruit follow when the main course has been cleared. Each diner helps himself according to preference and appetite. You would be urged to pile a generous helping of rice onto your soup plate and then make your own selection from the little plates and bowls surrounding your main bowl. The idea is for you to combine each flavor of sauce with your choice of fish or meat, mix it with the rice, alternate with soup or a fresh vegetable and eat whatever you will until satisfied.

But if you're unaccustomed to the bite of tiny red chilies, fresh-ground curry or peppery sauce—watch out!

Looking beyond the rice bowl to those side plates, each of which may be adapted to serve as a main course for an American meal, you will inevitably find fish or other seafood in some form. It may be there in the shape of butterfish in ginger sauce, shrimp salad, curried sea bass or sweet-and-sour sole; or it may not be apparent at first glance. But if it is there in no other form it will be there in one or more of the somewhat compellingly flavored Thai sauces such as *nam pla, nam prik* and others. *Nam pla* is a particularly ubiquitous sauce, turning up undisguised in its own sauce container or partially hidden in a number of dishes—and only partially, for its taste is noticeable. There are several versions of *nam pla,* but essentially this very popular fishy sauce has, as its foundation, shrimp that have first been dried and salted and then thoroughly pounded and a mixture of lime juice, sugar and garlic. This concoction is served with fresh fish and in curries or in any dish that the Thai cook might choose to use it in.

Another form of seafood is the fish-crisp, a delicate little fried shellfish ball that is as light as a feather and is usually made of prawns or other shellfish. It is often eaten almost plain, punctuated with a sweet-sour sauce that the Thais regard as semihot but that may seem a little hotter than that for those unaccustomed to it. These small crisps, called *tord mun gung,* are sometimes used to flavor fried rice, or they may be eaten with a squeeze of lime juice.

Thai cooks are expert in the art of frying. Fine noodles of rice flour are lightly fried with snippets of meat, onions and egg batter, then sprinkled with sugar and *nam pla* and fried a second time in deep fat to a delicate brown. Similarly, tiny pellets of meat are wrapped in jackets made of rice flour, then fried to a light crispness. *Mee krob* is a Thai favorite, a dish of crisp fried noodles with tiny chunks of shrimp, crab, pork, chicken and bean curd.

And then there will be curry, for in a Thai meal the meat dishes almost invariably include a tingling concoction that must be called curry for want of a better word. According to the Thais, the word "curry" as used in the Western world is a misnomer, a vague label for something that isn't curry at all, a description of something hot rather than something that is actually a subtle mingling of a variety of spicy flavors. The Thais produce at least twenty-five varieties of hot meat dishes, each with its own descriptive name, but each having to fall into the category of curry because there are not enough translatable names to go around. But store-bought curry powder—that's not curry!

Twenty-five assorted curries, each with a different mix of spices . . . The paste used as the basis for each of these *real* curry dishes is freshly pounded each day at home by the diligent housewife. According to the dish for which it is made, the curry mixture may vary from biting, peppery-hot to almost cool, and from sweet to sour, and from sweet-and-sour to bitter. Twelve, thirteen, sometimes more ingredients go into the making of each curry paste; such ingredients as chili peppers, peppercorns, caraway seeds, coriander seeds, cinnamon, roasted shallots, cardamom, nutmeg, mace, garlic, turmeric, mustard seeds, cumin powder, saffron; and when the time comes to prepare the curried dish it is not simply a question of stewing up a pot of meat and stirring in the paste. No, indeed! Bite-sized pieces of meat are simmered slowly in water or perhaps coconut milk with a touch of *nam pla* until nearly cooked, at which time the curry paste is added along with fresh coconut cream. Should the cook have any tamarind, *makrut* or *horapa* leaves on hand, she will add small quantities of these as well. As she cooks, she taste-tests; adds some sugar, a little more *nam pla*, perhaps a sprinkle of cardamom, a few drops of lime juice. When the meat is chopstick-tender and seasoned to the cook's satisfaction, it is transferred to a serving dish and adorned with tamarind leaves or mint and several red and green chilies to improve the color scheme and add yet more bite.

And that, in Thailand, is curry.

It might be represented on your Thai dining table by *masaman curry*, with its basic ingredients of beef or chicken, peanuts, coconut cream, and a curry paste beginning with "7 to 10 dried hot chili peppers according to taste . . ." Your own taste might call for less, for when you are the cook you are the mother of your own kitchen.

Pork is a very popular meat and may be used in a curry, but more often it is used in small quantities to enrich a fish dish or to flavor a soup, or it may be minced with the yolk of hard-cooked eggs, lightly seasoned "according to taste," replaced in the firm egg whites, then fried crisp and served up as *waning-moon eggs. Sweet pork*, too, often appears on the Thai menu. This dish consists of small, tender slices of pork simmered in water flavored with fish sauce to which a caramel sauce of palm sugar is added. Further slow simmering results in a meat dish of a velvety texture and sweet unusual taste.

Another Thai favorite is *kai priew wan*, a sweet-and-sour chicken dish made with chicken breasts and livers, cucumbers, carrots, noodles, tomatoes and onions, flavored with sugar, soy sauce and vinegar. Thais are also very fond of salads and greens, though few of their salads feature what we might think of as traditional ingredients. *Yam koong*, for example, is a shrimp salad with peppers, garlic, nuts, soy sauce and coconut cream.

Then again there is the rice, for this is served not only as the cen-

36

ter dish but in many ways. One of the best-known Thai rice dishes is *khao pad,* fried rice with diced pork, crab meat and garlic.

One of the side dishes offered to you might be *ma haw*—galloping horses—rambutans or oranges stuffed with chopped pork and peanuts. When you dip into the soup bowl you may ladle out a serving of *leg of pork* (*tom yum*) soup, or prawns and mushroom soup, or perhaps the tapioca soup called *kaeng chud saku.*

For there is always soup. Every Thai table has its tureen, set over a charcoal warmer so that the soup will stay hot throughout the meal. Bland or clear soups are served when the side dishes are rich, and more elaborate soups when they are light. The basic stock, even for the tapioca soup, is nearly always chicken, but Thai cooks achieve innumerable variations with their own choice of extra ingredients. The addition of chili sauce creates one variation; it makes a hot soup doubly hot. Little seasoned balls of meat, kidney, liver, chicken and duck are frequently added for greater variety; and fresh mushrooms, shrimp, rice noodles and soybeans provide yet other harmonies of flavor. One of the most delicious and unusual Thai soups is made from fresh pineapple.

Which brings us to sweets and fruits. When the main meal has run its course the sweet dishes are brought on. Typically, there might be a candied sweetmeat, a pudding or custardlike dessert, a soft fruit jelly or a liquid sweet.

Thai sweets are very often made with coconut. The American housewife is at a disadvantage here, for the perfection of a coconut dessert demands a juicy young nut freshly cut out of its green outer casing. One of the tastiest of such desserts has coconut both as content and container. The top of a baby nut is cut off and the milk is removed to be whisked together with egg and sugar. This mixture is then poured into the coconut, the top is replaced and the nut is popped into the oven for baking. The tender nutmeat and the creamy filling mingle flavors; the resulting custard is light and delicate, and the coconut flesh can be spooned out like soft white of egg. For the American cook who is unable to find the recommended young green coconut, it may be of comfort to know that a similar dish can be made by substituting a young pumpkin for the coconut container and filling it with homemade coconut custard (*see Sankhaya*).

Another favorite sweet, although again perhaps beyond the reach of the Western housewife, deserves mention because it is such a favorite of the Thais and because it is so very ambrosial. Traditionally supposed to have been served to the Buddha after he had fasted for many weeks, this *green rice cream* is made from the fresh green heads of unripe rice, sweetened and then boiled in jasmine-scented water. When soft it is pressed through a fine sieve, and what emerges is a smooth jellylike substance of a lovely jade-green shade. It is served with thick coconut cream that has been slightly salted for contrast with the sweetness. Certainly a dish fit for a Buddha! And there is yet another sweet morsel considered so delicious by the Thais that they call it *forget to swallow*. It is little more than a combination of coconut milk, rice flour and cream, but the flavor is well worthy of the name.

A Thai specialty is the liquid dessert. These sweets are not truly liquid, but neither are they anything like as solid as, say, apple pie or even custard. One that can easily be made in any kitchen is sweet tapioca with cream; another is bananas stewed in coconut milk. Some are made of strained fruits. A Thai hostess would surely serve you one of these, but she would also offer a variety of fruit. There would be an assortment of colors, tastes, scents and textures, and all skins, pips and stones are removed before serving so that all you have to do is eat the fruit and enjoy it.

Unlike some of their Oriental neighbors, Thais eat three regular meals a day and regard punctuality as a virtue. That, at least, is a familiar starting point for an unfamiliar dining experience!

RICE

BOILED RICE

4 *cups rice*   6 *cups water*

Half fill a large pot with the rice. Pour in the measured water. Bring to a boil. Remove all the scum and boil the rice for 10 more minutes. Cover tightly and continue cooking over a very low heat until all the water has been absorbed (about 20 minutes). Well-cooked rice will look dry and fluffy and will feel soft when it is pressed flat.

KHAO PAD
Fried Rice

1 *tablespoon finely minced garlic*   1 *cup canned or frozen crab meat*
¼ *cup lard or bacon fat*   *or cooked shrimp*
1 *cup finely diced Chinese roast*   4 *cups cooked rice (cold)*
   pork   *Pepper to taste*
1 *egg, beaten*
   Soy sauce

In a saucepan or large frying pan brown the garlic in the lard and add the pork. Pour the egg over the pork and garlic and stir quickly so the egg does not set. Add the soy sauce, crab meat and rice. Stir well, tossing lightly. Remove from heat and spoon onto a hot serving platter. Sprinkle with pepper to taste. Serve hot.

HORS D'OEUVRE

BREAD TOPPED WITH PORK, BEEF OR SHRIMP

1 cup coarsely ground raw pork,
    beef or shrimp
2 tablespoons finely chopped
    onions
1 teaspoon salt

½ teaspoon pepper
2 eggs
7 slices thin white bread, crusts
    removed, quartered
   Lard or vegetable shortening

In a bowl mix the pork with the onions, salt, pepper and eggs and spread on each quarter of bread. Melt the lard in a skillet and heat until very hot. Lower the heat and fry the bread, meat side down, until brown. Turn and brown on the other side. Remove from the skillet and drain on paper towel. Arrange on a platter and serve hot.

MA HAW
Galloping Horses

5 cloves garlic
2 or 3 tablespoons lard
   About 2½ pounds mixed lean
    and fat pork, finely chopped
3 tablespoons coarsely ground
    roasted peanuts
2 tablespoons sugar

Nam pla to taste (see Glossary)
2 small fresh pineapples or 8 large
   navel oranges
  Coriander leaves (Chinese parsley)
  Chilies, cut in slivers

Crush the garlic and fry in the hot lard in a large frying pan until light brown. Add the pork, peanuts, sugar and nam pla. Peel and core pine-apple and cut into pieces 1-inch square. (If using oranges, separate into the natural sections, cutting them open on the back, and lay them flat on a serving dish, skin side down.) Place 1 teaspoon pork mixture on pineapple square or orange slice and decorate with the coriander leaves and chilies.

CURRIES

MASAMAN CURRY
Beef or Chicken

1 3-pound roasting chicken or 2½ pounds beef
4 cups coconut cream (see Glossary
1 cup unsalted peanuts
Nam pla (see Glossary) to taste

Masaman curry paste to taste (see next recipe)
1 2-inch stick cinnamon
15 cardamoms
Pulp from 3 tamarind pods (see Glossary)
Juice of 1 lime
Light brown sugar to taste

Cut the chicken or beef into 2-inch cubes. Simmer the meat in a covered saucepan with the coconut cream, peanuts and nam pla until tender. Remove the meat and set it aside; continue to cook the cream mixture over low heat until it is reduced by one third. Stir in the curry paste and add the meat, cinnamon and cardamoms. Cover and simmer until the mixture is smooth and slightly thickened. Season with more nam pla, the tamarind pulp, lime juice and sugar to taste. Stir and remove from heat. Serve over long-grained white rice, steamed or fried, with a side dish of finely minced raw red or green chilies. Whole roasted white onions (½ pound) may be added to the sauce before serving.

MASAMAN CURRY PASTE

7 to 10 dried hot chili peppers
½ teaspoon black peppercorns
1 teaspoon caraway seeds
2 tablespoons coriander seeds
1 stick cinnamon
5 cardamom seeds
1 tablespoon grated lemon rind
5 cloves

½ teaspoon ground nutmeg
1 pinch mace
2 tablespoons peanut oil
1 teaspoon salt
8 or 9 minced shallots
5 cloves garlic, finely chopped
½ teaspoon shrimp paste or
    ¼ teaspoon anchovy paste

Remove and discard the seeds from the chilies and chop the chilies very fine. Put the chilies in a saucepan with the peppercorns, caraway and coriander seeds, cinnamon, cardamom seeds, lemon rind, cloves, nutmeg and mace, and cook over medium heat until slightly browned. Remove from pan and pound to a paste in a mortar. Add oil to pan. Add salt, shallots, garlic and shrimp paste and sauté. Combine all ingredients, blend.

41

KAENG KAREE KAI
Yellow Chicken Curry

1 chicken
7 cups cream made from meat of
    2 coconuts (see Glossary)
    Curry paste to taste (see next
    recipe)
2 tablespoons nam pla (see
    Glossary)
1 teaspoon monosodium glutamate

1 teaspoon makrut leaves, chopped
    (see Glossary)
1 teaspoon salt
2 cups fresh green chilies,
    chopped
1 cup horapa leaves, chopped
    (see Glossary)

Cut the chicken meat from the bones and cut the meat into small pieces; set aside. Cut the bones into larger pieces and set aside. Put the cream into a stewpan, stirring until it boils. Let boil for 5 minutes. Remove half of this boiled cream and put aside. Continue boiling the remaining cream for 15 minutes longer. Put the chicken meat and bones into the boiling cream. Boil for 10 minutes. Add the curry paste, monosodium glutamate, makrut leaves and the remaining half of the coconut cream. Stir and cook over medium heat until chicken is very tender. Remove cover. Season to taste. Add the green chilies and the horapa leaves. Remove from heat. Discard bones. Serve hot.

CURRY PASTE

7 to 9 big dried chili peppers,
    minced, according to taste
1 teaspoon peppercorns
1 teaspoon caraway seeds
½ teaspoon finely grated lime
    rind
1 teaspoon coriander root or
    seeds broken up

2 tablespoons sliced onions
1 teaspoon salt
1 tablespoon finely grated lemon
    rind
1 teaspoon turmeric
2 tablespoons sliced garlic

Put all the ingredients in a mortar and pound until smooth. (You may use a blender, adding a little water to ease grinding.) Use either fresh or dried. Sufficient for 2 pounds of meat. Store in a covered jar.

SOUPS

KAENG CHUD SAKU
Tapioca Soup

4½ cups chicken stock
 ¾ cup minced raw pork
     Dash of nam pla (see
        Glossary) or soy sauce to
        taste

 ½ cup small or instant tapioca
 ¾ cup canned or frozen crab
        meat
     Pepper to taste
 5 or 6 lettuce leaves, slivered

In a saucepan bring the stock to a boil and stir in the pork. Season with the fish or soy sauce. Add the tapioca and simmer until the pork is cooked. (If you use instant tapioca, cook the pork in the stock for 10 minutes before adding the tapioca.) Flake the crab meat, add to the stock and bring to the boiling point again. Adjust seasoning with more soy sauce and pepper. Remove from heat. Pour into individual bowls and decorate with the lettuce. Serve hot.

LEG OF PORK SOUP
Tom Yum

With a sharp pointed knife, remove the bones from a leg of pork. Scrape the skin well and wash. Remove the meat and fat from the bones. Mince this meat and fat together until very fine. Now mix with garlic that has been pounded with coriander roots or seeds and pepper or peppercorns. Season with nam pla (*see Glossary*) or monosodium glutamate, stuff into the leg, then secure the opening. Boil in stock with 1 stalk lemon grass (*see Glossary*) beaten and cut into 2 or 3 pieces. When the meat is thoroughly cooked, take it out of the stock, cool, cut in thick slices and place in a serving dish. Strain the stock through a cloth. Reheat. Season with more monosodium glutamate, little chilies and lime juice. Add a lime, cut up. Pour this seasoned stock over the meat. If desired, fried crushed garlic may also be added. Sprinkle with pickled coriander leaves. Serve hot.

PORK WITH BAMBOO SHOOTS SOUP

2½ *pounds bamboo shoots*
2½ *pounds pork cut from the*
     loin
10 *cloves of garlic, pepper,*
     coriander seeds

Stock to cover meat and vegetable
Nam pla (see Glossary) to taste
Palm sugar (see Glossary) or light
brown sugar, to taste

Slice the bamboo shoots very fine. Boil in salted water till the bitter taste is all gone and the vegetable becomes light yellow in color. Drain thoroughly and set aside. Cut the pork into small pieces, 1½ inches square. Put the pieces in a saucepan. Pound the garlic, pepper and coriander seeds together and add to the meat. Mix thoroughly. Add the stock, bamboo shoots, nam pla and sugar. Cover and boil until the pork is tender. Remove from heat. Serve hot.

CHICKEN AND MUSHROOM SOUP

2 *cups fresh whole or 1½ cups*
    canned mushrooms
1 *fresh chicken*
    Stock to cover
    Garlic

Pepper
Coriander root or seeds
Lard or chicken fat
Nam pla (see Glossary)

Trim fresh mushrooms and slice if desired; set aside. Cook the chicken in the stock, then remove the meat (reserving bones) and cut it into small pieces; set aside. Return the chicken bones to the pot and let simmer for 2 or 3 hours. Drain off the stock and put it aside; discard the bones. Pound together the garlic, pepper and coriander. Sauté this mixture in hot lard. Add the chicken meat, giblets and nam pla, mixing well. Add the stock and bring to a boil. Then add the mushrooms. Cover the pot and bring to a boil again for a few minutes. Remove from heat. Serve very hot in individual cups.

SIDE DISHES

TORD MUN GUNG
Fried Shrimp Balls

4 *large cloves garlic*
¾ *teaspoon salt*
½ *teaspoon pepper*
1 *pound raw shrimp, peeled and*
  chopped

Vegetable shortening or corn oil
  for frying
1 *cup tomato sauce, home-made*
  or canned

Using a mortar and pestle, pound the garlic, salt and pepper together. Add the shrimp and pound again into a paste. (A blender may be used with a little water added. Follow directions for grinding vegetables.) Form into medium-sized balls. Fry in deep hot vegetable shortening, turning occasionally, for 10 to 15 minutes or until brown. Remove and drain on paper towel. If the shrimp balls must be kept until serving time, keep them warm between two plates. To reheat, return to same hot fat in which they were fried for about 3 minutes. Serve hot with tomato sauce poured over them.

FRIED BEAN SPROUTS, CABBAGE OR BROCCOLI

½ *pound bean sprouts, fresh or*
  canned, or cabbage or
  broccoli
6 *cloves garlic*
3 *tablespoons lard or bacon fat*

½ *cup raw pork cut from loin in*
  thin slivers
¼ *pound raw shrimp, peeled and*
  deveined
Nam pla (see Glossary) to taste
Sugar and pepper to taste

If the bean sprouts are fresh, clean and wash well; set aside. If canned, rinse quickly and drain well on a paper towel; set aside. (When using cabbage, shred and blanch it, then follow the same method. Broccoli should be cut into small sections.) Crush the garlic and brown in the lard in a large frying pan. Add the pork and cook over medium heat, stirring, until done. Add the shrimp, seasonings to taste and bean sprouts, making sure the pan is very hot before adding or they will lose too much moisture. If you prefer bean sprouts tender rather than crisp, cook longer over low heat with pan covered. Remove from heat. Put into a serving dish and sprinkle with pepper. Serve hot.

MAIN DISHES

PLA PRIEW WAN
Sweet-and-Sour Fish

1 *large whole sea bass, 1 to 2*
    pounds
1 *cup white flour*
1 *teaspoon salt*
1 *tablespoon olive oil*

⅓ *cup water*
Vegetable shortening or corn
    oil for deep frying
Parsley or sliced hot green
    chilies to garnish

Clean and dry the fish. Score diagonally on both sides, cutting deeply to the bone. In a bowl blend the flour, salt and olive oil thoroughly, adding the water a little at a time to make a thick smooth batter. Have ready a deep skillet with hot shortening. Coat the fish with the batter and fry it until brown. Turn and brown other side. Remove and drain well on a paper towel. Place the fish on a platter. Pour Nam Priew Wan (Ginger Sauce) (*see next recipe*) over it and garnish with parsley or hot green chilies.

NAM PRIEW WAN
Ginger Sauce

8 *to 10 dried Chinese mushrooms*
2 *tablespoons finely chopped*
    scallions
¾ *cup water*
4 *tablespoons white or red pickled*
    ginger

3 *tablespoons sugar*
3 *tablespoons white vinegar*
1 *tablespoon soy sauce*
1 *tablespoon cornstarch, mixed*
    with 1½ tablespoons water

Soak the mushrooms in a bowl of warm water for 15 minutes or until soft. Squeeze the excess water out of them and chop them finely. Place them in a saucepan with the scallions, water, ginger, sugar, vinegar and soy sauce and boil for 5 minutes. Add the cornstarch mixed with water to the boiling sauce. Stir until thickened. Remove from heat.

HAE GUN
Shrimp Rolls

2 *bean-curd leaves (see Glossary)*	2 *teaspoons salt*
4 *or 5 heaping tablespoons pork*	1 *teaspoon ground pepper*
fat, diced fine	4 *tablespoons flour*
2 *pounds whole raw shrimp*	2 *eggs*
3 *cloves garlic*	*Oil for deep frying*

Sprinkle the dry bean-curd leaves well with water and put aside on a plate until quite soft. In a bowl pour boiling water on the pork fat. Drain through a sieve and set aside. Shell and wash the shrimp and drain them well in a sieve. Put the shrimp in a large bowl and mince thoroughly with the peeled garlic. Add the salt, pepper and flour and mix well. Beat and add the eggs to the shrimp. Add the prepared pork fat and mix well again. Divide into 2 portions and shape each portion into a roll similar to a sausage, using the bean-curd leaves as the wrapper. Steam for about 10 minutes or until well cooked. Cool on a wire rack, then cut crosswise or diagonally as preferred. Fry in hot oil until brown and crisp. Remove and drain on a paper towel. Serve with sweet-and-sour sauce (*see next recipe*).

SWEET-AND-SOUR SAUCE

4 *heaping tablespoons finely*	1 *cup granulated sugar*
chopped Chinese mushrooms	1 *cup vinegar*
4 *heaping tablespoons finely*	1 *cup Chinese soy sauce*
chopped sweet red pickled	1 *cup water*
ginger (see Glossary)	4 *tablespoons corn flour*
2 *heaping tablespoons minced*	
scallions	

Soak the mushrooms and then wash them thoroughly before chopping them. Place in a saucepan with the ginger, scallions, sugar, vinegar, soy sauce and ½ cup of the water. Blend the remaining ½ cup of water with the flour. Stir into the sauce. Cook over medium heat, stirring, until thickened and smooth. Salt to taste. Remove from heat. Serve hot.

MEE KROB
Crisp Fried Noodles

4 bunches Chinese or Thai rice vermicelli (see Glossary)	3 tablespoons finely cut bean curd (see Glossary)
1 pound vegetable shortening or lard, heated in deep pan	1 tablespoon soy sauce and/or 1 tablespoon nam pla (see Glossary)
4 scallions, cut in 1-inch lengths	1 tablespoon lime or lemon juice
4 cloves garlic, crushed	4 eggs
6 raw shrimp or 3 prawns, peeled, deveined, cut into small pieces	Vinegar to taste
3 heaping tablespoons each pork, chicken and crab meat	2 tablespoons sugar

Scald the vermicelli in boiling water, drain and spread to dry on a large flat plate. Fry in portions in the hot shortening until crisp and golden, turning only once or twice. Remove, drain on paper towels, and set aside. Transfer ¼ cup of the hot shortening to a large skillet. Add the scallions and garlic and cook until soft but not brown. Add the shrimp and meats, bean curd, soy sauce and nam pla (if you are using the latter) and lime juice, stirring constantly. Break in the eggs 2 at a time and stir the mixture until dry. Then add the fried vermicelli broken into pieces. Season to taste with vinegar, sugar and more soy sauce and nam pla. Remove from heat and spoon onto a hot serving dish and serve at once, garnished with finely cut chilies, chopped coriander or parsley leaves, pickled garlic, grated orange rind or chives.

SWEET-AND-SOUR PORK OR SHRIMP

2 cups thinly sliced lean pork or chopped shrimp	6 or 8 small cucumbers, peeled and cut lengthwise into 8 pieces
Flour	
Vegetable oil or lard for frying	4 firm medium tomatoes, cut into small pieces
¼ cup lard	
1 clove garlic, chopped	½ cup stock
1 large onion, peeled, cut in half and sliced	2 tablespoons sugar
	2 tablespoons vinegar
4 green chili peppers, cut into narrow strips	4 tablespoons light soy sauce

Dust the pork with the flour. Fry until crisp in hot oil in a deep pan. Remove and drain well on a paper towel. Keep the meat warm. Heat ¼ cup lard in a second pan, brown the garlic lightly, then add the onion, chili peppers, cucumbers, tomatoes and pork. Pour the stock over the ingredients and cook over medium heat for 5 minutes. Add the sugar, vinegar and soy sauce. Bring to a boil and salt to taste. Remove from heat. Serve hot.

YAM YAI
Vegetable Salad

A few drops lime juice
2 tablespoons finely shredded boiled pork skin
2 tablespoons boiled pork (heart, liver and shoulder)
¼ cup chopped boiled shrimp
½ cup bean sprouts
½ cup wun sen (see Glossary)
1 tablespoon black mushrooms
1 tablespoon steamed squid cut into long shreds (optional)
2 tablespoons boiled chicken breast cut into long shreds
2 tablespoons peeled, very finely chopped garlic
2 tablespoons sliced seeded cucumbers

2 tablespoons shredded turnip
2 hard-cooked eggs, sliced
2 eggs well beaten and fried, pancake style, like a very thin omelet, then shredded very fine
½ cup chopped mint leaves
¼ teaspoon salt
Coriander roots
Freshly ground black pepper
Garlic
Vinegar
Lime juice
Soy sauce
Shredded chilies
Pickled coriander leaves

Add the lime juice to the pork skin and squeeze gently with the tips of the fingers. Then wash the skin well in hot water and set aside. Pour hot water over the pork and shrimp. Drain well and set aside. Remove the roots from the bean sprouts and parboil the sprouts. Drain and set aside. Cut the wun sen into short pieces, parboil, drain and set aside. Soak the mushrooms in cold water until they are puffed up and then parboil. Drain and set aside.

Put the squid and chicken in a large bowl. Add to the bowl everything that has been set aside, plus the garlic, cucumbers, turnip, eggs and mint leaves. In another bowl pound together the salt, coriander roots, peppercorns and garlic. Add the vinegar, lime juice and soy sauce, stirring well. Just before serving, pour the sauce over the ingredients in the other bowl and mix well. Serve with the chilies and coriander leaves sprinkled on top.

YAM OF BEEF

About 2½ pounds beef (filet)
10 sprigs coriander or parsley
2 stalks lemon grass (see
  Glossary)
Lime rind, grated

5 cloves garlic
Sugar
Nam pla (see Glossary)
5 small chilies, crushed
Lime juice
Red chilies, shredded

Roast the beef in a 300° F. oven for 45 minutes, or until still rare. Pick the coriander leaves (or parsley) from the stems (discarding the stems) and soak in cold water. Drain, dry well and set aside for garnish. When the beef is cold, slice as thin as possible and place in a large bowl. Shred the lemon grass and an equal amount of lime rind very fine. Add to the beef. In another bowl crush the garlic and chop coarsely. Add the sugar, nam pla, chilies and lime juice. Mix well and pour over the beef, again mixing well. Spoon onto a serving dish. Decorate with the coriander leaves and red chilies. Serve cold.

ROAST LOIN OF PORK

Plain: Simmer a pork loin in water until tender. Pound together (or use a blender) coriander roots, garlic and pepper and rub the meat liberally with this. Roast in a 350° oven until brown and crisp—about 30 minutes per pound.

Dressed: With a sharp knife separate the meat from the bones of loin, stopping just before the bottom of the ribs so that the meat is still securely held to the end of the bones. Thrust 2 or 3 flat sticks between the bones and the meat to hold the meat away from the bones.

Peel a pineapple, reserving both the rind and the meat.

Pound together (or use a blender) coriander roots, garlic and pepper. Rub over the meat. Place meat in a flat baking pan, rib side down. Cover with the pineapple rind. Bake in a 350° oven for 30–35 minutes, or until it is almost done. Remove the rind. In a bowl mix together light soy sauce, vinegar and granulated sugar. Sprinkle some of this mixture over the roast and return to oven for browning. Repeat the sprinkling once or twice while browning. When done, place the roast on a platter and decorate tastefully with the pineapple meat and cucumbers cut into pieces, and red chilies cut to look like flowers.

Pour the remaining sauce into the baking pan, mixing it with the gravy. Spoon up some of the gravy, heat in a saucepan, pour into a sauceboat and serve with the roast.

FRIED MEAT BALLS

3 *coriander roots or seeds*
5 *cloves garlic*
5 *peppercorns*
⅓ *teaspoon grated nutmeg*
½ *cup each finely chopped or*
ground beef and lean pork
or 1 cup finely chopped or
ground pork
1 *egg, beaten*

⅓ *cup finely diced hard pork fat*
1 *teaspoon each chopped*
coriander leaves or lettuce
or parsley and scallions
2 *teaspoons nam pla (see*
Glossary)
Flour
Lard for frying

In a bowl pound together the coriander roots, garlic and peppercorns. Add the nutmeg and meats. Pound to a paste (or use a blender with a little water to make mixing easy). Then add the egg, the pork fat, coriander leaves, scallions and nam pla. Mix well and form into small balls. Coat the balls lightly with flour and fry in the hot lard until they are brown. Remove from lard and drain on paper towels. Serve hot.

PU CHA

4 *boiled crabs*
1 *teaspoon each pounded garlic,*
coriander roots and pepper
1 *large egg, separated*

3 *or 4 tablespoons coconut cream*
(see Glossary)
Nam pla (see Glossary)
Coriander leaves
Lard for deep frying

Shell the crabs. Clean, dry and set aside the body shells. In a bowl mix together the crab meat, garlic, coriander roots, pepper, the beaten white of the egg and the coconut cream. Season with nam pla. Fill the crab shells with this mixture. Brush the top of the mixture with the beaten egg yolk. Decorate with the coriander leaves, then steam until done (about 20 minutes). Before serving, deep fry in deep hot lard until brown. Remove from fat and drain. Serve hot.

SWEETS

KHANOM NIEO

Cook ½ cup glutinous rice (*see Glossary*) as you would regular rice, then pound it to a paste (or use food mill). Press paste flat in a cake pan, about ⅓ inch thick. Place pan in a large shallow pan of boiling water to steam for 5 to 8 minutes. Remove from the heat and leave till it is completely cold. Cut into fingers or diamond shapes of an even size and coat with grated coconut. Serve with a light sugar sirup.

KLUAY CHUAM
Bananas Stewed in Sirup

½ cup sugar   4 medium bananas
1 cup water

Dissolve the sugar in the water. Strain through a cloth into a big pan or cooking pot. Add the peeled bananas cut into pieces. Bring to a boil without covering, then continue to cook gently, sprinkling two or three times with cold water, and removing any scum that forms. When the bananas look bright and clear and the sirup begins to thread, about 200° F., place the bananas on a plate. Serve hot, either with coconut cream (*see Glossary*) seasoned with a pinch of salt or alone.

KLUAY KHEAK
Bananas Fried in Batter

2 cups boiled taro (*see Glossary*)   4 teaspoons granulated sugar
3 cups grated coconut   1¼ teaspoons salt
1 cup coconut milk (*see   6 ripe bananas
    Glossary*)   Fat for frying
10 tablespoons flour

In a bowl mash the taro well. Add the coconut, coconut milk, flour, sugar and salt. Mix thoroughly. Peel the bananas, slice them in half lengthwise and coat with the batter. Deep fry in hot fat till brown. Serve hot. Quartered sweet potatoes and taro sliced raw may be used as well as bananas.

52

MED KHANOON
Jackfruit Seeds

3 cups mung beans (see Glossary) 1 cup coconut cream (see
   or split green peas   Glossary)
                                 About 2 pounds sugar

Crush the beans and wash well, removing the skins while washing them, then soak in cold water overnight. In the morning boil the beans in a covered pot until they are soft. Drain and place over very low heat. When cooked, pound or mash the beans well. In a bowl blend together the coconut cream and the sugar. Add to the beans and mix well. Cook and stir until the mixture is thick and leaves the side of the pot. Remove from heat and cool. Beans thus prepared may be made into many different desserts. Here is one such.

Form the above cooked bean mixture into the shape of jackfruit seeds (1½" or 2" oblong balls). In a large saucepan dissolve sugar in water and boil to a thin sirup. Coat each "seed" with beaten egg yolk and cook over medium heat in the sirup for 8 minutes. Drain and put on a dish. Make "threads" with additional beaten egg yolk and cook in the sirup. When the threads are well cooked, remove from the sirup and scatter them over the "seeds" for decoration. Pour some of the sirup over all. Serve hot or cold. This dish should keep for a few days. Reheat each time in the same sirup.

KHANON RUA

1 cup egg yolks (duck if possible) 10 teaspoons flour (for hen eggs,
2 cups very fine sugar   only 4 teaspoons flour)

Stir the egg yolks and sugar in a bowl for about 1 hour, stirring in one direction only, never turning back. Grease little boat-shaped cake pans or corn-shaped muffin pans and warm them in the oven. Just before baking sift the flour into the eggs and mix lightly. Half fill the pans with the above mixture and bake in a 300° F. oven until the cakes are golden brown. Remove from pans and cool on a wire rack. *Rua* means "boat."

THONG MUAN
Rolled Gold

1 cup each flour and coconut milk (see Glossary)
2 eggs

½ cup sugar
¼ cup water mixed with 1 tablespoon lime juice

Mix all the ingredients thoroughly in a bowl and bake the batter in a greased iron made for the purpose. This iron can be bought in Chinese stores. The purpose of the iron is to press the batter very thin. The iron looks like two round flat irons that press together.

FOY TONG
Golden Shreds

6 eggs
1 cup sugar

¾ cup water

Separate eggs, strain yolks through a fine strainer. Add only the egg white that clings to the shells. In a saucepan blend together granulated sugar and water and boil to a sirup. Pour a small amount of the egg yolk, unbeaten, through a funnel or cone made of heavy aluminum foil with a small hole at the bottom into the boiling sirup. Let cook until shreds are well formed, then remove the shreds from sirup with a fork, lay them on a flat plate and fold them into a square or an oblong shape. Continue until all the egg yolk is used up, taking care that the shapes are of a uniform size. For crisp golden shreds, turn the heat up under the sirup and when the yolk mixture is well cooked, form the shreds into round little cakes instead of square or oblong shapes. They will get hard when cold.

TAKO HAEO

¼ cup rice flour
¼ cup arrowroot flour
2 cups scented water (see Glossary)
2 cups granulated sugar
¾ teaspoon salt
12 water chestnuts
3 tablespoons rice flour
2 cups coconut cream (see Glossary)

In a bowl mix the rice and arrowroot flours with the water, sugar and salt. Strain through a piece of thin cloth (cheesecloth) into a saucepan. Peel and cut the water chestnuts into small pieces. Add to the flour mixture. Stir over low heat for about an hour or until the mixture is thick and holds its shape, then turn out onto a plate. Sprinkle the surface with the 3 tablespoons of rice flour and then cover with the coconut cream. Serve hot or cold.

TAKO MADE OF CORN

¾ cup palm sugar (see Glossary)
3 cups coconut milk (see Glossary)
1 tablespoon cassava flour (see Glossary)
½ cup rice flour
½ teaspoon salt
1 cup grated uncooked corn
1 cup thick coconut cream (see Glossary)

In a bowl dissolve the sugar in the coconut milk. Add the cassava and rice flours and salt and strain through thin cloth (cheesecloth) into a saucepan. Stir over low heat for 20 minutes, or until it is almost cooked. Add the grated corn and stir for a few more minutes. Spoon onto a plate or a glass dish. Cover the whole surface with the coconut cream.

SANKHAYA

1 cup palm sugar (see Glossary)
1 cup coconut cream (see Glossary) made with scented water (see Glossary)

3 eggs, beaten
1 pumpkin or 3 green young coconuts

In a bowl dissolve the palm sugar in the coconut cream. Add the eggs and mix well. Cut the top from the pumpkin (or the coconuts) so that it may be replaced as a cover. Scoop out all the undesirable parts inside the pumpkin. (If coconuts are used, peel off the outer husks and scrape the shells well before cutting off the tops. Pour off the coconut liquid.) Pour the custard through thin cloth (cheesecloth) into the prepared pumpkin set in a tin or enamel dish the same size as the pumpkin to keep it from breaking while baking. (No dish is needed for the coconuts.) Replace the top and bake in a 350° F. oven about 1 hour—until well cooked. Serve hot or cold. If preferred, less sugar may be used.

This Sankhaya custard may be baked in a baking dish. In that case a little milk must be added to the custard before baking it. Place the baking dish in a pan of water in a 300° F. oven for 25 minutes. If you wish a firmer custard, add more eggs. The custard may be served hot or cold as is or with glutinous rice (see Glossary) and coconut cream.

KHANOM BUA LOI

In a bowl knead glutinous rice flour and scented water (see Glossary) to a dough. Form into little balls about ¼ inch in diameter. In another bowl dissolve palm sugar (see Glossary) in coconut milk (see Glossary) and strain through a thin cloth (cheesecloth) into a saucepan. Bring to the boiling point. Add the prepared balls and continue boiling for 15–20 minutes, or until they are well cooked. Remove from the sirup and place on a serving dish. Uncooked coconut cream (see Glossary) is often poured over the balls just before serving. Serve cold.

Saku Bua Loi: Made by using boiled saku instead of the balls made of flour. Fresh cassava root is sometimes pounded fine and used instead of the glutinous rice flour dough.

KLUAY BUAT CHEE
Bananas Stewed in Coconut Milk

10 *bananas*
1½ *cups coconut milk (see Glossary)*
½ *teaspoon salt*

2 *tablespoons sugar, or more*
½ *cup roasted mung beans (see Glossary)*

Peel the bananas. Cut each one crosswise into 4 to 6 sections. Place in an enamel cooking pot with the coconut milk, salt and sugar to taste. Bring to a boil, then sprinkle with the peeled mung beans, partially pounded. Remove from heat. Serve hot.

This dish is rarely tasted by visitors because it is considered too common to be presented. Even in Thailand it is never served to invited guests. However, it is easy to make and can be very tasty, provided the coconut milk is very thick and if possible is made with scented water (*see Glossary*). Use bananas that are really ripe and free from rough handling. Do not boil too long or the milk will not look nice. Thai nuns are dressed in white; hence the name of this dish, which means "Nun Bananas."

SWEET TAPIOCA WITH CREAM

3 *cups scented water (see Glossary)*
½ *cup tapioca*
½ *cup palm sugar (see Glossary)*

1 *cup coconut cream (see Glossary)*
Pinch of salt

In a saucepan bring the water to the boiling point. Add the tapioca and stir until well cooked. Add the sugar and boil for a while, stirring well. Remove from heat. Pour over it the coconut cream to which a pinch of salt has been added. For variety, add to the cooked tapioca the flesh of young coconuts, grated corn or boiled mung beans (*see Glossary*). Glutinous rice (*see Glossary*) or cassava flour (*see Glossary*) may be substituted for the tapioca.

BURMA

Burma is a warm and lovely land of rugged mountains and river valleys, of vast expanses of rice fields and rich teak forests that reach far up the mountainsides. It is a land of enormous mineral wealth, abundant in petroleum, silver, tin and exquisite gem stones such as sapphires, rubies and jade. The well-watered soil supports cattle, sheep, pigs, goats and water buffalo and produces, in quantity, sesame, peanuts, pulses, corn, millet, sugar, beans, fruit and vegetables. Yet for all this—all this wealth of natural resource—its principal product, principal export and principal food is . . . rice. And in view of the profusion of produce, it comes as a bit of a surprise to discover that there is not a great deal of variety in the everyday diet of the Burmese people. Elaborate foods and complicated menus are largely reserved for festivals and ceremonials and, although the occasional novel item appears on the workaday menu, the daily fare is almost unvaryingly simple.

Yet it is piquant, and of great appeal to the gourmet with a true appreciation for curry. On the whole, Burma's food is very similar to the foods of its near neighbors—the Indians, Thais, and Malays—with some touches that are purely Burmese. Virtually every meal consists of rice and curry—not even curry and rice, but rice and curry. The curries are nearly all hot and spicy, although they tend to be less biting than those of India and Thailand, and an occasional curry dish will even be quite mild. Like most peoples in hot climates the Burmese prefer tangy foods. Burma is said to have three seasons only: the hot season, the rainy season and the fairly cool season. Summer temperatures (March through May) may soar above 100 degrees; all seasons tend toward high humidity. And when it rains, as it often does between June and October, the rain may continue for days and days . . . long, warm, very humid days. Truly a curry country!

The Burmese usually start their day with an awakener of coffee and bread. As a rule they will eat a fairly large brunch-type meal between nine and eleven in the morning, and then have nothing (except perhaps a very light snack) until the evening meal at five or six o'clock. It is simply too hot to eat in the middle of the day.

The full-course, well-served Burmese meal consists of several curries, boiled rice, salad, sometimes a soup, occasionally a dessert. Your Burmese hostess will invite you to seat yourself at a table that is literally covered with small dishes, which, when their lids are removed, reveal several different kinds of curry and a variety of aromatic sauces. There is also, you observe, an enormous bowl of rice, or several little ones. Now you help yourself to whatever you wish, to whatever looks the most appetizing to you. Almost certainly there is a meat curry, or a meat-and-vegetable curry, and possibly a chicken curry, and probably one with prawns, shrimp or some other type of seafood. There might even be others as well. Surrounding the curries will be the sauces, all different but nearly all based on one variety or another of *nga-pi*, dried and fermented fish or shrimp . . . a pallid description of a sort of gustatory bombshell. One must tread lightly and take a very small serving of this favorite Burmese delicacy; an unsuspecting soul who takes too generous a helping is due for something of a shock. The taste for *nga-pi* is one that takes a very long time for Westerners to acquire; it is *strong*. Most of us think it is quite awful, and then again some of us eventually conquer our prejudice against its obtrusive, pungent, acrid taste and learn to enjoy it very much in moderation. It may be just as well to learn to like it if one wishes to eat truly Burmese foods in Burma, because it turns up remorselessly in all manner of sauces and dressings, but it may be omitted from Western menus or replaced in recipes with anchovy paste.

Appetizers are rarely served, but soups are quite popular. If you have a choice between taking (or making, when it comes your turn to cook Burmese) soup of the *hingyo* or of the *chin-ye-hin* type, by all means choose the *hingyo*. *Chin-ye-hin* soups are strong and sharp, almost acid to the taste, and are not really palatable to most newcomers to the Burmese table.

After the soup you help yourself to rice, and on the rice you put a helping of two or three of the curries. You will find them to be quite hot, for they have been cooked in a liberal blend of sesame oil, pepper, onions and spices. If the meal is really well prepared you will enjoy the subtly differing flavor of the various curries, and you will find the meal in general to be a mosaic of contrasting, interesting tastes. You will think at first that the curries are very similar to those made in India, and then perhaps you will be slightly puzzled by a difference in texture. This is due to the Burmese use of coconut milk in their curries, something that Indians seldom use. It adds a delightful smoothness to the Burmese dishes, taking away from the cutting edge of the hottest curries. With the curries you will try some sauce—being very cautious of the quantity until you are sure just how much you like *nga-pi.*

There will be vegetables too, also served with a strong, sharp *nga-pi*-based sauce. Some may have been cooked rapidly in oil; others are served uncooked. There may be cucumbers with green mango, and there will almost certainly be a mixed green salad. The salad dressing preferred by the Burmese is *nga-pi-yet,* and you will very soon discover that you have met it before in slightly different guise. It is that ubiquitous, strongly fishy-flavored *nga-pi* again, mixed with garlic, onions and chilies; and you have to be made of quite stern stuff to be able to take it.

When you are a guest, the trick to eating Burmese food is to take a sample of each dish until you find the ones you like, then help yourself to more of the latter and blend them according to your own taste. When you are a hostess, the thing to do is adapt the Burmese menu to the known tastes of your guests. You will probably prefer to concentrate on a single not-too-tangy soup, one or two really good curries of contrasting contents, a large bowl of rice and a simple green salad with a dressing of your own choice. For your first venture into Burmese cooking you might try, for example, a shrimp-and-pumpkin soup; a dish of *ne myit hin,* which is a curry of shrimp and bamboo shoots, and one of *chet-glay hin,* a chicken curry; or *ah mhae tha hin,* a ground beef curry, and perhaps *sha nga boung,* an unusual but tasty meal of fish croquettes in coconut cream. You will serve rice, naturally, with any Burmese meal, and either vegetables or salad, and perhaps a simple fruit dessert or something on the order of *ohn htamin,* which is coconut rice. The Burmese people are not great dessert eaters, but they do enjoy fruit, which they serve fresh or in a simple dessert such as bananas in a sirup of coconut cream. On occasion, instead of fruit they will have a sweet dish based on tapioca, semolina or rice and coconut; but fresh fruit remains the favorite.

Coffee or tea may be served to round out the meal. In some parts of Burma the practice is to add some favorite grain or cereal to the tea until it has the consistency of thick soup; but my own feeling is that authenticity is sufficient when it stops short of cereal-thickened tea—and *nga-pi.*

SOUPS

FISH SOUP

1 2-pound fish (sea bass, mackerel   ¼ teaspoon black pepper
      or other)   ¼ cup rice
2 quarts water   ½ cup chopped celery
1 teaspoon salt   ¾ cup thinly sliced cabbage
2 small onions, sliced   ½ teaspoon monosodium
4 tablespoons soy sauce   glutamate

Wash the fish and remove the head, skin and bones. Place the head,
skin and bones in a saucepan with the water, salt and onions. Bring to
a boil, then lower the heat and simmer about a half hour. Cut the fish
into small pieces and mix well in a bowl with the soy sauce and the
freshly ground black pepper and set aside while the soup stock is cooking. When the stock is finished, strain, return to heat and bring to a boil.
Add the rice and cook over medium heat for 20 minutes, then add the
fish (undrained) and mix well. Simmer for 20 minutes and add the
celery, cabbage and monosodium glutamate. Cook for another 10 minutes. Remove from heat. Serve hot.

PUMPKIN OR SQUASH SOUP

1 cup uncooked shrimp, shelled   4 cups pumpkin or winter
      and deveined   squash, cut into small, thin
6 cups beef broth   pieces
1 large onion, chopped fine   ¼ teaspoon ground dried
2 teaspoons anchovy paste   chili peppers
2 cloves garlic, minced   Salt to taste

Cut the shrimp into very small pieces and add to the beef broth in a
saucepan. Add the onion, anchovy paste and garlic and bring to a boil.
Now add the pumpkin or squash, chili peppers and salt. Continue cooking over lowered heat for 15 minutes. Remove from heat. Serve hot.

CURRIES

CHICKEN CURRY

2 *small fryers, cut up*
2 *teaspoons curry powder*
2 *tablespoons soy sauce*
   Pinch of saffron
2 *large onions, chopped fine*
½ *teaspoon ground dried*
   chili peppers

3 *cloves garlic*
¼ *cup oil*
2½ *cups water*
1 *teaspoon cinnamon*
1 *heaping teaspoon salt*
3 *bay leaves*

Clean the chickens and dry. Combine the curry powder, soy sauce and saffron and rub over the chicken. Set aside. Pound the onions, chili peppers and garlic very fine (blender may be used). In a deep pan, heat the oil and brown the onion mixture. Add the chicken and sauté lightly. Add the rest of the ingredients, cover and simmer about 1 hour or until tender. Remove from heat. Serve hot.

GROUND BEEF CURRY

3 *tablespoons oil*
1 *cup minced onions*
3 *cloves garlic, minced*
¼ *teaspoon ground dried*
   chili peppers
1 *teaspoon powdered ginger*

2 *teaspoons salt*
   Pinch of saffron
2 *pounds ground beef*
½ *cup boiling water*
3 *tablespoons soy sauce*

Heat the oil in a large skillet and sauté the onions and garlic until soft. Add the chili peppers, ginger, salt, saffron and beef. Cook over medium heat for 5 minutes, stirring constantly. Add the water and soy sauce and mix. Continue cooking over low heat until the water is absorbed. Remove from heat. Serve hot.

SHRIMP CURRY

1½ cups sliced onions
¼ cup oil
½ cup minced onions
2 pounds uncooked shrimp,
    shelled and deveined
1 teaspoon ground dried
    chili peppers

¾ teaspoon saffron
2 tablespoons minced garlic
2 tablespoons powdered
    ginger
2 teaspoons salt
2 cups coconut cream (see
    Glossary)

In a large skillet brown the sliced onions in the oil. Add the minced onions, shrimp, chili peppers, saffron, garlic, ginger and salt. Mix thoroughly and sauté for several minutes. Add the coconut cream and mix. Continue cooking over low heat until the coconut cream is thoroughly hot but not boiling. Remove from heat. Serve hot with rice.

FISH IN COCONUT CREAM

1 teaspoon ground dried
    chili peppers
2 pounds fish filet, cut small
1 medium onion, chopped
1 heaping teaspoon powdered
    ginger
3 cloves garlic, minced
2 tablespoons lemon juice

1½ teaspoons salt
1 tablespoon cornstarch
½ teaspoon turmeric
1 medium onion, sliced
¾ cup oil
1 cup coconut cream (see
    Glossary)

In a bowl pound until very fine (electric blender can be used) the chili peppers, fish, chopped onion, ginger and garlic. Add the lemon juice, salt, cornstarch and turmeric and mix well. Shape into small patties or balls and set aside. In a large skillet brown the onion slices in the heated oil. Remove the onions and set them aside. Add the fish patties to the oil and brown, then remove. Pour off all the oil except 1 tablespoon. Add the coconut cream to the skillet, bring to the boiling point and add the fish patties. Simmer over low heat for 15 minutes. Remove from heat. Serve hot with the browned onions.

TOMATO CURRY

4 tablespoons oil
1 pound onions, sliced very thin
1 teaspoon salt
½ teaspoon turmeric
3 cloves garlic

½ teaspoon ground dried
   chili peppers
2 teaspoons anchovy paste
5 tablespoons water
6 cups tomatoes, quartered

Into the heated oil in a skillet stir all the ingredients. Simmer very slowly for 20 minutes, or until everything is tender. Remove from heat. Serve hot.

SIDE DISHES

CUCUMBER DISH

6 medium cucumbers
½ cup vinegar
2 teaspoons salt
¾ cup oil
5 medium onions, sliced
   very thin

5 cloves garlic, sliced
1½ teaspoons sugar
¾ teaspoon black pepper,
   freshly ground
1 teaspoon turmeric

Wash and peel the cucumbers, cut lengthwise and remove the seeds. Slice crosswise and place in a saucepan. Cover with boiling water and half of the vinegar and boil until the cucumbers are transparent. Drain and place in a bowl. Sprinkle with the salt and set aside. Heat the oil in a skillet and brown the onions and garlic, then remove from the oil and set aside. Add the sugar, pepper, turmeric and the remainder of the vinegar to the oil. Mix well and pour over the cucumbers, mixing lightly until well coated. Set aside to cool. Before serving, cover with the browned onions and garlic.

RICE WITH COCONUT MILK

2 *cups sliced onions*
4 *tablespoons oil*
2 *cups uncooked rice*

4 *cups coconut milk (see*
Glossary)
1½ *teaspoons salt*

Sauté the onions slowly in the hot oil in a skillet until golden brown, stirring often. Add the rest of the ingredients and enough water to barely cover the rice. Cover and simmer very slowly until tender. Remove from heat. Serve hot.

SWEET

BANANA DESSERT

2 *tablespoons water*
1 *cup sugar*
6 *large firm bananas*

Pinch of salt
1⅓ *cups coconut cream*
(see Glossary)

In a saucepan cook the water and sugar over low heat until a sirup forms. Peel the bananas and place in a deep saucepan. Pour the sirup over the bananas. Bring to a boil. Add a pinch of salt to the coconut cream and add to the bananas. Simmer until the liquid is absorbed. Keep turning the bananas often while cooking. Remove from heat. Serve hot.

INDIA
PAKISTAN

The cookery of the India-Pakistan subcontinent is far more than the cookery of a single nationality or of recent civilization. It is an intricate art with its roots in time-honored custom, in centuries of change, in the various nationalities of the inhabitants, in climatic conditions, in individual and national taste—and in religion. Indeed, it is clear that the influence of the Hindu and Mohammedan religions is pivotal in the dietary practices of the peoples of these lands. The vast majority of Pakistanis are Moslems, who do not eat pork, ham or bacon; the vast majority of Indians are Hindus, who do not eat beef. It is perhaps in the spirit of compromise that the Indians and Pakistanis both have so many mutton offerings on the menu. Still, because of the differences in religious custom, the American housewife looking for representative recipes will find many fine Pakistani dishes featuring beef, and a number of superb Indian dishes containing mutton, chicken or seafood—or no meats at all. She will also find, on Indian and Pakistani menus alike, plenty of dishes containing that multitude of spices known as Indian curry.

Many people hesitate to try the foods of India-Pakistan because they fear that the famous curry will be "too hot" for them. It may be so, if they sample indiscriminately; Indian curry can be very hot indeed. But that isn't always the case. Indian cooking can also be very delicate in flavoring. In fact, Indian cooks feel that seasoning is the most important aspect of cooking, unlike the Chinese and Japanese, who regard the meticulous chopping or slicing of the food and the swift cooking time as of at least equal importance to the seasoning. And the Indian emphasis on seasoning has very obviously led to the excellence and variety of their curries. Certainly, when it is prepared right, a good curry dish is subtle and pleasing and just hot enough to be tasteful—"hot enough" for the taster, that is, and tastes do vary enormously.

Curry seasoning, in India as in Thailand, is no packaged powder stored in a can or jar. It is a mixture of many, many spices ground daily by the chef. The ingredients and proportions are dependent on the taste and judgment of the chef or cook and on the requirements of the particular dish. Cinnamon, ginger, pepper, cloves, chili, garlic, cardamom, coriander and aniseed are the most widely used spices and herbs, but they are by no means used in all curry mixtures.

Since the standard for curry is not just its heat but its complex and infinitely varying flavor, we can expect to find a curry so mild and pleasing that even a noncurry eater can enjoy it. We will not be disappointed, for while it is true that many Indian curries *are* quite hot—to our unaccustomed tastes—many others are only mildly spicy. A great many people in India and Pakistan themselves prefer a gentle to a biting curry. Many delicious and completely authentic Indian curries can be made with a minimum of pepper and no ground chilies at all; they are nonetheless genuine. An excellent curry can be made with a blend of turmeric, salt and *garam-masala,* the latter a finely ground mixture of coriander, caraway, cloves, black peppercorns, cardamom and cinnamon. This can be purchased ready-made from any store that sells Indian groceries. All you do is add your own salt and turmeric. (I might add here that there are also plenty of perfectly authentic Indian gourmets who do not care for the onions and garlic that so many of their countrymen seem to love. When a recipe calls for these items and you don't happen to like them, you, too, can feel quite free to leave them out.)

Garam-masala is also convenient for those people who are somewhat deterred by the passionate emphasis on fresh spices and the daily grind of preparing new curry. They can add what they wish—chili, more pepper, and so on—but at least they don't have to grind everything separately. Fresh ingredients are important, but it is not necessary to overdo things in a frantic effort to prepare "real" Indian food. Even a conscientious Indian chef will sometimes buy his curry mix completely ready-made, and so can you, provided you can be sure you are getting genuine Indian curry powder.

Essentially there are four important factors in the making of a fine curry dish: quality of ingredients; genuineness of the freshly made or recently store-bought Indian curry; discretion in using quantities of curry that are appropriate to the dish; and care in making the gravy. The gravy must always be rather thin; it should never, for instance, be thickened with flour. If it does require thickening at all, it is best either to add a little milk or to evaporate the excess juices by cooking as long as necessary with the lid off the pan.

What else goes into the curry dish is, as often as not, mutton. American housewives will find that young lamb, seldom if ever used in India, is excellent in a curry. So are fish and other seafood, particularly crab and prawns and lobsters, and chicken and beef.

A popular hot-and-sour curry is *vindaloo,* much relished in the west of India. Its basic ingredient may be mutton (or lamb), pork, fish or prawns, but whatever it is, preparation method and tangy taste remain the same: the meat and a quantity of spices are marinated for some time before cooking—at which time even *more* ground spices are added. The result is a striking dish that's even hotter than it is sour.

Curries of the north are less hot, less juicy (that is, made with less gravy), but richer. Among these are the various *korma* curries, the *korma* curry being basically a thick, rich braised meat dish. Another popular curry is the very unusual (to us) *kabob* curry, which is made of bite-sized pieces of meat skewered together with garlic, onions, chili and ginger and then barbecued. Also delicious are *seekh kabobs,* which are made of finely ground meat with spices, bound in egg batter, then fixed to a skewer for barbecuing.

Visitors to India, and guests at your table, take readily to *koftas,* a sort of spicy meat croquette; and few are able to resist *tandoori,* which is barbecued spiced chicken, meat or fish. Then there are the *do pyaza* dishes, which are meat preparations with a double dose of onions, and *roghan josh,* the tender mutton curry with a hint of saffron.

Rice, wheat, lentils and milk form the basis of the diet preferred by that large group of Indians who are vegetarians. Many simple but tasty dishes can be made from milk products like curds (yogurt) and cottage cheese, and from various cereals and vegetables. A plain but delicious meal can be made of thinly grated vegetables—

cooked or raw—mixed with beaten curds and garnished with salt, pepper and green coriander leaves. This is known as *pachadi*. Somewhat heartier is *khichri*, or *kitcheree*, a flavorsome mixture of lentils and rice that is popular even among nonvegetarians.

Ghee is a word that crops up frequently in Indian recipes. It is clarified butter, and most foods are prepared in it. The Indian chef prefers it to regular butter because it is free from moisture and impurities and does not burn or blacken during cooking. Oil is sometimes used, too, but such animal fats as lard and drippings are generally avoided. However, in Western versions of Indian food, it is perfectly permissible to substitute one's own choice of fat or oil for the *ghee*.

Rice is the core of most Indian and Pakistani cooking, with some exceptions. A *pulao* (also called *pellao*, and *pilau*) is a seasoned rice dish which sometimes includes meat or poultry and other desired ingredients, cooked in butter and spices. *Biryani* is a closely related but somewhat richer rice preparation, which is always colored and flavored with saffron or turmeric, consisting of layers of parboiled rice alternating with layers of rich meat or vegetable curry, baked and then topped with crisp-fried onions, sultana raisins, nuts and sliced boiled eggs.

Of breads and pancakes there are many. The *chapati* is a kind of dry pancake or flat bread made of unfermented wheat dough; it is round in shape, paper-thin and somewhat resembles a tortilla. *Chapaties* are eaten at meals with meat, lentils or cooked vegetables. Not unlike them are *parathas*, which are fried breads made of unleavened wheat flour. They look rather like small shallow dishes, and they may be served plain or filled with a vegetable. *Poori*, or *puri*, is deep-fried wheat bread, round, crisp and slightly puffy. *Loochi* is the Bengal version of *poori*. It is made of refined wheat flour, *ghee* and water blended into a dough and then deep-fried. Popularly, fried eggplant is served with it. Another favorite type of bread is *nan*, a dry bread made from a slightly leavened dough and baked—traditionally—in a mud oven. *Samosas* are tasty appetizers of finely chopped, and sometimes curried, meat or fish or vegetables wrapped in a thin pastry and deep fried. And the *dosa*, a specialty of the south, is a type of savory pancake made with a fermented batter of ground lentils and rice.

Some of the favorite sweet dishes are *halwa, kheer, doodh pak, barfi, jalebi* and *payasam*. *Halwa* is a very sweet and most delicious dessert dish that comes in several varieties. Sometimes it is made of lentils, semolina or wheat; and sometimes it is prepared with carrots, pumpkin, rice, bananas, nuts and so on, together with butter, milk and sugar. *Kheer* is a puddinglike preparation of milk and the cook's choice of flavoring ingredients, and *payasam* is a milk pudding made with vermicelli or lentils. *Doodh pak* is a rich rice pudding; *barfi* is something like fudge; and *jalebi* is a golden-crisp sweet ring filled with sugar sirup, an exotic sort of doughnut.

As for liquid refreshments coffee and tea are widely used as hot drinks, and during the summer months there are many delicious cold fruit drinks to choose from. A particularly refreshing drink is made from sugar-cane juice, lemon juice and ginger. *Lassi* is another popular beverage; it is beaten yogurt diluted with water and then either sweetened or salted according to one's taste. Iced tea or milk are appropriate substitutes on the American dining table.

When it comes to serving the Indian or Pakistani meal, the Westerner is faced with a choice between the traditional and the modern. The traditional custom, especially in the Punjab, was to start the meal with a sweet dish, but this custom is changing. The modern order of service starts the meal with one dish of curry, preferably juicy, accompanied by rice *pulao*. With the curry comes the inevitable Bombay duck; and then there are the *puppadums,* chutneys and Indian pickles: Bombay duck, as the gourmet world has long known, is not duck at all, but a thin white fish. It is sometimes served fresh and appears in a number of dishes, but it is better known salted, dried and served as a taste contrast to the curry and rice. *Puppadums*, or *pah-pahds*, are savory wafer biscuits, and the chutneys are a sweet and pungent delight.

The varieties of chutney are endless and delicious. The green chutneys are widely favored and are made with freshly ground coriander leaves, onions, salt and green chilies, sometimes with the addition of coconut and lemon juice or tamarind. Mint, date, mango, lemon, mixed fruit and coconut chutney are only a few of the other chutneys made. Fortunately for us, a good prepared chutney is purchasable where Indian foodstuffs are sold.

After the curry and rice come the other vegetable and meat dishes, which are eaten with one of the varieties of plain breads such as *chapaties, pooris* or *parathas*. Then comes the dessert, and finally a bowl of fresh fruit. That is the modern way. But the traditional way of serving the food—with the exception of the sweets-first custom— still has much charm and convenience. It is to have a brass or nickel-plated *thali,* or medium-sized round tray, for each person. On it are arranged three or more shiny bowls filled with various foods. *Chapaties* (or other bread) and rice are placed directly in the *thali*. Now comes the difficult part. Although most townspeople use knives, forks and spoons at home, and although all city restaurants and hotels do supply cutlery, yet it is still customary for a great number of Indian folk to eat with their fingers. This is by no means considered bad manners; it is tradition. The diners sip the juicy foods directly from the small metal bowls and gather up the rest of the food with morsels of crisp bread.

For the convenience of the Western housewife, a compromise plan may be used: Cutlery, by all means; no round trays with small bowls on them, but a large dinner plate at every place; and *all* dishes but desserts presented at the same time for the diner to make his own selection. There should be only one stricture in regard to the serving dishes: It is never correct to pour the curry over the rice before serving or to serve rice as a border to a curry dish. The curry and the rice must always be served in separate dishes, so that those who prefer to eat them separately may do so.

Disconcerting though it may be, the Indian housewife, as a rule, is exceptionally good at *guessing* the amounts of various ingredients to be used in any recipe; she uses weights and measures only when an extra-large quantity of food is to be prepared. I would say that this is a prime example of how the finest of Oriental chefs seem to cook by instinct—or, at least, with the experience born of long practice—rather than by rote. Many of them simply do not measure; least of all do they describe their recipes in terms of the precise measurements to which cookbook readers are accustomed. To make things even more difficult for the Western housewife, when Indian chefs *do* attempt to pass on their culinary secrets in what I might call measured terms, we discover that these terms have little relationship to those used in the American kitchen. I have tried to translate them as closely as possible into Western measures, but you may in some cases have to vary measurements slightly in accordance with your own preference. This will almost certainly be true in the cases of butter and seasonings; here, even more than usually, your own cooking judgment must be your final guide.

74

INDIA

BASICS

GHEE

Ghee, which is clarified butter, is widely used in Indian cooking and can be made the following way. (Margarine can be prepared the same way.) Place the desired amount of butter in a saucepan and simmer slightly less than 2 hours. Strain through a fine cloth (cheesecloth) and store in glass jars. It will keep very well for quite a long time. It often crystallizes as it stands but this does not harm it.

GARAM-MASALA

A blend of several spices used in a great many recipes. This can be prepared beforehand and kept in a jar until needed.

24 *large cardamoms*
 2 *ounces coriander seeds*
 2 *ounces black peppercorns*

1½ *ounces caraway seeds*
 ½ *ounce whole cloves*
 ½ *ounce ground cinnamon*

Remove the skin from the cardamoms. Add to the coriander seeds, peppercorns, caraway seeds and cloves. Place in a coffee grinder and grind until fine but not powdery. Add the ground cinnamon and mix in thoroughly. Store in an airtight jar.

HERBS

Herbs are used in many dishes, and the amount used in the recipes should depend on individual taste. If you are using dried herbs instead of fresh herbs, the amount should be greatly reduced.

RICE

Rice, one of the basic foods in India, is served in various forms. The two most popular preparations are *pulao* and *biryani*. In *pulao*, the rice is fried in *ghee* (clarified butter) or vegetable oil and cooked in hot water or a meat stock. A bouquet of cardamom, bay leaves and cinnamon is added. Usually, the name of a particular *pulao* is derived from the meat, vegetable, fruit and so forth added to it. Thus you have mixed vegetable *pulao*, meat *pulao*, egg *pulao* and so on. A well-prepared *pulao* is never greasy or too highly seasoned.

Biryani is a delicious richer preparation. The rice is partially cooked; a curry is then prepared with vegetables, meat or chicken and cooked with butter or *ghee* and spices. The rice and the curry mixture are placed in a pan in layers. Milk and fat are sprinkled over it. For a richer *biryani*, the amount of *ghee* can be increased. An airtight lid is placed on the pan. The *biryani* is then baked for 20 minutes to a half hour. When done it is served with crisp-fried onions, sliced boiled eggs and fried nuts.

PULAO
Fried Rice

2 medium onions	½ teaspoon saffron steeped in
½ pound ghee or butter	¼ cup warm water
2 cloves garlic, chopped	(optional)
2 sticks cinnamon	1½ teaspoons salt
12 whole cardamoms	Kettle of boiling water
½ teaspoon whole allspice	4 ounces raisins
2 cups rice	2 ounces blanched almonds, lightly fried in butter

Slice the onions and put in the hot ghee in a deep pan with a tight-fitting lid. Add the garlic and the spices. Fry until the onions are soft but not brown. Add the rice and, mixing it lightly, continue to fry over low heat for 5 minutes. Add the saffron and water and salt. Add a sufficient amount of boiling water to stand about 2 inches above the rice. Cover the pan and cook over very low heat until all the water has been absorbed and the rice is thoroughly cooked (each grain separate). Remove from heat. Before serving, lightly mix in the raisins and almonds. Serve hot.

BHAT
Plain Boiled Rice

2 cups rice
8 cups boiling water

2 teaspoons salt

Add the rice to the boiling water in a large heavy pot with a tight-fitting lid. Add the salt. Stir the rice with a fork to prevent it from sticking to the bottom of the pot. Cover the pot and allow to boil rapidly for approximately 15 minutes. Test a grain of rice with your teeth or a thumbnail to see if it is sufficiently cooked. When the rice is done place it in a colander and pour a cup of cold water over it. This will separate the grains. Allow to drain thoroughly. Put back in pot and allow to steam for a few minutes. Serve hot.

KOFTAS PULAO
Minced Meatballs and Rice

1 pound finely minced beef
1 medium onion, minced
¼ teaspoon chopped garlic
1 teaspoon garam-masala (*see* Basics, p. 75)

Salt to taste
1 egg
1 tablespoon flour
2 tablespoons butter or fat
   Pulao (Fried Rice) (*see* p. 76)

Mix all the ingredients except the butter and pulao together and shape into balls the size of walnuts. Slowly fry in the butter. Prepare the pulao and place the meatballs in it. Cover and cook over low heat until the meatballs are done (about 15 minutes). Serve hot.

MATTAR PULAO
Peas and Rice

2 tablespoons butter
¼-inch stick cinnamon
4 whole cloves
½ teaspoon caraway seeds

1 cup rice
2 teaspoons salt
1 cup fresh peas
3 cups boiling water

Melt the butter in a large saucepan and add the cinnamon, cloves and caraway seeds. Sauté on low heat for 2 or 3 minutes. Now add the rice, salt and peas. Stir the mixture and continue to fry for several more minutes. Add the boiling water, stirring constantly. Cover the pan, turn the heat very low and cook for 45 minutes. Remove from heat. Serve hot.

KHICHRI
Rice and Lentils

1 cup rice
½ cup lentils
4 cups boiling water
1 teaspoon salt
   Pinch of ground coriander
   Ground ginger to taste

3 whole cloves
2 tablespoons garam-masala (see
   Basics, p. 75)
4 tablespoons butter
2 medium onions, chopped

Boil the rice and lentils in the water with the salt and spices. When cooked, set aside to drain. Melt the butter in a saucepan, add the chopped onions and fry until brown. Add the rice and lentils and simmer for 5 minutes. Remove from heat. This dish is good served hot with pickles or yogurt.

YAKHMI PULAO
Rice Pulao with Lamb or Chicken

The Soup
2 pounds lamb cut into very
   small pieces or 3 to 3½
   pounds chicken

3 cups water or enough to cover
   meat or chicken
1 large onion, sliced
1 teaspoon salt

Place all the ingredients in a pot and bring to a boil. Lower the heat and simmer until the meat or chicken is tender. Remove the meat or chicken from the soup. Put the soup in another container until needed. Use the same pot to cook the following:

The Rice
½ cup butter
1 medium onion, sliced
1 teaspoon mixed herbs
   and spices

½ teaspoon salt
½ teaspoon turmeric
4 whole cloves
1 cup rice

Heat the butter and fry the onion until golden brown. Add the spices, salt, turmeric and cloves. Mix well and fry for several minutes. Add the rice and fry for 2 or 3 minutes. Add the soup and cook over medium heat for 20 minutes. Add the meat or chicken, mix and cook gently, covered, over low heat until the chicken or meat and rice are done. If there is not enough soup, boiling water may be added. Remove from heat. Serve hot with vegetable dishes.

MURGHI CHAWAL
Chicken with Rice

1 3-pound chicken, cut up
1 medium onion, sliced
2 cups rice
6 whole cloves
6 whole cardamoms
½ stick cinnamon

½ cup butter
1 teaspoon salt
½ cup raisins
¼ cup slivered blanched
   almonds

Place the chicken in a pot with the onion and just enough water to cover the chicken. Cook until tender. In another pot fry the rice with the spices in the butter for 6 or 7 minutes, stirring constantly. Add the chicken stock and onion to the rice. The liquid should be about 2 inches above the rice. If insufficient, add boiling water. Salt to taste. Continue to slowly simmer over low heat until the rice is cooked and all the liquid has been absorbed. Remove from heat. Before serving add the raisins and almonds. Serve hot. Platter may be garnished with hard-cooked eggs and fried onions.

LAMB OR MUTTON BIRYANI

2 pounds meat, cut small
½ cup yogurt
½ teaspoon saffron
1 tablespoon warm water
1 cup butter
2 large onions, sliced
½ ounce cinnamon
1 ounce green ginger, ground

½ ounce cumin seeds
½ ounce ground cloves
½ ounce cardamom
1 small garlic, minced
3 teaspoons salt
4 cups rice (2 pounds)
5 cups water

Soak the meat in the yogurt in a bowl for 30 minutes. In a cup steep the saffron in the warm water. Melt the butter in a large saucepan and fry the onions until brown. Put in the meat with the yogurt and add all the spices, garlic and salt. Fry the meat until it is a rich brown color. Add the rice to the meat and continue frying. Add the water and stir. Cover and let cook until the rice and meat are done. Add the saffron during the last half hour of cooking. Remove from heat. Serve hot.

MACHHI PULAO
Fish with Rice Pulao

2 tablespoons butter	2 teaspoons salt
1 teaspoon ground turmeric	2 teaspoons lemon juice
2 teaspoons garam-masala (see	1 pound fish filet cut into
Basics, p. 75)	small pieces
1 small bunch fresh parsley,	1 medium onion, chopped
chopped	1 cup rice
½ teaspoon chili powder	3 cups hot water

Put 1 tablespoon of butter in a frying pan and heat. Add the herbs and spices and 1 teaspoon of salt and let crackle in the hot butter for 3 or 4 minutes. Pour in the lemon juice and stir. Turn heat up a little higher and carefully add the pieces of fish to the hot mixture and fry on both sides. Keep spooning the herb-and-spice mixture over the fish until well coated. (Be careful not to break the pieces of fish.) Fry about 5 minutes and remove the fish from the pan.

In another frying pan sauté the onion in the remaining tablespoon of butter. When the onion is soft but not brown, add the remaining salt and the rice. Mix together and continue frying over very low heat for 5 minutes. Add the gravy mixture from the other frying pan and mix thoroughly. Pour in the hot water and bring to a boil. Cover and cook for 25 minutes over very low heat. Stir the rice and top with the pieces of fish. Cover and cook for another 10 minutes. Remove from heat. Serve hot.

CURRIES

This national dish of India has so many variations that it would be impossible to list them all here. Most people are afraid to try curries, thinking of them as too "hot." This is not so. Curry can be made hot, medium or mild. Many people in India do not care for hot foods and their curries are mildly spiced, but still delicious. A properly prepared curry is a subtle and pleasing dish and just hot enough to suit the individual taste. Each particular dish varies with the proportion of spices used. Chili, pepper and salt are cooked with the food and never added after serving.

The Indian homemaker mixes her curry paste from day to day, grinding and pounding the different spices and herbs on a curry stone. However, we can achieve an excellent curry by buying the best quality of genuine Indian curry powder and using it properly.

MURGH SADAH
Chicken Curry

2 tablespoons butter or fat
2 onions, thinly sliced
2 cloves garlic, cut fine
1 teaspoon ground turmeric
2 teaspoons garam-masala (see Basics, p. 75)
½ teaspoon ground ginger

½ teaspoon ground chili (optional)
2 tablespoons chopped fresh parsley
2 teaspoons salt
1 3 to 3½ pound chicken, cut up

Heat the butter in a large saucepan and add the onions and garlic. Sauté for several minutes, then add the herbs, spices and salt. Mix well and fry for a few more minutes. Be very careful not to burn the contents. Now add the pieces of chicken to this curry mixture and fry for 5 minutes. Add a small amount of water to make a rather thick gravy. Cover the pan and slowly simmer until the chicken is done (about 20 minutes). Remove from heat. Serve hot. Very good when served with a rice pulao and vegetables. Also very good with a few drops of lemon juice sprinkled over it.

MURGHI KHASA
Special Chicken Curry

1 3 to 3½ pound chicken, cut up
2 medium onions, finely minced
3 tablespoons vinegar

1½ teaspoons ground turmeric
1 clove garlic, finely minced

Place the chicken in the above ingredients in a bowl to marinate for 2 hours. Get the following ingredients ready.

4 tablespoons butter or fat
1 large onion, minced
6 whole cloves
1 small piece cinnamon
6 whole cardamoms

1 clove garlic, thinly sliced
1 piece of fresh or pickled ginger, sliced
1 teaspoon salt

Place the butter in a large pan, add the onion and sauté until partially done. Add the cloves, cinnamon, cardamoms, garlic, ginger and salt. Mix well and continue to simmer over very low heat for 5 more minutes. Add the chicken with the marinade. Mix lightly and thoroughly. Cover the pan and simmer over very low heat until the chicken is cooked. Remove from heat. Serve hot.

MURGH MASALLAM
Spiced Chicken

1 3- or 4-pound chicken, cut up
  Ground red chili to taste
5 large tomatoes, peeled and
    cut into small pieces
2 medium onions, minced
1 medium garlic, minced
1 teaspoon ground turmeric
1 teaspoon cumin seeds

4 whole cloves
1 small piece cinnamon
1 small piece ginger
2 whole cardamoms
1 teaspoon molasses
  Salt to taste
  Butter

Rub the chicken pieces with the red chili. Put the chicken, tomatoes, onions, garlic and the spices into a heavy saucepan. Add the molasses and salt. Add enough water to cover and dot with a generous amount of butter. Cover with a tight-fitting lid and cook over low heat until tender. Uncover, turn heat slightly higher and cook for a few more minutes. Remove from heat. Serve hot.

TANDOORI MURGH
Barbecued Spiced Chicken

3 1 to 1½ pound fryers
2 cups plain yogurt
2 teaspoons chili powder
6 cloves garlic
1 teaspoon black pepper
½ teaspoon ground hot
    red pepper
6 tablespoons vinegar
1 tablespoon minced papaya
2 teaspoons ground ginger

2 teaspoons ground coriander
2 teaspoons ground cumin seed
3 green cardamoms, powdered
3 cooking cardamoms, powdered
  Juice of 1 lime
3 teaspoons salt
½ cup melted butter or more
  Thin lemon slices
  Coriander leaves

With a sharp knife cut several slits on the breasts and legs of the chickens being careful not to separate any of the joints. (Chickens may be split or cut in quarters if preferred.) In a large bowl, mix all the other ingredients except the butter, lemon slices and coriander leaves. Marinate the chickens in this mixture for 6 or 7 hours or overnight in the refrigerator. Drain, brush with the melted butter and broil over charcoal. Brush with more butter from time to time. Remove from grill. Serve hot, garnished with thin lemon slices and coriander leaves.

BUDHUK KORMA
Duck Korma

1 4 to 5 pound duck, cut up	1 teaspoon ground turmeric
1 cup yogurt	⅛ teaspoon chili powder
½ teaspoon ground cumin seeds	¼ teaspoon black pepper
1 tablespoon ground coriander	

Place the duck in a bowl with the above ingredients and let stand for 3 hours to marinate. When ready to proceed, prepare the following:

2 tablespoons of butter or fat	3 cardamoms
1 medium onion, sliced	1 small piece of cinnamon
1 clove garlic, sliced	Lemon juice to taste
3 cloves	Salt to taste

Melt the butter in a large pot and sauté the onion, garlic and spices. Add the duck and the marinade and stir well. Cook slowly over low heat with the pot covered until the duck is cooked. Add the lemon juice and salt to taste. Remove from heat. Serve hot.

MADRAS EGG CURRY

2 tablespoons chopped onions	2 medium ripe tomatoes,
1 clove garlic, sliced very thin	chopped fine, or
4 tablespoons butter or fat	1 teaspoon tomato paste
1 tablespoon curry powder	Water
	Salt to taste
	Lemon juice to taste
	6 hard-cooked eggs, whole

In a saucepan lightly sauté the onions and garlic in the butter for 3 or 4 minutes. Add the curry powder, mix well and continue to sauté for 3 more minutes. Add the tomatoes and enough water to make a rather thick gravy. Add the salt and lemon juice to taste and simmer for 10 minutes. Now add the eggs and heat thoroughly. Remove from heat. Serve hot.

EGG CURRY WITH EGGPLANT

Make Madras egg curry (*see recipe p. 83*). Slice 1 small, peeled egg-plant into ¼ inch slices and partially cook in the gravy before the eggs are added. Then cook all together. Remove from heat. Serve hot.

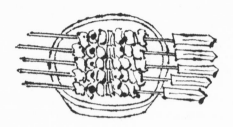

KABOBS

SEEKH KABOBS KHASA

1 pound ground lamb or beef round	½ teaspoon pepper
	½ teaspoon chili powder
Small piece ginger, minced	1 tablespoon split-pea flour
1 medium onion, minced	(see Glossary)
2 tablespoons chopped coriander leaves or parsley	2 teaspoons lemon juice
	3 cloves garlic, chopped fine
1 teaspoon salt	6 small skewers
½ teaspoon cinnamon	2 tablespoons yogurt
½ teaspoon ground cloves	

Combine the meat with the minced ginger, onion and herbs in a bowl. Mix in the salt, spices, chili powder, flour, lemon juice and garlic. Knead for several minutes and then roll out on a board until a smooth dough is formed. Divide into six portions and wrap around each skewer like a small frankfurter. Brush the yogurt generously over them like a paste, and then roast them. Keep turning almost constantly until they are well roasted on all sides. Remove from skewers and serve hot with curry and a fresh mint chutney.

SHAMI KABOBS

The Patties

2 teaspoons butter
1 medium onion, minced
1 clove garlic, chopped fine
½ teaspoon chili powder
   (optional)
  Small piece ginger
1 tablespoon chopped fresh mint
1 heaping teaspoon salt
½ teaspoon turmeric

2 tomatoes, sliced
1 pound lean lamb or beef,
   ground
1 tablespoon split peas
¼ cup warm water
2 teaspoons lemon juice
1 teaspoon garam-masala
  Lemon wedges or chutney

In a saucepan sauté lightly in the butter the onion, garlic flakes, chili powder, ginger and the herbs. Add the salt and turmeric and mix in; then add the tomatoes. Fry for several minutes and then add the meat and split peas. Continue frying for 5 minutes. Add the water and bring to a boil. Then lower the heat and cook for 40 to 50 minutes. Add the lemon juice and the garam-masala, mix and then mash the meat well. Remove from heat, let cool and then thoroughly mash again. Shape into patties of convenient size.

The Batter

2 tablespoons split-pea flour
   (see Glossary)
3 tablespoons milk

⅛ teaspoon salt
  Small amount of oil for frying

Mix the split-pea flour with the milk. Add the salt and beat until smooth. Heat the oil in a frying pan. Coat each patty thoroughly in the batter and fry over medium heat until brown and crisp. Drain on a paper towel. Serve hot with lemon wedges or a bowl of chutney.

MADRAS CURRY KABOB

1 *pound lean beef or lamb,
  cut into 1-inch pieces*
4 *small skewers*
8 *small button onions*
8 *thin slices of green ginger*
4 *tablespoons butter or fat*
2 *tablespoons minced onions*

3 *fresh or pickled chilies, chopped*
2 *cloves garlic, thinly sliced*
1 *tablespoon curry powder*
2 *teaspoons tomato paste*
  Beef stock or water
  Salt to taste
  Lemon juice to taste

Place the beef on the skewers alternately with the button onions and the slices of ginger. Pack tightly together. Melt the butter in a saucepan and gently sauté the onions, chilies and garlic. Add the curry powder, mix and simmer for a couple of minutes. Mix in the tomato paste. Gradually add enough beef stock to make a rather thick gravy. Add salt to taste and lemon juice if desired. Place the full skewers in the gravy, cover the pan and simmer slowly until the meat is tender. Remove from heat and remove meat from skewers. Serve hot.

VINDALOOS

For people who prefer a hot curry, *vindaloos* are ideal. They are made with more chilies than are the regular curries and the liquid is vinegar. The meats used are more on the fatty side: pork, fatty beef, duck, etc. To save a lot of time and work, some of these recipes call for a dry *vindaloo* mixture that is available and is excellent when mixed into a paste with vinegar.

LAMB VINDALOO

¼ *ounce ginger*
1 *teaspoon turmeric*
½ *ounce mustard seeds*
½ *teaspoon chili powder*
4 *tablespoons vinegar*
2 *pounds lamb, cut into
  small pieces*

¾ *cup butter or fat*
3 *cloves garlic, minced*
1 *cup chicken stock or broth*
1½ *pounds whole, peeled potatoes*
2 *medium tomatoes, chopped*

Grind the spices together in a bowl and mix in half of the vinegar. Add the meat, mix and let stand for an hour. Melt the butter in a large saucepan and fry the meat with the garlic. Add the remaining vinegar and a little stock. Simmer slowly over low heat. When the meat is about half cooked, add the potatoes and tomatoes and continue cooking until all the ingredients are tender. Remove from heat. Serve hot.

BEEF VINDALOO

1 teaspoon finely chopped garlic
3 level tablespoons finely chopped
    onions
2 whole red chilies or
    1 teaspoon ground red chili
4 tablespoons ghee or butter
    Vinegar—enough to make a
    paste

2 tablespoons vindaloo
    mixture
1½ pounds fatty beef, cut into
    serving pieces
Salt to taste
Water

In a large pan sauté the garlic, onions and chilies in the ghee for 3 or 4 minutes. (If using dry red chilies, cut in half and remove seeds before sautéing.) Add the vinegar to the vindaloo mixture to make a paste. Add the paste to the ingredients in the pan and mix well. Continue cooking over low heat for 5 more minutes. Add the beef, salt and a very small amount of water. Mix all the ingredients thoroughly. Cover the pan with a tight lid and simmer until the beef is tender. Remove from heat. Serve hot.

PORK VINDALOO

3 tablespoons chopped onions
½ teaspoon chopped garlic
½ cup butter or fat

3 tablespoons vindaloo mixture
    (see Glossary)
2 pounds pork, cut up
1 teaspoon salt

In a large pan sauté the onions and garlic in the butter until the onions are golden. Add the vindaloo mixture (which has been made into a paste with vinegar). Mix very well and cook over very low heat for about 3 minutes. Watch carefully because this burns very easily. Add the pork and salt, mix thoroughly. Cover the pan and cook over low heat until the pork is tender. If necessary, add a small amount of water to make a thick gravy. This dish requires constant watching to prevent burning. Remove from heat. Serve hot.

CHICKEN VINDALOO

1 pound unpeeled whole small
   potatoes
3 cloves garlic
3 medium onions
2 tablespoons chopped
   fresh herbs
2 teaspoons garam-masala
½ teaspoon ground ginger

½ teaspoon chili powder
2 teaspoons salt
2 tablespoons vinegar
1 2 to 3 pound chicken
½ cup butter or fat
½ teaspoon ground turmeric
3 or 4 medium tomatoes, sliced
2 cups hot water

Boil the unpeeled potatoes until half done. Cool, peel, cut in half and set aside. Chop the garlic, onions and herbs together, put them in a bowl and add the garam-masala, ginger, chili powder, salt and vinegar. Mix well. Cut the chicken into small pieces, removing most of the bones, and put in another bowl. Add half of the seasoning mixture to the chicken and let marinate for 2 hours in the refrigerator. In a large saucepan, fry the remainder of the seasoning mixture in the butter. Add the turmeric and tomatoes and fry for a few miuntes. Add the chicken, mix well and fry for 10 minutes. Now add the hot water and bring to a boil. Cover the pan, lower the heat and cook until the chicken is almost tender. Add the potatoes and continue cooking until all is tender. If needed, add a little more hot water. Remove from heat. Serve hot.

DUCK VINDALOO

2 medium onions, chopped
1 clove garlic, sliced thin
¼ cup butter or fat
3 tablespoons vindaloo mixture
   (see Glossary)

2 fresh red chilies, seeds removed,
   or 1 teaspoon ground red chili
1 4 to 5 pound duck, cut up
   Salt to taste

In a large skillet fry the onions and garlic in the butter until they are a golden brown. Add the vindaloo mixture (made into a paste with vinegar) and the chilies and mix well. Cook over low heat for 5 minutes. Add the duck, salt and a small amount of water, stir thoroughly. Cover and simmer until the duck is completely done. Remove from heat. Serve hot.

FISH

Indians prepare fish in many interesting ways. Fried fish is a great favorite as are curried fish dishes. Many kinds of fish can be used: mackerel, haddock, halibut, eels, cod, fresh herring and so forth. A hot fish curry is made with generous amounts of chilies and onions and is cooked in oil. The milder curries are usually made with coconut milk.

FISH CURRY

3 *cloves garlic, minced*
2 *medium onions, minced*
2 *tablespoons snipped parsley*
3 *tablespoons olive oil or fat*
2 *teaspoons salt*
1 *teaspoon ground turmeric*
2 *teaspoons dry coconut*

1 *teaspoon garam-masala*
½ *teaspoon chili powder*
2 *medium tomatoes or 1 small*
    can tomato paste
1 *tablespoon lemon juice*
1 *pound fish filet, cut into*
    bite-size pieces

In a saucepan gently sauté the minced garlic, onions and parsley in the olive oil. Add the salt, turmeric, coconut, garam-masala and chili powder. Mix thoroughly and fry for several minutes. Slice the tomatoes (or use tomato paste) and add to the pan. Sauté slowly until tender. When soft, mash the tomatoes in the gravy and then add the lemon juice. Continue cooking over medium heat for 5 more minutes, then add the fish. Very carefully mix and cover the fish with the gravy. Bring to a boil, then cover the saucepan and simmer for 10 minutes. Don't overcook the fish. Remove from heat. Serve hot. This is excellent with rice.

EEL CURRY

2 medium onions
1 clove garlic
4 tablespoons butter or fat
1 tablespoon curry powder
2 medium tomatoes, peeled and
    chopped, or 2 teaspoons
    tomato paste

Water
Salt to taste
2 1-pound eels, cut into 2-inch
    pieces
Lemon juice, if desired

Slice the onions and garlic very thin and fry in a saucepan in the butter for 3 minutes, then add the curry powder. Continue to cook for 3 more minutes over low heat, mixing well. Slowly add the tomatoes and enough water to make a thick gravy. Add salt to taste. Add the eels and simmer gently, uncovered, until the eels are cooked. Do not mix but shake the pan every once in a while. If desired, a little lemon juice may be added. Remove from heat. Serve hot.

FRIED FISH

2 pounds fish filets
1 teaspoon chili powder
    Pinch of ground turmeric

1 ounce each of garlic, ginger and
    coriander leaves, ground up
    together
    Oil or butter for frying
1 lemon

Wash and score the fish. Mix all the spices and rub over the fish. Fry in the oil until a light golden brown. Remove and drain on a paper towel. Squeeze lemon over fish and serve hot.

VEGETABLES

ALOO MATTAR
Peas and Potatoes

1 pound potatoes, uncooked
1 pound fresh peas, uncooked
1 cup butter
¼ ounce ground turmeric
½ ounce ground coriander
¼ ounce chili powder

1/16 ounce powdered ginger
1/16 ounce ground cumin
    Salt to taste
1 pound tomatoes
1 cup plain yogurt

90

Peel and cut the potatoes into small pieces. Shell the peas. Melt a small amount of the butter in a large pan and lightly fry the potatoes and peas, then remove them from the butter. Add the spices and salt to the butter and fry for a few minutes. Cut the tomatoes into small pieces and add to the butter together with the potatoes and the peas. When the ingredients are soft, add the yogurt, which has been beaten first. Keep hot until ready to serve.

CARROTS AND PEAS

6 *scallions, thinly sliced*	1 *teaspoon ground turmeric*
2 *teaspoons butter*	½ *teaspoon chili powder*
2 *tablespoons chopped herbs*	½ *pound carrots*
1 *teaspoon garam-masala*	1 *cup fresh peas, shelled*
2 *teaspoons salt*	2 *teaspoons lemon juice*

In a saucepan sauté the scallions in the butter with the herbs for several minutes. Add the garam-masala, salt, turmeric and the chili powder. Leaving these ingredients to simmer, scrape the carrots, cut into small pieces and add to the saucepan. Fry lightly for several minutes, then cover the pan and continue cooking over medium heat for another 15 minutes. Add the peas, mix thoroughly and continue cooking in the covered pan over very low heat until the carrots and peas are dry and tender. About 5 minutes before removing from the heat, add the lemon juice. Serve hot with other curried dishes.

CABBAGE CURRY

2 *pounds firm cabbage*	½ *teaspoon chili powder*
1 *tablespoon butter*	*(optional)*
1 *medium onion, chopped*	2 *teaspoons salt*
1 *teaspoon ground turmeric*	1 *teaspoon garam-masala*

Shred the cabbage into medium-sized pieces. Wash well and set aside to drain. In a large heavy frying pan melt the butter and fry the onion. Add the turmeric, chili powder and salt. Mix well and add the cabbage to the frying pan without stirring; the cabbage will shrink during cooking. Stir gently with a fork to prevent crushing. Cook for 15 minutes over medium heat. When excess fluid is absorbed, cover the frying pan and continue to cook over low heat until the cabbage is tender, then remove the cover and quickly fry until the curry is rather dry. Add the garam-masala and mix in well. When finished the curry should be very dry and not mushy. Remove from heat. Serve hot.

91

EGGPLANT

2 *large eggplants*	½ *pound tomatoes*
½ *cup butter*	2 *tablespoons chopped coriander*
2 *medium onions, chopped fine*	*leaves or parsley*
Small piece ginger, chopped	1 *cup yogurt, beaten*
1 *teaspoon garam-masala*	¼ *pound fresh peas, cooked*
½ *teaspoon ground turmeric*	*Hard-cooked eggs, to be*
Salt to taste	*used as garnish*
½ *teaspoon chili powder*	

Boil the eggplants and carefully remove the skins. (The whole eggplant should be soft before removing the skin.) Mash well and set aside. Melt the butter in a saucepan over low heat, add the onions and ginger and fry gently until golden brown. Add the garam-masala, turmeric, salt and chili powder and mix well. Cut the tomatoes into small pieces and add to the pan with the chopped fresh herbs. Continue frying until the mixture is dry, then add the eggplant and the yogurt and cook over low heat until almost dry and fairly solid. Keep stirring the mixture while cooking. Add the cooked peas and serve piping hot. Garnish with the hard-cooked eggs. Very good when served with meat dishes or other vegetables.

MUSHROOM CURRY

1 *pound mushrooms*	2 *teaspoons salt*
6 *small whole potatoes*	1 *teaspoon ground turmeric*
1 *tablespoon butter*	*Small amount chili powder,*
2 *medium onions, chopped*	*if desired*
4 *teaspoons fresh snipped chives*	2 *large tomatoes, sliced*
or basil	1 *tablespoon lemon juice*
Small piece ginger, chopped	1 *teaspoon garam-masala*

Rinse the mushrooms in cold water, drain well and cut brown part off the bottom of the stems. Cut mushrooms into halves or, if large, into quarters. Peel the potatoes. Melt the butter in a saucepan and fry the onions, herbs and ginger for about 5 minutes. Add the salt, turmeric and chili powder. Fry for 2 more minutes, then add the sliced tomatoes, mushrooms and whole potatoes. Mix thoroughly and cook for 30 minutes over medium heat. If you want liquid, cook covered; if not, cook uncovered. Add the lemon juice and the garam-masala and simmer gently for 10 minutes. Remove from heat. Serve hot.

DRY CURRIED CAULIFLOWER

1 *medium head cauliflower*
5 *small potatoes*
2 *tablespoons butter*
1 *small onion, sliced*
¼ *ounce ground ginger*

1½ *teaspoons ground turmeric*
2 *teaspoons salt*
½ *teaspoon chili powder*
1 *teaspoon garam-masala*

Slice the cauliflower into thin slices about 2 or 3 inches long. (Keep some of the stalk with the flower.) Wash and set aside to drain. Peel and wash the potatoes and cut into small pieces. Using a deep frying pan, melt the butter and fry the onion and the ginger, then add the turmeric and mix in. Place the slices of cauliflower and the potatoes in the frying pan and fry for 10 minutes. Add the salt and chili powder. Cover the pan and cook over low heat until tender, stirring often and gently with a fork to prevent crushing. When tender remove the cover and cook until excess fluid is gone, then add the garam-masala and cook for 5 more minutes. Remove from heat. Serve hot. This dish is delicious with all curried recipes.

BANANA CURRY

1½ *pounds bananas, not*
     quite ripe
2 *teaspoons butter*
½ *teaspoon ground turmeric*
½ *teaspoon caraway seeds*
     (optional)

1 *teaspoon salt*
½ *teaspoon chili powder*
     (optional)
½ *teaspoon garam-masala*
1 *tablespoon milk*
1 *tablespoon lemon juice*

Peel the bananas and cut them into pieces about an inch long. In a heavy frying pan melt the butter, add the turmeric and caraway seeds and fry for a few minutes. Add the pieces of banana, the salt and chili powder and simmer slowly for 5 to 8 minutes. Then add the garam-masala and milk. Stir carefully to avoid crushing the bananas. Add the lemon juice and simmer for about 10 more minutes or until all the excess liquid is gone. The bananas should be tender but not mashed or broken. Remove from heat. Serve hot with curried vegetables or meat dishes.

RAITA
Whipped Yogurt

Raita is a dish made with whipped, seasoned yogurt mixed with sliced vegetables, either raw or parboiled. Yogurt is widely used and very popular in India, and it is served in many ways. One of the favorite yogurt dishes is *raita*. The yogurt is beaten, then salt and pepper, green chilies, chopped coriander leaves and other spices are added to taste. To this mixture is added sliced tomatoes or diced potatoes or shredded cucumbers. *Raita* is served cold and is garnished with paprika and snipped parsley.

BREADS

In the north, wheat and wheat products are the staple food. The *chapati*, or *phulka*, is a wheat bread made of unfermented dough. It is round and very thin and looks like a tortilla. This bread is usually eaten with lentils, cooked vegetables and meat. A very popular form of *chapati* is called *nan*, which is a dough that is slightly leavened, flattened out and baked dry. It goes very well with *tandoori* recipes such as spiced barbecued chicken. Another variation is the *paratha*, which is fried shallow and can be served plain or stuffed with vegetables. In the south, rice flour generally is used to make the breads.

CHAPATI

Chapaties can be made with whole wheat flour or half white flour and half whole wheat flour with excellent results.

1½ cups whole wheat flour	½ cup butter
2 cups white flour	Cold water
1 teaspoon salt	

Sift the flours and salt together into a bowl. Add the butter and, using your hands, rub it into the flour. Add enough cold water to form the dough. Knead well by hand for several minutes. Cover and let stand for 1 hour. Again knead well, using a little cold water if necessary to work the dough. Divide the dough into small balls the size of a walnut and roll out each ball into a thin round pancake shape. Cook on a hot greased griddle until the chapati is slightly brown but not hard. Turn and cook the other side. Now turn again and press down the sides of the chapati, which will make it puff up. Serve hot, with or without butter.

A sweet chapati can be made by using this same recipe. Dissolve 6 tablespoons of brown sugar in a small amount of water and add to the dough before kneading.

PARATHA

3 cups whole wheat flour	¼ cup butter (to rub into flour)
½ teaspoon salt	Water
	½ cup butter

Prepare the flour, salt and the ¼ cup butter the same as for Chapati (see recipe above). Cover and let stand for 1 hour. Using a little water and a little of the ½ cup of butter, knead well until quite soft. Break off pieces of dough one at a time. Roll each piece of dough into a disc, using a little flour if needed. The dough should not be rolled out too thin (no less than ¼ inch). Brush melted butter over it, fold it in half and again apply butter. Fold again into a triangle or a round shape. Then roll it out again, still fairly thick, and fry on a hot griddle, using PLENTY of butter on both sides, until a golden brown. Serve hot.

STUFFED PARATHAS WITH POTATO FILLING

4 medium potatoes	1 teaspoon garam-masala
2 teaspoons butter	2 teaspoons salt
1 medium onion, minced	½ teaspoon chili powder
Small piece chopped ginger	2 teaspoons lemon juice
2 tablespoons chopped	Parathas (see recipe above)
fresh herbs	Melted butter

Boil the potatoes; when cool, peel and mash them. Melt the butter in a frying pan and add the onion, ginger and herbs and sauté for a few minutes. Add the garam-masala, salt, chili powder and the lemon juice. Now add the mashed potatoes, mix well and fry for 3 minutes. Remove from heat and set aside to cool.

Prepare the parathas. Spread some melted butter on a paratha, place a spoonful of the seasoned potato in the center and cover with another paratha. Pressing the edges together, seal all around. Fry on a hot, greased griddle for 1 minute, then add butter around the edges and fry, turning, until both sides are crisp and brown. Serve hot. Different seasoned stuffings may be used, such as peas, cauliflower, raw grated radish, cabbage or lentils.

POORI
A Form of Deep-Fried Round Wheat Bread

1½ cups whole wheat flour
2 cups self-rising flour
   Salt to taste

2 tablespoons butter or
   shortening
Warm water
Oil for deep frying

Sift the flours and salt together into a bowl and mix in the butter. Add enough warm water to make a firm dough. Knead and set aside, covered, for a half hour. Knead well, shape into balls and roll out to a thin round shape, 6 to 8 inches in diameter. Heat the oil and fry each round separately and quickly, turning, until well done on both sides and a light-brown color. They should puff up. Drain well on a paper towel and serve hot.

STUFFED POORI
Cauliflower Filling

   Poori (see recipe above)
2 cups finely chopped cauliflower
2 teaspoons salt
¼ teaspoon ground cloves
¼ teaspoon ground cinnamon
¼ teaspoon ground cardamom
¼ teaspoon pepper

½ teaspoon ground cumin
¼ ounce grated ginger, dried or
   fresh
½ teaspoon ground chili
   (if desired)

Prepare the poori dough as in the recipe above, rolling them out smaller and a little thicker.

Chop the flowerets and the tender part of the stalks of the cauliflower. Mix the remaining ingredients in a bowl with the chopped cauliflower. Put a little stuffing between each two pooris and seal the edges. Fry as regular pooris. Pooris may be stuffed with the same ingredients as parathas.

LOOCHI, OR LUCHCHI

The Bengal variety of poori, or fried bread.

1 cup white flour
1 teaspoon salt
1 tablespoon butter

6 tablespoons
   warm water
Oil for deep frying

Sift the flour and salt together into a bowl. Add the butter and mix it in. Add the warm water and make a firm dough. Knead well and pound for several minutes. Now divide the dough into 6 pieces and shape into balls. Using a little flour, roll each ball out into a thin round pancake shape. Deep fry each one separately and quickly in the hot fat. Drain thoroughly on a paper towel. May be served either warm or cold.

CHUTNEYS

In India the chutneys, a delightful assortment of pickled and fresh condiments, are an essential part of most meals. Those Westerners who are familiar only with mango chutney would be amazed at the number and variety of chutneys prepared in India. Hot and mild, sharp and sweet, chutneys are prepared to suit every palate. However, in India they are often made hot with chilies and are used rather sparingly. They are served with rice and curry dishes. Indians use a curry stone to grind chutneys; the American cook can use a regular mortar and pestle (*see Glossary*).

FRESH MINT CHUTNEY

1 bunch mint leaves	Minced garlic
1 sprig coriander leaves	Ground ginger
Juice of ½ lemon	Fresh green chilies } to taste
Pinch of sugar	Salt

Wash the mint and coriander leaves. Grind until they form a fine paste. Add the lemon juice and the seasonings to taste. Store in a jar in a cool place. Serve cold.

CORIANDER CHUTNEY

1 small bunch fresh coriander leaves	Salt to taste
	2 ounces dried coconut
¼ ounce fresh green chilies	1/16 ounce garlic
⅛ ounce fresh ginger root	Pinch of sugar
	Juice of ½ lemon

Wash the coriander leaves and set aside to drain. Wash the green chilies and ginger and drain. Grind all the ingredients except the lemon juice until rather soft. Add the lemon juice. Store in a jar. Serve cold.

DATE CHUTNEY

1 pound dates
1 ounce dried green chilies
½ ounce green ginger
¼ ounce garlic

1 cup vinegar
½ cup sugar
½ teaspoon salt

Pit the dates and then grind them with the chilies, ginger, garlic and some of the vinegar. With the remainder of the vinegar and the sugar make a sirup. Add the ground ingredients and the salt and cook in a saucepan over low heat until the mixture is thick. Remove from heat, allow to cool and store in a jar. Serve cold.

TOMATO CHUTNEY

1 ounce dried green chilies
1 small piece green ginger
2 cloves garlic
½ cup vinegar

1 pound ripe tomatoes
2 cups sugar
½ teaspoon salt

Grind the chilies, ginger and garlic together. Add some of the vinegar and mix well. Scald the tomatoes and remove the skins. Slice the tomatoes, put in a saucepan, add the rest of the vinegar and boil until the tomatoes are soft. Add the ground ingredients, the sugar and salt. Boil gently until the mixture is of the desired consistency. Allow to cool and store in a jar. Serve cold.

GOOSEBERRY CHUTNEY

1½ pounds firm fresh
    gooseberries
  2 ounces sweet preserved ginger
 12 cloves garlic
  2 cups sugar
1½ teaspoons chili powder

2 teaspoons garam-masala
2 teaspoons salt
1 teaspoon caraway seeds
    (optional)
1 cup malt vinegar

Wash and drain the gooseberries. Mince the ginger and garlic very fine. Place the gooseberries in a large saucepan, add the ginger and garlic, sugar, chili powder, garam-masala, salt and caraway seeds. Then add the vinegar, bring to a boil and continue to boil over low heat for 20 to 30 minutes. Using a wooden spoon, stir often to prevent sticking to the

98

bottom of the pan. Remove the chutney from the heat before it gets too thick; it thickens as it cools. After it has thoroughly cooled, store in a jar. Serve cold.

MIXED FRUIT CHUTNEY

½ *pound cooking plums*
½ *pound cooking apples*
½ *pound pears or apricots*
12 *cloves garlic*
¼ *ounce fresh ginger root*
2 *teaspoons garam-masala*

1 *teaspoon caraway seeds*
  (optional)
2 *teaspoons salt*
2 *tablespoons raisins*
1½ *teaspoons chili powder*
½ *cup brown sugar*
8 *ounces vinegar*

Wash, dry and pit the plums and cut into small pieces. Peel and core the apples and the pears and cut into small pieces. Mince the garlic and ginger. Put the cut fruit in a large saucepan with the garlic and ginger. Add the garam-masala, caraway seeds, salt, raisins and chili powder, then the brown sugar and vinegar. Bring to a boil and continue to boil over medium heat for 35 minutes. Using a wooden spoon, stir often and slightly crush the fruit with the spoon. Remove from the heat and set aside to cool thoroughly before placing in jars. Serve cold.

SWEETMEATS

The usual sweet dishes served with an Indian meal are *halwa* and *kheer*. There are many other delicious sweetmeats that are served, but because making them is complicated they are usually bought and not made at home.

Halwa: Halwa can be made with pumpkins, carrots, semolina, lentils or wheat. The ingredients are fried well in butter and then cooked in a sirup. Sometimes *khoa* (dried milk) is added to make a richer *halwa*. Before serving, it is garnished with raisins, chopped almonds, saffron, cardamoms and pistachios.

Kheer: Kheer is made by adding vermicelli, rice, carrots or semolina to a large amount of milk and then letting it simmer until it is rich and thick. When it is removed from the heat sugar and nuts are added.

CARROT KHEER

¼ pound carrots
 3 cups milk
¾ cup sugar
 6 tablespoons butter

2 tablespoons raisins
3 tablespoons chopped mixed nuts
1 teaspoon dried coconut
1 teaspoon grated nutmeg

Wash, scrape and grate the carrots. In a large heavy frying pan bring the milk to a boil. Add the carrots and keep boiling over medium heat, stirring often, until the mixture thickens (about 45 minutes). Add the sugar and, stirring constantly, cook over medium heat for 20 minutes. Add the butter, lower the heat and continue stirring for 15 minutes or until most of the butter has been absorbed. Add the well-washed raisins and mix in thoroughly. Butter a shallow dish and pour the mixture into it. Garnish with the mixed nuts, coconut and nutmeg. Allow to cool, then cut into squares.

CARROT HALWA

1 quart milk
1 pound carrots
1 cup sugar
4 tablespoons raisins

1 tablespoon golden sirup
     (available in gourmet food
     shops)
6 tablespoons butter
1 teaspoon nutmeg
     Slivered almonds for garnish

Bring the milk to a boil in a large heavy saucepan. Wash, scrape and grate the carrots. Place the grated carrots in the boiling milk and cook over medium heat for about 1¼ hours. Stir frequently to prevent sticking to the bottom of the pan. When the mixture is very thick, add the sugar, raisins, sirup and butter. Mix well, then pour into a deep frying pan. Stirring frequently, keep the mixture gently boiling until it begins to solidify. Generously butter a serving dish. The halwa is done when it has the desired thickness and is a deep-orange color. Remove from the heat and spread it on the buttered dish. Garnish with the nutmeg and the almonds. This can be served hot or cold and it will keep for several days.

PUMPKIN HALWA

1 *pound pumpkin (weighed after*
  peel and seeds are removed)
¼ *cup milk (slightly less)*
¾ *cup brown sugar*
4 *tablespoons raisins*

1 *tablespoon slivered almonds*
2 *teaspoons shredded coconut*
6 *tablespoons butter*
½ *teaspoon nutmeg or*
  crushed cardamom seeds

Grate the pumpkin. Using a heavy frying pan bring the milk to a boil. Add the pumpkin to the milk and boil rapidly for 10 minutes, constantly stirring and mashing. The mixture should now be rather dry. Add the brown sugar, which should moisten the pumpkin and milk. Continue boiling rapidly for 8 more minutes. Now add the raisins, almonds and coconut. Mix thoroughly, then add the butter. Cook over medium heat until the halwa is completely dry, about 7 or 8 minutes. Pour onto a buttered serving dish and garnish with the nutmeg. Serve hot or cold.

RICE KHEER

5 *cups milk*
1 *cup rice*
  Sugar to taste
¼ *cup raisins*

¼ *teaspoon saffron*
¼ *teaspoon cardamom seeds*
7 *tablespoons slivered almonds*

In a large heavy saucepan bring the milk to a boil and add the rice. Simmer over low heat for 3 or 4 hours. When the rice is about half done, add the remaining ingredients. Mix and pour into buttered pan. Bake in 350° F. oven for 20 minutes. Remove from heat. Serve hot or cold.

DRINKS

In northern India the favorite hot drink is tea. Spiced tea flavored with mint, lemon grass or crushed cardamom is also popular in Bombay and Kashmir.

Coffee is the favorite drink in southern India, which is well known for its excellent coffee beans. After the coffee has been roasted and ground it is percolated through stainless-steel or brass filters, sometimes overnight for good strength. It is then heated and served with diluted milk in proportion of one tablespoon of coffee to a cup of milk.

One of the cold drinks served is *nimboo pani,* which is lemon juice sweetened with sugar and served with soda or water. Another drink is *lassi,* which is beaten yogurt diluted with water and then either sweetened or salted. In the south the *lassi* is varied with the addition of onions, ginger or chilies called *sambaran* and it is a very popular drink there.

Chilled mango juice is delicious and is a summer favorite. Along the coastal areas, where the coconut groves are, the juice of green coconuts is a great favorite. It is considered a very safe and refreshing drink for travelers.

In the north, flavored milk is served, like almond milk, spiced milk or *keser* milk. Sweet lime juice, tomato juice, mango sherbet, apple juice and orange juice have also become popular drinks. These are served plain or diluted with soda or water.

PAKISTAN

MAIN DISHES

OVEN KABOBS
Pakistani Style

2 *pounds lean ground beef*	¼ *teaspoon ground cloves*
¼ *teaspoon ground cardamom*	¼ *teaspoon black pepper*
¼ *teaspoon ground cumin*	¼ *teaspoon ground ginger*
¼ *teaspoon red pepper*	1 *tablespoon yogurt*
1 *large onion, chopped*	*Salt to taste*

Mix all the ingredients thoroughly in a bowl. Form into small balls or flatten into 3-inch patties about 1 inch thick. Arrange on a cookie sheet and broil about 3 inches from source of heat. Broil 5 minutes on each side. Remove from broiler. Serve hot. Delicious accompanied by pea pulao (*see next recipe*) and a green salad.

PEA PULAO

1 small onion, sliced	4 black peppercorns
2 tablespoons butter or vegetable oil	2 bay leaves
	Salt to taste
4 cardamoms, ground	1½ cups water
¼ teaspoon ground cumin	1 cup rice
1 stick cinnamon	1 package frozen peas

Sauté the onion in the butter together with the spices in a saucepan for 5 minutes. Add the salt, water and rice and cook over medium heat until about half the water has been absorbed by the rice. Add the frozen peas. When most of the water has been absorbed, place in a covered casserole and put in the oven at 300° F. for 15 minutes. Remove from the oven. Serve hot.

MURGH KORMA
Chicken Korma

2 large onions, sliced	1 1-, 2-, or 3-pound chicken, cut into pieces
½ cup butter or oil	
2 teaspoons ground coriander	1 teaspoon salt
¼ teaspoon ground ginger	¼ teaspoon garlic salt
¼ teaspoon ground turmeric	2 tablespoons yogurt
1 bay leaf	About 2 cups water
⅛ teaspoon ground red pepper	

In a large frying pan sauté the onions in the butter until a golden brown. Add the coriander, ginger, turmeric, bay leaf and red pepper and cook briefly over medium heat. Add the chicken and brown it. Add the salt, garlic salt, yogurt and about 2 cups of water. Simmer, covered, until sauce thickens and chicken is tender. More water may be necessary. Remove from heat. May be served hot with rice and eggplant in sour cream (see next recipe).

EGGPLANT IN SOUR CREAM

1 *small eggplant*
3 *tablespoons butter*

¼ *teaspoon chili powder*
Garlic salt to taste
1 *cup sour cream*

Peel and cut the eggplant into ½-inch cubes and sauté in the butter in a frying pan until soft and golden brown. Remove from heat. Add the chili powder and garlic salt to the sour cream and pour over the eggplant. Mix well and chill before serving. This dish goes well with almost any Pakistani entrée.

CHICKEN CURRY

¾ *cup butter*
2 *large onions, sliced*
2 *cardamoms, crushed*
1 *inch cinnamon stick*
1 *tablespoon ground ginger*
2 *tablespoons ground cumin*
1 *teaspoon ground turmeric*

¼ *teaspoon red pepper*
¼ *teaspoon ground coriander*
2 *ripe medium tomatoes, sliced*
1 *frying chicken, 3-3½ pounds,*
  cut into pieces
Salt to taste
½ *cup lukewarm water*

Melt the butter in a large pan; add the onions, cardamom and cinnamon stick. Cook over medium heat until the onions are browned, then add the remaining spices and tomatoes. Stir the mixture constantly until the tomatoes are done. Add the chicken, salt and water. Keep the heat low and cook until the chicken is tender. For additional gravy, add a small amount of water and cook the mixture 2 or 3 minutes longer. Remove from heat. Serve hot.

KIMA
Spiced Ground Beef

1 *large onion, chopped*	½ *teaspoon chili powder*
3 *tablespoons butter*	¼ *teaspoon black pepper*
1 *pound lean ground beef*	¼ *teaspoon red pepper*
2 *fresh medium tomatoes, diced*	½ *teaspoon garlic salt*
1 *tablespoon curry powder*	*Salt to taste*
1 *teaspoon paprika*	1 *can of peas (8½ ounces)*

Sauté the onion in the butter in a heavy skillet until golden brown. Add the beef and tomatoes and cook over moderate heat for 15 minutes. Add the spices, salt and peas as well as the liquid from the can. Cover and simmer for 30 minutes. Remove from heat. Serve hot.

SHRIMP CURRY

3 *pounds shrimp, cooked,*	¾ *cup butter*
shelled and deveined	2 *large onions, sliced*
8 *cloves garlic*	2 *teaspoons curry powder*
3 *small green chilies*	1 *teaspoon ground turmeric*
3 *large ripe tomatoes*	*Salt to taste*

Dry the shrimp thoroughly. Grind the garlic and peppers together. Remove the skin from the tomatoes by dipping them in boiling water and cut them into quarters. Melt the butter in a pan over low heat and add the onions and garlic-and-pepper mixture. When the onions are golden brown, add the curry powder and turmeric (blended with water to form a paste), stirring well. Add the tomatoes with salt to taste and stir steadily over low heat until the water has evaporated. For additional sauce, add ¼ cup warm water before adding the shrimp. Add the shrimp, mixing it in well, and cook over low heat for about 5 minutes. Remove from heat. Serve hot.

LAMB CURRY

½ cup butter
2 large onions, sliced
6 cloves garlic, crushed
1 teaspoon ginger
½ teaspoon cinnamon
¾ teaspoon ground cumin
¼ teaspoon red pepper

¼ teaspoon ground turmeric
1 tablespoon ground coriander
2 pounds lamb, cut into small
   pieces
2 cups water
Salt to taste

Melt the butter in a large pot; add the onions and garlic. Cook over medium heat until the onions are browned, then add the spices and sauté for 3 minutes. Add the lamb and sauté for 10 minutes. Add the water and salt. Keep the heat low and cook until the meat is tender. If needed, add more water. Remove from heat. Serve hot.

SEEKH KEBOB
Pakistani Barbecue

1 slice white bread
2 tablespoons yogurt
1 medium onion, chopped
1 whole green chili
½ teaspoon ground cumin
¼ teaspoon ground cloves

⅛ teaspoon each black pepper
   and red pepper
1 pound ground beef
Salt to taste
4 skewers

Soak the bread in the yogurt in a bowl and make a paste. Combine with the remaining ingredients and let the mixture stand for 1 hour. Mold the mixture into elongated balls, thread on the skewers and broil until brown. Serve hot.

SWEETS

JALEBI
Pastry

2 cups flour
   Water, as needed
½ cup sugar

½ teaspoon saffron
1 drop rose water (see Glossary)
3 tablespoons butter

In a bowl make a thin batter of the flour and water; let it stand overnight, tightly covered. It will ferment. Put the sugar in a saucepan and add just enough water to make a thick sirup. Add the saffron and rose water and heat the sirup slightly. Place the batter in a pastry bag and squeeze into a skillet in which the butter has been melted, forming circles, figure 8s or any other desired design. Fry the pastries thoroughly, remove from the skillet and place in the warm sirup, soaking each pastry through. Remove from the sirup and place on absorbent paper before serving. Serve hot or cold.

CARROT HALWA
Carrot Dessert

1 pound carrots
   Milk
2 tablespoons butter
   Pinch of saffron

2 whole cloves
4 whole cardamoms
1½ cups sugar
24 almonds, slivered

Wash, scrape and grate the carrots. Cook them in milk to cover in a saucepan over low heat until reduced to paste. In another pan, heat the butter, add the saffron, cloves, cardamoms and carrot mixture. Sauté until light brown. Add the sugar and continue stirring until it is well dissolved and the carrots are golden brown. Stir in the almonds. Transfer the mixture to a bowl and chill before serving.

FIRNI
Rice Pudding

1 quart milk
¼ cup long-grained rice
1 cup sugar

¼ cup slivered almonds
1 cup pistachio nuts, sliced fine

Heat the milk in a saucepan to near boiling point and add the rice. Reduce heat, cover and let the mixture simmer slowly, stirring occasionally. When the mixture begins to thicken, add the sugar and mix well. Simmer another minute and remove from heat. When cool, pour into a large bowl, decorating the top with the slivered almonds and pistachios. Chill before serving.

CHINA

Great lasting civilizations always produce great arts, and in China, which has a history stretching back almost five thousand years, the preparation of food is truly a great art. Chinese cuisine is among the finest in the world. Many gourmets consider it superior to that of France. Perhaps this is because the Chinese have a deep respect for food, epitomized in their saying that "it is better for a man to wait for his meal than the meal to wait for the man"—a saying that, incidentally, also reveals a respect for man and his right to enjoy a meal at its peak of flavor, texture and aroma.

The people of China are multitudinous. Neither they nor their country can be described as rich. Because of this, the diet that they have evolved over the course of the centuries is heavily reliant upon such foods as rice, noodles and vegetables, which are inexpensive but filling and lend themselves to countless methods of preparation and varieties of seasoning. Again, because China is not rich, meats such as pork, liver, beef, duck, chicken and lamb may be bought by the ounce, so that even poor households may have at least a mouthful each of several different kinds of meat at any one meal. Thus, small quantities of meat or poultry add zest and variety to a meal, rather than bulk, and produce a meal of several differently flavored main dishes rather than just one main dish containing a little bit of this and a little bit of that all jumbled together. The Chinese cook often achieves very delicate nuances of flavor by using a large variety of ingredients in very small quantities in several harmonious dishes, thus turning an initial disadvantage into an asset. Virtually the only flesh ingredient that appears in more than minimal quantities and tiny pieces is fish. It may even be served whole. Seafood, more than any meat, supplies the protein in the Chinese diet and plays a big part on the Chinese menu.

Animal fats are rarely used, and dairy products are virtually non-existent. Still, meals are generally well balanced, low in calories and high in nutrients. Meats and vegetables are diced, chopped or sliced paper-thin so that long hours over the fire are unnecessary. Food, swiftly cooked, comes right out of the pan to the dining table and then, just as swiftly, onto the diner's plate, so that the precious vitamin content is preserved almost intact. It was long, long ago that the Chinese realized the food values of green vegetables—long before the West made that discovery—and the necessity for maintaining those values through rapid cooking and prompt serving. What appears on the Chinese dinner table, even the humble one, is not only flavorsome but nutritious.

The art of Chinese cookery is a meticulous one, and in some ways it is complex. But there is an essential logic and simplicity about its principles, and it can quite easily be mastered by those with a little patience and a great love for food. Even a beginner can produce authentic dishes without difficulty in an ordinary kitchen, using no more than ordinary skills and ordinary utensils.

"Quick-cooking" is one of the keynotes of the Chinese cuisine. The Chinese style is to take time over the preparation and as little time as possible over the cooking. It is the cook and not the diner who cuts the food; it is he who slices, chops, shreds, minces, dices or crushes the ingredients in the kitchen before cooking, with the twofold advantage of reducing the foods to quick-cooking size and sparing the diner the tedium of cutting up his own food. Nor does the Chinese diner add his own salt, pepper, spices or what he will. The cook does this before serving, in the belief that the seasoning can be truly effective only when added during the cooking process. Only during cooking, according to the cook, does seasoning become properly wedded to the ingredients so that seasoning and ingredients together present a harmonious whole.

This "wedding" of ingredients is another keynote of Chinese cooking. To the Chinese chef, good cooking depends on the relationship between the various ingredients and seasonings rather than on the character of the individual elements—although the latter is by no means to be ignored. Harmony is the central principle, harmony of taste, aroma, color and general appearance. To achieve this, the cook must take care to select the right ingredients, blend them appropriately and use accurate timing in the cooking process. If he ignores any one factor he will not achieve a harmonious whole; he will fail to provide the total experience that the Chinese expect of a meal.

He starts with a selection of fine ingredients. He continues by cutting them into appropriate sizes and shapes for short cooking time and attractive appearance. He cooks them in a special way, in particular combinations that emphasize freshness of flavor, offset richness, brighten blandness. The quick top-of-the-stove cooking method he employs ensures that there is a delicate blending or overlapping of flavors rather than a loss of flavor identities. His object is to retain the original flavor of the main ingredients and enhance it in every possible way, while at the same time retaining and enhancing the textural qualities. Food texture should be appropriately delicate, tender, smooth, soft or crisp; it must never be mushy or rubbery. Meat must always be extremely tender, vegetables crunchy and crisp, poultry juicy to the point of melting. In some dishes it is important for the inside and outside textures to be different. A sweet-and-sour fish, for instance, must be delicately tender inside and crispy crackling on the outside.

To the Chinese, an essential part of harmony in a meal is contrast and variety. Several main dishes are provided to avoid monotony and to pique the appetite; Chinese second helpings need not be a repetition but a fresh new taste. A rich dish may be offset by a light and delicate one, a cold dish balanced with a hot, a tiny ingredient set against a big one, a highly seasoned dish counteracted by a bland dish, a sweet contrasted with a salt, a smooth food followed by a crisp one. No single dish is the featured attraction. All are equally important.

There are several different schools of Chinese cooking. The Cantonese school, which has achieved the greatest popularity among Americans, is characterized by its sweet-and-sour pork, steamed fish, steamed dumplings, chicken velvet, Cantonese lobster and sautéed beef with oyster sauce. It is mostly stir-fried (sautéed) and typifies the quick-cooking method that preserves the succulence, flavor and texture of the meats and vegetables.

Szechuan meals are inclined to be oily, and they are notably peppery; hot pepper is used very freely. What is more, most dishes are liberally seasoned with small red chilies, which are so smolderingly hot that they make ordinary pepper seem bland in comparison. The deep-fried crispy duck is very good though, as is the spiced cabbage with pork. Honan food is somewhat similar, but richer. It, too, is spicy and hot, or sweet and sour, and tends toward exotic dishes. The carp is fine, and the garlic, chives, leeks and scallions so liberally used are no problem for the Western palate, but the regional specialties are unlikely ever to be in great demand outside the Orient. The pride, the delicacy, of Honan cuisine is bear's paw, with elephant's nose running a close second.

The dishes of Hunan are slightly different, although also highly seasoned. Hunan specialties include unusual chicken dishes going by such names as beggar's chicken, paper-wrapped chicken and the like. The Peking, or Mandarin, school, as well known as that of Canton although somewhat less popular in America, concentrates on meat, duck and breads. The most famous dish is the Peking roast duck. Others that are widely known and liked are the spring rolls (egg rolls), fish in sweet-and-sour sauce, Chinese-style pancakes, baked sesame-seed cakes, the steamed breads that take the place of the rice of the South and the "firepot," or chafing dish, concoctions.

The Shanghai food style is salty and is outstanding for fish and shellfish dishes of all kinds and for its noodles. Also popular are the tiny meat-filled dumplings that may be either boiled or fried and then served with sharp mustard and sweet fruit sauce. On the whole the food is rich, and tangy sauces are much used.

The people of Fukien are fond of broths and souplike dishes, crisp spring rolls, seafood and their red fermented bean paste. Much of the cooking in Taiwan is Fukienese, and it is superb.

As if these various styles of cooking did not present enough variety, there is also the Mongolian style—a sort of self-service barbecue in which excellent meat is the essential ingredient.

All these regional differences make for infinite variety in the Chinese cuisine, so that there really is something for every taste. It is impossible to say how many different dishes there are. Some authorities say four thousand and some say fourteen thousand. But whatever the figure, there is no doubt that Chinese food offers plenty of choice.

The Chinese say that there are seven items essential to housekeeping: oil, soy sauce, vinegar, fuel, rice, salt and tea. To these important items the gourmet chef would add: young garlic, fresh ginger root, scallions, leeks and chives; cooking wines (used in small quantities for many dishes but in fairly liberal amounts for such specialties as drunken chicken or duck); sugar, cornstarch and monosodium glutamate; peppers, fermented black beans, sesame, anise, coriander and the "five-spice powder" that consists of aniseed, clove, cinnamon bark, fennel and Szechuan pepper; Chinese parsley, or fresh coriander; water chestnuts, dried Chinese mushrooms, bamboo shoots, snow peas, *bok choy* (a kind of cabbage) and celery cabbage; oyster sauce and *hoisin* sauce, the latter a sort of Chinese ketchup.

Stir-frying, which is similar to the sauté cooking of the West, is the most characteristic method of Chinese cooking. The fire must be very hot, and the oil (preferably peanut oil) must be sufficient to coat the food, but not so much that the food becomes fat-saturated or heavy with grease. The minimum amount of oil for effective cooking will permit all foods to retain their essential flavor and freshness. Pork, beef, lamb, white-meat poultry, shelled seafood and fresh young vegetables are the favored ingredients for stir-frying. All food materials must be cut into bite-sized pieces for rapid cooking. Meats should be cut against the grain, crisp leafy vegetables and carrots should be cut on the diagonal, and such vegetables as onions and mushrooms should be cut straight. For very rapid cooking, vegetables should be shredded. All food should be stirred briskly throughout the cooking period—which is only a matter of a few minutes, and in fact only a minute or two for some vegetables.

Other cooking methods used by Chinese cooks—shallow frying, deep frying, clear simmering, braising, steaming, red stewing, roasting and barbecuing—are more or less self-explanatory but for red stewing, which is plain old stewing plus soy sauce. In other words, the food is simmered slowly in soy sauce as well as water, so that it achieves a reddish appearance.

Soup cooking is popular in cold weather and is often done at the table. Meat, poultry or fish is cut into paper-thin slices, dipped in a mixture of soy sauce, wine and cornstarch, and then plunged into a briskly boiling clear, thin stock or plain boiling water. In a minute or two the sliver of food is tender and tasty and ready for eating. The soup improves with the cooking; or if the liquid was plain water to begin with, that very quickly becomes soup. As the soup is eaten, more water is added, and then more solid ingredients; then the meat is eaten, soup is sipped, and the process goes on until the meat is finished. Vegetables can be added too, but they must be quickly

115

withdrawn from the pot or they will not only lose their own taste and texture but will slightly spoil the taste of the meaty stock.

The Western kitchen is more than adequately adapted to the preparation of Chinese meals. Although no special equipment is absolutely required, it would be the rare Chinese cook who would attempt a meal without a *wok* or two. The *wok* is the most versatile of cooking pots. It is a bowl-shaped metal pan, purchasable at Chinese specialty stores, that can be used for stir-frying, deep frying, simmering, steaming and even—if a big enough one is bought—for outdoor barbecuing. Another essential for the Chinese chef is the Chinese-style cleaver, a broad, heavy knife with a rectangular blade. This all-purpose knife can be used to cut, slice, chop, shred, crush and even mince all manner of meats and vegetables. Chopsticks, too, are important in the kitchen. They are useful for sorting, stirring and mixing ingredients as well as for conveying morsels of food from platter to pan and from pan to serving platter. There is no real need for any of these instruments in the American kitchen, but they are a great help, especially the *wok* and cleaver.

For authenticity and pleasure, chopsticks should be used at the dining table. They are not at all difficult to use after one has had a little practice. At the Chinese dining table—round, because it is more companionable and also because it makes it easier for everyone to reach all the serving bowls—each place setting consists of a small plate, a porcelain spoon, a small soup bowl, a tiny wine cup, a small saucer for soy sauce and a pair of chopsticks. At the usual family meal all the food is put on the table at the same time, and the number of dishes served is about the same as the number of people present. For a family of four to six, for instance, a meal is likely to include a meat dish of pork or beef, combined with harmonious ingredients; a seafood dish; a vegetable dish; an egg dish; rice; soup; tea; and fresh fruits.

Dinners for guests are a little more elaborate. For a sitting of eight to twelve people the meal starts with appetizers that are placed on the table before the guests are seated and consist of four cold dishes or one very large cold assortment that will include such delicacies as salted shrimps, perhaps, and cold kidneys as well as a variety of other meats and seafoods. (Westerners may prefer to substitute hot appetizers such as shrimp egg rolls, tiny fried dumplings and spareribs.) Then four hot stir-fried dishes will be served, followed by four steamed or braised dishes to be eaten with the rice.

116

Somewhere in between the main courses two sweet dishes may be served by way of contrast: sugared apple slices, perhaps, or lotus soup with glutinous rice dumplings. Then there will be two or more meat dishes, also to be eaten to the accompaniment of rice, and a closing bowl of soup—for, contrary to Western custom, the Chinese prefer to end the meal with soup.

A somewhat simpler but still quite festive meal might include one large mixed cold platter, four to six main dishes—including perhaps a sauté of crab meat, roast duck, steamed fish and thin-sliced meat and vegetables—and a sweet, the rice and a soup. Tea is served at the beginning and end of a meal. Desserts per se are seldom eaten, but if you as the hostess prefer a sweet dish at the end of the meal rather than somewhere in the middle you should certainly feel free to follow your own preference. But don't aim for anything heavy. A platter of cookies or a little fresh or preserved fruit is all that is needed to put the finishing touches to a Chinese meal. The amounts of each dish that you prepare for a meal must depend on the number of your guests and the number of dishes that you plan to serve them. The fewer the dishes, the greater the quantities; and the more the dishes, the less of each will you need to prepare. But never forget that the essence of the Chinese meal is variety and harmony. Take the trouble to prepare a single dish for each one of your guests and you are bound to satisfy them all.

RICE

CHINESE-STYLE FLUFFY RICE

1 cup rice   2 cups water

Bring the water to a boil in a saucepan and add the rice. When the water comes to a boil again, stir the rice once, then cover tightly and lower flame. Cook for 20 to 25 minutes without removing the cover. When the rice is dry and soft it is done. If necessary allow it to steam for 5 more minutes. Do not stir again. Uncover and serve.

SOUPS

HANG YANG WU
Almond Soup

⅓ cup Chinese almonds   ⅛ teaspoon salt
2⅓ cups cold water   ⅓ cup sugar
3½ tablespoons rice flour   About 1 cup cold water

The almonds should be blanched and ground fine. Soak the almonds in the cold water in a saucepan for 15 minutes, then bring to a boil, cover and simmer for 10 minutes. Mix the rice flour with the salt and sugar in a bowl and add enough water to make a smooth paste. Gradually add to the boiling almond water, stirring constantly. Bring to a boil again and continue cooking and stirring over medium heat for 5 more minutes. When it is thick, pour through a strainer. May be served hot or cold.

CHICKEN AND CUCUMBER SOUP

2 small cucumbers   4 cups rich chicken broth
1 chicken breast, skinned   3 tablespoons sherry
    and boned

Wash and peel the cucumbers, cut lengthwise and remove the seeds. Cut into thin slices. Cut the skinned and boned chicken breast into thin small pieces. In a saucepan bring the broth to a boil and add the cucumbers and chicken and continue to boil for 5 minutes, then add the sherry. Remove from heat. Serve hot.

BIRD'S NEST SOUP

¼ *pound bird's nest*
  (see Glossary)
1 *quart rich chicken broth*
  Salt and pepper to taste
2 *egg whites*
2 *tablespoons cornstarch*

1 *tablespoon cold water*
¼ *pound bamboo shoots, minced*
¼ *pound white mushrooms,*
  minced
2 *tablespoons cooked ham,*
  minced

Soak the bird's nest in warm water for 3 hours. Remove, wash several times and drain. In a saucepan bring the chicken broth to a boil and add the bird's nest, salt and pepper, and simmer for 5 minutes. Beat the egg whites and gradually add to the broth while stirring constantly. Mix the cornstarch with the cold water, add this to the boiling broth and keep mixing until it has thickened a little. Add the bamboo shoots and mushrooms and simmer for about 3 minutes. Garnish with the ham. Serve hot accompanied by a bowl of soy sauce.

EGG-DROP SOUP

3 *cups chicken stock*
2 *eggs*
  Salt to taste

½ *teaspoon monosodium*
  glutamate

In a saucepan bring the soup stock to the boiling point. Beat the eggs and add a dash of salt. Pour the eggs into the boiling stock very slowly, stirring constantly. Add the monosodium glutamate and mix well. Remove from heat. Serve hot.

CABBAGE SOUP

¾ *pound boned chicken or lean*
  pork
8 *cups chicken stock*
1 *medium head Chinese cabbage*

1½ *teaspoons salt*
1¼ *teaspoons pepper*
1½ *teaspoons monosodium*
  glutamate

Cut the chicken or pork into very thin small pieces. Place in a pot with the stock and cook over medium heat for 7 minutes. Cut the cabbage into

119

2-inch-wide strips and add to the soup with salt and pepper. Cook until the cabbage is tender, about 5 minutes, no more; don't let the cabbage get soft. Add the monosodium glutamate and stir. Remove from heat. Serve hot.

HOT-AND-SOUR SOUP

⅓ pound lean pork
4 Chinese mushrooms
   (see Glossary)
2 ounces bean curd
   (see Glossary)
3 cups chicken stock
1½ tablespoons soy sauce
2 tablespoons sherry

1 teaspoon salt
½ teaspoon pepper
1½ tablespoons vinegar
2 teaspoons cornstarch
1 tablespoon water
¼ teaspoon monosodium
   glutamate

Slice the pork, mushrooms and bean curd into long thin shreds. In a saucepan bring the stock to a boil and add the pork, mushrooms and bean curd. Gently simmer for 8 minutes, then add the soy sauce, sherry, salt, pepper and vinegar. Mix the cornstarch with the water and add to the soup. Continue cooking over low heat until the soup has thickened. Add the monosodium glutamate and mix well. Remove from heat. Serve hot.

SEAFOOD CONGEE

½ cup rice
8 cups water
½ pound filet of sole
1 cup shrimp
½ pound squid

4 scallions
2 tablespoons peanut oil
1 tablespoon light soy sauce
   Salt to taste
   Dash of white pepper

Rinse and drain the rice. In a large uncovered pot bring the rice to a boil in the water. Lower the heat, cover the pot and let the congee (see Glossary) simmer for 1 hour. Meanwhile, slice the sole thinly, shell and devein the shrimp, clean the squid and cut it into 1-inch pieces. Cut the scallions crosswise into ⅛-inch rings. After the congee has simmered for 1 hour, add the fish, shrimp and squid and boil for 2 minutes. Turn off heat and add scallions, the oil, light soy sauce, salt and pepper. Remove from heat. Serve hot.

120

HORS D'OEUVRE

EGG ROLLS

Pancake Batter
2 cups flour
1 teaspoon salt
6 eggs

2 cups water
Oil for frying

Sift the flour and salt together into a bowl, add the eggs and water and beat. The batter should be thin but not too thin. Set aside to stand for a few minutes. Heat about ½ teaspoon of oil in a small frying pan. Pour off excess oil because the pan should not be too greasy. Pour in about 2 tablespoons or a little less of batter and tilt the pan to spread it around. Fry over medium heat for less than a minute on each side. The pancake should be very thin and done on both sides but not brown. Set the pancakes on a board, side by side, and cover with a cloth or wax paper until ready to fill. Continue frying until the desired number is reached. If any batter is left it can be used for sealing the rolls.

Filling
1 cup canned water chestnuts
1½ cups canned bamboo shoots
½ pound roast pork
½ cup scallions
½ pound fresh shelled deveined
    shrimp
1 teaspoon salt

⅛ teaspoon pepper
1 teaspoon monosodium
    glutamate
1 teaspoon sugar
2½ cups chicken stock
Oil for deep frying

Drain the water chestnuts and bamboo shoots thoroughly and dry. Cut the chestnuts, bamboo shoots and pork into small narrow strips. Chop the scallions very fine. Mince the shrimp very fine. Mix all in a bowl with salt, pepper, monosodium glutamate and sugar. Add the stock and stir in. Spread each pancake with 1½ tablespoons of filling. Fold in three sides and roll up tightly, sealing with some batter or water. Fry the rolls in deep fat (365° F.) until a golden color. Remove and drain on a paper towel. Serve hot accompanied by duk sauce (*see Glossary*) and mustard.

EGG DUMPLINGS

¾ *pound pork*   1 *teaspoon salt*
 3 *scallions*   *Oil for frying*
 2 *slices ginger*   ½ *cup water*
 1 *tablespoon soy sauce*   1 *teaspoon sugar*
 6 *eggs*

Chop the pork very, very fine. Mince the scallions and ginger very fine. Combine the pork, scallions and ginger in a bowl, add one half of the soy sauce (1½ teaspoons) and mix well. Beat the eggs with the salt. In a large frying pan put 2 teaspoons oil and heat. Drop about a tablespoon of the egg in the middle of the pan as if making a pancake. At once place a teaspoon of the pork mixture in the middle of the egg, fold in half and press the edges together. Remove from the pan. Follow this procedure until all the ingredients are gone. Now replace all the dumplings in the pan and add the water, sugar and the rest of the soy sauce. Cover the pan with a tight lid and simmer for 15 minutes.

FISH AND SEAFOOD

SWEET-AND-SOUR FISH

 1 *3½-pound fish (white meat)*   1¾ *cups vinegar*
½ *cup flour*   2 *tablespoons cornstarch*
    Oil for deep frying   1 *medium onion, thinly sliced*
 1 *cup sugar*   2 *tablespoons chopped ginger*
 5 *tablespoons soy sauce*   *(optional)*

Clean the fish, but leave the head and tail on. Coat the fish well with the flour. Heat the oil and deep fry the fish until brown and crisp. Remove and drain on paper towels. To make the sauce, mix 3 tablespoons of oil, the sugar, soy sauce, vinegar and cornstarch in a saucepan. Place over medium heat, add the onion and ginger and boil for 5 minutes. Pour over the fish. Serve hot.

STEAMED BASS IN BROWN SAUCE

1 2-pound sea bass, whole
1 tablespoon brown bean sauce
   (see Glossary)
1 clove garlic, minced
½ teaspoon salt
¼ teaspoon pepper
¼ green pepper

1 cup water
1 teaspoon soy sauce
½ teaspoon monosodium
   glutamate
½ teaspoon sugar
1 tablespoon cornstarch
1 teaspoon cold water

Have the bass dressed and left whole. Mix the bean sauce with the garlic. Salt and pepper the fish and then spread the bean sauce and garlic over the fish. Place the fish in a long, shallow heatproof dish and put on a rack in a roasting pan that has a cover. Cut the green pepper into fine lengthwise slivers and scatter over the fish. Put boiling water in the roasting pan. Make sure that the boiling water will not overflow into the fish dish while steaming. Pour 1 cup of water around the fish for the stock. Put the cover on the roasting pan and steam for 30 minutes. Pour off the fish stock into a small saucepan. Add the soy sauce, monosodium glutamate and sugar. Mix the cornstarch with the cold water and add to the sauce. Bring to a boil and cook for 3 minutes. Place the fish on a serving platter, pour the sauce over it and serve with rice.

SHRIMP FOO YUNG

¾ cup mushrooms
¼ cup water chestnuts
6 eggs
1 cup raw shelled deveined
   shrimp, chopped
1 cup chopped onions

3 tablespoons soy sauce
Oil
4 tablespoons chicken bouillon
1 tablespoon cornstarch
¼ teaspoon sugar

Cut the mushrooms and water chestnuts into thin slices. Beat the eggs in a bowl, add the mushrooms, chestnuts, shrimp, and onions and beat until thick. Add 2 tablespoons soy sauce and beat again. In a shallow pan put a small amount of oil and heat. When the oil is hot add the mixture and brown on both sides. Remove, drain on a paper towel, and put on a plate. To make the sauce, mix together in a small saucepan the remaining tablespoon of soy sauce, the bouillon, cornstarch and sugar. Simmer over low heat, stirring until hot and smooth. Pour over the egg mixture and serve hot.

STEAMED EGGS WITH SHRIMP

4 eggs
1½ cups water
½ teaspoon salt
1 cup small raw shrimp

1 tablespoon oil
1 tablespoon light soy sauce
Dash of white pepper

Beat the eggs thoroughly in a bowl. Add the water and salt and beat to mix. Pour the mixture into an 8-inch pie plate. Shell and devein the shrimp and add to the egg mixture. Steam over water in a very gentle steam for 10 minutes. Sprinkle the oil, light soy sauce and white pepper on top and serve hot at once in its steaming plate.

SHRIMP WITH FRIED NOODLES

1 cup raw shelled deveined
    shrimp
1½ tablespoons oil or fat
½ pound shredded Chinese
    cabbage
15 water chestnuts, thinly sliced
½ teaspoon salt

1 teaspoon sugar
1 cup thinly sliced bamboo shoots
1 teaspoon monosodium
    glutamate
3 cups chicken stock or water
2 tablespoons cornstarch
3 tablespoons cold water

Cut the shrimp in half lengthwise. Heat the oil in a frying pan, add the cabbage and cook for 3 minutes. Add the shrimp, water chestnuts, salt, sugar, bamboo shoots, monosodium glutamate and stock. Cover and cook over medium heat for 10 minutes. Mix the cornstarch with 3 tablespoons cold water until smooth and add to the ingredients in the pan. Cook for 5 minutes. Serve hot over fried noodles.

To Cook Chinese Noodles
½ pound Chinese egg noodles
6 cups boiling salted water

3 tablespoons fat

Cook the noodles in the water for 3 or 4 minutes, then set aside to drain well. Heat the fat in a pan until very hot and fry the noodles until golden but not brown. (Canned fried noodles may be used if preferred.)

SHRIMPS IN HOT BROWN-BEAN SAUCE

1 *pound small raw shrimp*
3 *cloves garlic*
3 *thin slices ginger*

Hot brown-bean sauce
3 *tablespoons oil*

Shell and devein the shrimp. Chop the garlic and ginger coarsely. Make the hot brown-bean sauce. Heat the oil in a wok over high heat, add the garlic and ginger and sizzle for half a minute. Add the shrimp and stir-fry for 3 minutes. Add the sauce and cook over high heat, stirring for 2 minutes to allow the sauce to simmer and thicken. Remove from heat. Serve hot.

Hot Brown-Bean Sauce
  2 *tablespoons brown-bean sauce*
    (*see Glossary*)
  1 *tablespoon dark soy sauce*

  1 *teaspoon cornstarch*
  ¼ *cup water*
  ¼ *teaspoon sugar*

Combine all the ingredients in a cup and mix well.

SQUID IN VINEGAR SAUCE

1 *pound medium-sized squid*
  Vinegar sauce
8 *cups water*

1 *tablespoon oil*
2 *thin slices ginger*

Clean and wash the squid thoroughly. Slash a diamond pattern on one side of the squid and cut into 2-inch pieces. Make the vinegar sauce. In a large pot bring to a boil the water, oil and ginger. Add the squid and boil quickly for 2 minutes. Drain and place on a platter. Pour the vinegar sauce on top and serve hot or cold.

Vinegar Sauce
  2 *tablespoons white vinegar*
  3 *tablespoons light soy sauce*

  ½ *teaspoon sugar*
  1 *tablespoon sesame oil*

Combine all ingredients in a cup and mix well.

BRAISED ABALONE ON LETTUCE

1 12-ounce can abalone	8 cups water
2 scallions	4 tablespoons oil
Sauce	2 tablespoons salt
1 medium head lettuce	

Drain the abalone and reserve the juice for the sauce. Slice the abalone into ⅛-inch pieces. Cut the scallions into 2-inch lengths. Make the sauce. Separate and wash the lettuce leaves. In a large pot bring to a boil the water, 2 tablespoons of the oil and the salt. Add the lettuce leaves and boil quickly for 1 minute. Drain and place the leaves on a large platter and keep them warm. Heat the remaining 2 tablespoons of oil in a wok over medium heat, add the scallions and abalone and stir-fry for 1 minute. Add the sauce and bring to a boil. Cook over medium heat, stirring, for 1 minute to allow the sauce to thicken. Remove from heat. Pour the mixture over the lettuce and serve hot.

Sauce

Abalone juice	¼ teaspoon salt
¼ cup water	Dash of white pepper
1 tablespoon cornstarch	

Combine all the ingredients in a cup and mix well.

BRAISED BEAN CURD WITH CRAB MEAT

6 fresh bean curd squares	2 thin slices ginger
(see Glossary)	1 cup crab meat, fresh or frozen
3 tablespoons oil	

Cut the bean curd into ¼-inch cubes. Make the sauce (see below). Heat the oil in a wok over medium heat. Add the ginger and sizzle for half a minute. Add the bean curd and crab meat and bring to a simmer. Add prepared sauce and cook over medium heat, stirring, for 3 minutes to allow the sauce to simmer and thicken. Remove from heat. Serve hot.

Sauce

¼ cup oyster sauce	2 teaspoons cornstarch
(see Glossary)	½ teaspoon sugar
2 tablespoons dark soy sauce	¼ cup water

Combine all the ingredients in a cup and mix well.

SCALLOPS AND FRESH MUSHROOMS

4 *scallions*
2 *thin slices ginger*
1 *pound fresh scallops*
¼ *pound fresh mushrooms*

Sauce
3 *tablespoons oil*
1 *tablespoon rice wine*

Cut the scallions into 2-inch lengths. Cut the ginger into thin strips. Wash and halve the scallops. Wash and slice the mushrooms into ¼-inch pieces. Make the sauce. Heat the oil in a wok over high heat. Add the scallions and ginger and sizzle for half a minute. Add the scallops and wine and stir-fry for 2 minutes. Add the mushrooms and cook over high heat, stirring, for 1 minute. Add the sauce and cook, stirring, for half a minute to allow the sauce to simmer and thicken. Remove from heat. Serve hot.

Sauce
2 *tablespoons light soy sauce*
1 *teaspoon cornstarch*
¼ *cup water*

¼ *teaspoon salt*
½ *teaspoon sugar*

Combine all the ingredients in a cup and mix well.

NOODLES IN CRAB-MEAT SAUCE

10 *cups water*
8 *ounces Chinese noodles*
Sauce

2 *tablespoons oil*
1 *cup crab meat, fresh or frozen*
Dash of white pepper

In a large pot bring the water to a boil. Add the noodles and cook, stirring, in the boiling water for 5 minutes or until the noodles are soft. Drain, place on a large platter and keep them warm. Make the sauce. Heat the oil in a wok over medium heat. Add the crab meat and pepper and stir-fry for 1 minute. Add the sauce and cook over medium heat, stirring, for 1 minute to allow the sauce to simmer and thicken. Pour the crab meat and sauce over the noodles and serve hot.

Sauce
2 *tablespoons light soy sauce*
1 *tablespoon cornstarch*
1 *cup water*

1 *tablespoon sesame oil*
½ *teaspoon salt*

Combine all the ingredients in a cup and mix well.

POULTRY

CHICKEN WITH CHESTNUTS

1 *pound dried chestnuts, shelled*
1 *6-pound chicken, whole*
2 *tablespoons oil*
3 *scallions, each cut into*
    4 or 5 pieces

3 *tablespoons sherry*
6 *tablespoons soy sauce*
3 *pieces fresh ginger*

Simmer the chestnuts in 5 cups of water in a saucepan for 2½ hours. Put the chicken in a pot with the oil and 2 cups of water and bring to a boil. When boiling, add the scallions. Add the sherry, soy sauce and ginger. Cover the pot and cook over low heat for about 1 hour until the chicken is tender. Add the chestnuts and water and cook, covered, for 20 more minutes. Remove from heat. Serve hot.

FRIED CHICKEN WITH WALNUTS

⅓ *cup blanched walnuts*
1 *cup oil*
1 *chicken breast, diced*
1½ *teaspoons cornstarch*

2 *tablespoons soy sauce*
  Scant teaspoon sugar
1 *teaspoon salt*
6 *large mushrooms*

Fry the walnuts in the oil until golden brown. Remove from heat and drain on several layers of paper towels. Put a small amount of oil in a frying pan and when the oil is hot add the diced chicken. Mix and cook over high heat until all pink is gone from the meat, several minutes. In a bowl mix the cornstarch with a little cold water until smooth, add the soy sauce, sugar and salt and mix thoroughly, then pour over the chicken. Soak the mushrooms in hot water for 15 minutes, then dice them and add to the frying pan. Stir the mixture constantly until the mushrooms are tender. When done remove from heat, add the fried walnuts and mix well. Serve hot.

STEAMED CHICKEN

2 *whole boned chicken breasts*
6 *scallions*
8 *cloud ears* (*see Glossary*)
4 *thin slices ginger*
1 *teaspoon cornstarch*
¼ *teaspoon salt*

1 *tablespoon oil*
3 *tablespoons light soy sauce*
1 *teaspoon rice wine*
½ *cup water*
½ *teaspoon sugar*

Chop the chicken breasts into bite-sized chunks. Cut the scallions into 2-inch pieces. Soak the cloud ears in warm water till soft. In a large bowl mix all the ingredients together thoroughly. Pour into an 8-inch pie plate and steam over water in a continuous steam for 20 minutes. Serve hot.

COLD CHICKEN WITH GINGER AND SCALLIONS

6 *cups water*
2 *whole chicken breasts*

1 *teaspoon salt*
Sauce

Bring the water to a boil in a pot. Add the chicken breasts and simmer for 20 minutes. Lift out and cool. Remove the meat from the bones and discard the bones. Shred the meat with fingers to bite-sized slivers. Arrange the meat on a platter and sprinkle with salt. Make the following sauce.

Sauce
6 *thin slices ginger*
6 *scallions*

4 *tablespoons oil*

Chop the ginger and scallions finely. Heat the oil in a skillet till bubbling and add the ginger and scallions. Pour this at once over the chicken and serve.

CHICKEN WITH PINEAPPLE

½ cup water chestnuts
⅓ cup celery
½ cup bamboo shoots
1 1-pound chicken breast
1 tablespoon oil
1 cup shredded Chinese cabbage
2 teaspoons salt
⅛ teaspoon white pepper

½ teaspoon monosodium
   glutamate
2 teaspoons sugar
1½ cups chicken stock
1 can chunk pineapple, drained
2½ teaspoons cornstarch
¼ cup cold water

Slice thinly the water chestnuts, celery and bamboo shoots. The chicken breast must be freshly cooked but not overcooked. Cut from the bone and slice into very thin diagonal strips. Heat the oil in a pan and fry all the vegetables for 3 minutes. Add the salt, pepper, monosodium glutamate and sugar and mix very well. Add the chicken stock and bring to a boil. Add the pineapple and chicken. Mix the cornstarch with water until smooth and add to the pan, mix and cook all over medium heat for 3 or 4 minutes. Remove from heat. Serve very hot in a covered bowl.

CHICKEN-AND-CHINESE-MUSHROOM RICE

2 chicken breasts
6 mushrooms
2 thin slices ginger
1 teaspoon cornstarch
½ teaspoon salt
3 tablespoons light soy sauce

2 tablespoons oil
½ teaspoon sugar
1 tablespoon rice wine
2 cups rice
3½ cups water

Chop the chicken breasts into bite-sized chunks. Soak the mushrooms in water till soft, discard the stems and quarter the caps. In a bowl mix all the ingredients except the rice and water. Wash and drain the rice. Place the rice in a pot and add the water. Bring to a boil uncovered. Continue boiling uncovered for about 5 minutes or until all the water disappears except for bubbles on the rice. Spread the chicken mixture on top, tightly cover the pot, turn the heat to low and cook for 20 minutes. Remove from heat. Serve hot.

ROAST DUCK .

1 6-pound duck
2 scallions, cut into small pieces
1 tablespoon brown bean sauce
  (see Glossary)
2 cloves garlic, finely minced
1 teaspoon cinnamon
1 teaspoon monosodium
  glutamate

1 tablespoon brown sugar
⅛ teaspoon pepper
2 teaspoons salt
1 tablespoon sherry
1 cup chicken stock or water
1 tablespoon soy sauce
1 tablespoon honey
1 tablespoon cold water

Wash and clean the duck and drain. In a bowl thoroughly mix the scallions, bean sauce, garlic, cinnamon, monosodium glutamate, brown sugar, pepper, salt and sherry. Add to the chicken stock in a pot, mix well and bring to a boil for 1 or 2 minutes. Have needle and thread ready to sew up the duck. Tie the neck with string. Pour the seasoned stock into the duck and sew the opening. Mix the soy sauce with the honey and cold water. When well mixed rub all over the duck, making sure the skin is thoroughly covered. Place the duck in a roasting pan, cover and roast for 50 minutes in a 450° F. oven. Remove the cover from the pan and while continuing to roast turn the duck until all sides are crisp and brown. Baste with the liquid in the pan. When the skin is crisp and the duck is tender, serve at once.

MEATS

ROAST PORK

1 tablespoon sherry
2 teaspoons salt
3 tablespoons sugar

2 tablespoons soy sauce
½ teaspoon ground cinnamon
1 2-pound pork tenderloin

In a bowl mix the sherry, salt, sugar, soy sauce and cinnamon. Cut the pork in half the long way. Thoroughly rub the seasoned mixture into the meat on all sides, cover tightly and set aside in a cool place for 1½ hours. Uncover and set aside to drain. Preheat oven and roast the pork for 1 hour or more at 350° F. Meat should be thoroughly cooked and tender. Good served hot or cold. May be shredded and used for cooked pork recipes.

GOLDEN PORK BALLS

2 scallions	1 egg, beaten
3 thin slices ginger	1 tablespoon cornstarch
1 pound ground pork	½ teaspoon salt
1 tablespoon rice wine	1 cup oil
3 tablespoons light soy sauce	¼ pound fresh watercress

Chop the scallions and ginger finely. In a bowl mix well all the ingredients except the oil and watercress. Divide the mixture into 12 portions and shape into balls. Make the batter. Heat the oil in a flat skillet. Dip the pork balls in the batter, then fry about 4 minutes in the oil or until golden brown. Remove and drain on a paper towel. Line a large platter with the watercress and place the golden pork balls on top. Serve hot.

Batter
  3 tablespoons cornstarch   ¼ cup water

BRAISED PORK CHOPS

4 pork chops	1 teaspoon cornstarch
2 tablespoons dark soy sauce	½ teaspoon sugar
2 tablespoons rice wine	2 tablespoons oil
3 cloves garlic, chopped fine	¼ cup water

In a small bowl dissolve the cornstarch in the water. Cut each pork chop into 3 pieces; there should be a piece of bone with each piece of meat. In a bowl marinate the pork for half an hour in the dark soy sauce, wine, garlic, cornstarch and sugar. Heat the oil in a wok over high heat. Add the pork and brown for 2 minutes on each side. Add the water, bring to a boil, cover the wok and braise the pork for 5 minutes or until the water all but boils away. Remove from heat. Serve hot.

STEAMED GROUND BEEF WITH
WATER CHESTNUTS

½ cup water chestnuts
2 thin slices ginger
1 pound ground beef
2 teaspoons cornstarch
¼ cup water

2 tablespoons light soy sauce
1 tablespoon oil
½ teaspoon sugar
½ teaspoon salt
Dash of white pepper

Chop the water chestnuts coarsely and the ginger finely. In a large bowl mix all the ingredients together well. Spread the mixture in an 8-inch plate. Steam over water in a continuous steam for 10 minutes. Serve hot at once.

CHINESE MINCED BEEF

3 tablespoons oil
2 cloves garlic, chopped fine

½ cup coarsely chopped onions
1 pound ground beef

Make the sauce. Heat the oil in a wok over high heat. Add the garlic and onions and sizzle for 2 minutes. Add the beef and stir-fry for 2 minutes to break up any lumps. Add the sauce and cook over high heat, stirring, for 1 minute to allow the sauce to simmer and thicken. Remove from heat. Serve over hot fluffy rice.

Sauce
4 tablespoons dark soy sauce
1 tablespoon cornstarch
½ cup water

1 teaspoon sugar
½ teaspoon salt

Combine all the ingredients in a cup and mix well.

BEEF IN BLACK-BEAN SAUCE

2 *cloves garlic*
4 *tablespoons fermented black*
   beans (see Glossary)
1 *pound flank steak*
2 *tablespoons dark soy sauce*

1 *teaspoon rice wine*
½ *teaspoon sugar*
2 *teaspoons cornstarch*
  Sauce

Chop the garlic and black beans coarsely. Slice the steak into ⅛-inch-thick strips. In a bowl marinate the steak for half an hour in the dark soy sauce, wine, sugar and cornstarch. Make the sauce. Heat the oil in a wok over high heat. Add the garlic and black beans and sizzle for 1 minute. Add the steak and stir-fry for 3 minutes. Add the sauce and cook over high heat, stirring, for half a minute to allow the sauce to simmer and thicken. Remove from heat. Serve hot at once.

Sauce
  1 *tablespoon dark soy sauce*
  1 *teaspoon cornstarch*

½ *cup water*

Combine all the ingredients in a cup and mix well.

VEGETABLES

BRAISED BAMBOO SHOOTS AND CHINESE MUSHROOMS

  2 *cups sliced bamboo shoots*
12 *Chinese mushrooms*
    (see Glossary)
    Sauce

2 *tablespoons oil*
2 *thin slices ginger*

Slice the bamboo shoots in ⅙-inch pieces. Soak the mushrooms in water till soft, discard the stems. Make the sauce. Heat the oil in a wok over medium heat. Add the ginger and sizzle for half a minute. Add the bamboo shoots and mushrooms and stir-fry for 1 minute. Add the sauce, bring to simmer and braise for 5 minutes. Remove from heat. Serve hot.

Sauce
  2 tablespoons dark soy sauce   ¼ teaspoon salt
  2 teaspoons cornstarch   ½ teaspoon sugar
  ½ cup water

Combine all the ingredients in a cup and mix well.

CHINESE BROCCOLI SALAD

  2 bunches fresh broccoli   1 tablespoon salt
 10 cups water   Sauce
  2 tablespoons oil

Cut the broccoli into two parts: the flower part and the stem part. Cut the flower part into small bite-sized clusters. Peel the tough skin off the stem and quarter the stem lengthwise. Slant-cut each quarter into 2-inch pieces. In a large pot bring to a rapid boil the water, oil and salt. Add the broccoli and boil quickly for 1 minute. Drain the broccoli, rinse in cold water, drain and place on a large platter. Make the sauce. Pour over the broccoli, toss and serve.

Sauce
  2 tablespoons light soy sauce   ¼ teaspoon salt
  2 tablespoons white vinegar   1 tablespoon sugar
  2 tablespoons sesame oil

Combine all the ingredients in a cup and mix well.

STIR-FRIED GREEN BEANS WITH GARLIC

  1 pound fresh green beans   ½ teaspoon salt
  6 cloves garlic   1 tablespoon light soy sauce
  4 tablespoons oil   1 teaspoon sugar

Remove the ends and string from the green beans and cut in half crosswise. Crush and chop the garlic coarsely. Heat the oil in a wok over high heat. Add the green beans and garlic and stir-fry for 5 minutes. (The heat should be very high and the skin of the green beans should be singed slightly.) Add the salt, light soy sauce and sugar. Stir to mix. Remove from heat. Serve hot.

SWEETS

ALMOND COOKIES

2½ cups flour
  1 teaspoon baking powder
1½ cups sugar
  2 cups finely ground blanched
     almonds

1 cup butter or shortening
1 egg
2 tablespoons water
30 whole almonds

Sift the flour, baking powder and sugar into a bowl. Add the ground almonds, mix well. Cut in the butter and work it in by hand. Add the egg and 1 tablespoon water and knead. Use a little more water if needed but not too much. Knead thoroughly. Break off small pieces of dough, about tablespoon size, shape into balls and place on a greased cookie sheet. Press down slightly and put an almond in the center of each cookie. Bake in a 375° F. oven for about 5 minutes, then lower heat to 325° F. and bake until a golden-brown color, about 8 to 12 minutes.

STEAMED SPONGE CAKE

⅔ cup pastry flour
¼ teaspoon baking powder
  Pinch of salt

2 egg whites, beaten
½ cup sugar
2 egg yolks

Sift the flour, baking powder and salt together into a bowl. Beat the egg whites until stiff, then gradually add the sugar and continue beating until very stiff. In a separate bowl beat the egg yolks until lemony and carefully fold into the whites. Carefully fold the dry ingredients into the egg mixture. Grease an 8-inch cake pan or 12 custard cups, fill and place on a rack in a large pan and add water to just below the rack. Water must not touch the pan or cups. Cover and let steam for about 20 minutes until the cake is set. Serve hot or cold.

EIGHT PRECIOUS PUDDING

1 cup glutinous rice
   (see Glossary)
1½ cups water
  ½ cup sugar

3 tablespoons lard
   Preserved pineapple bits
   Several red cherries, cut in half

Cook the rice in a covered saucepan with the water until the rice is done. Cool the rice slightly and add the sugar and lard and mix well. Generously grease a deep bowl with more lard. Place the pineapple and cherries around the bottom of the bowl. Put the cooked rice in the bowl and press down firmly. Steam on a rack over boiling water (high heat) for a half hour. Remove and unmold onto a serving dish. Serve hot.

ASSORTED FRUITS

1 small can pineapple chunks
1 can mandarin oranges
8 slices preserved red ginger

1 dozen preserved kumquats
1 can litchi nuts
8 maraschino cherries

Drain the pineapple chunks and mandarin oranges. Fill a bowl with shaved ice in the shape of a mound. Arrange the pineapple chunks, oranges, ginger, kumquats and litchi nuts over the ice. Decorate with the cherries.

THE PHILIPPINES

When a Filipino throws a party his friends and neighbors are more than likely to say of him, *"Siya'y nagbuwal baka,"* or "He killed a cow." This is a traditional saying but it is usually an understatement. One cow might seem sufficient to us, but if the party-giver were truly following the native custom of munificent party-throwing the chances are that he would have killed not just one cow but several cows, a number of pigs and probably quite a few chickens.

For Filipinos love to eat on a grand and glorious scale, and they love to eat with friends.

The various regions of the tropical archipelago that is the Philippines háve their own specialties, ranging from hot and spicy to rich and heavy. In all, the Philippine cuisine is a rather unusual combination of traditional, or native, Filipino, Chinese, Japanese, Spanish and American foods. "Oriental-tropical" is perhaps the most accurate way to describe the average Filipino diet—that is, what most Filipinos eat most of the time.

Everyday fare in the Filipino household is quite simple: rice, fish, vegetable stew, fried meats or meat sautéed with potatoes or shrimp and vegetables. Lard is used liberally in preparation of much of the food. The kitchen, no matter how humble, is always stocked with staple spices and condiments such as cloves, garlic, onions, black pepper, paprika or achiote seeds, oregano, dried laurel leaves, *toyo* (soy sauce), *patis* (fish sauce), vinegar and coarse salt.

Breakfast for rural folk, at six or seven o'clock in the morning,

139

may consist of something like the following: boiled rice, fried or boiled fish, sliced onions and tomatoes and rice cakes with ginger tea. In Manila, where they eat a little later or at least have a second breakfast around ten o'clock, the morning staple is *pan de sal*. This is a small bun or roll that is usually eaten with liberal quantities of margarine, butter or guava jelly, and dunked in the sweet thick black coffee preferred by most Filipinos. A particularly nice breakfast dish for those who have time for more than a fast cup of coffee is scrambled eggs mixed with chopped onions and tomato, and dried pork or beef strips flavored with vinegar, salt and garlic.

Lunch is likely to consist of soup, fried shrimp, a stew of pork, shrimp or vegetables, with rice on the side, and *pancit. Pancit* is a dumpling-like dish of Chinese origin that contains chopped shrimp or pork and vegetables and a touch of *kalamansi*, a small green citrus fruit that is variously used to make a refreshing drink and to bring out the full flavor of a number of foods . . . a sort of liquid monosodium glutamate.

Then there is the midmorning or midafternoon snack called the *merienda*. It may consist of no more than coffee and cookies, or it may be considerably more substantial, but it is always *there* . . . particularly if the main meal may be a little late.

Dinner may, typically, feature *adobo*. This is a highly spiced concoction of pork and chicken seasoned with vinegar, garlic, black pepper, salt, laurel and onion. In one version the meats are fried to a crisp brown, and in another—*pampango*—they are served up in quantities of rich gravy.

For dessert the average family turns frequently to the banana, which comes in many varieties and is eaten as a fresh fruit or cooked up into some excellent desserts; or to some other fruit, cooked in sirup with anise; or to the native taffy. Plain water is often used as a thirst quencher with meals, although milk or the rich, aromatic hot chocolate of the Philippines is also frequently encountered.

But all this is for everyday. In Philippine life there are many days that are more than simply everydays, and on those days the Filipinos will kill the cow and the chickens and the pigs and come up with—fiesta.

On every celebratory occasion there will be a feast of many courses . . . roast suckling pig, roast kid with brains served in the skull as an entrée (not a pretty picture, perhaps, but delicious to the taste), hams, chickens, pork cutlets, prawns, crabs, chicken-liver pies, fruits and sweetmeats of every description.

The tender suckling pig, the *lechón*, roasted whole on a bamboo spit over charcoal, is the national fiesta favorite. This is how the Filipino prepared it centuries ago, and this is how he does it still: He kills the pig swiftly, shaves and cleans it, and then lets it stand for an hour or two while he prepares a bed of live charcoal in the ground. He stuffs the pig with either tamarind leaves or banana leaves (which impart a special flavor) or boiled rice and then thrusts a bamboo pole through the length of it. Then he rests the pole over the glowing charcoal, each end on a specially prepared bamboo stand so that he can rotate the pig slowly while it is roasting. Every once in a while he bastes the pig with water, turns it, bastes again and turns. The *lechón* cannot be hurried; it must roast slowly, slowly, and the cook must be a very patient man.

Lechón is not properly *lechón* unless it is served with its characteristic thick liver sauce, which is a concoction of pig's liver that has been roasted dry, pounded fine and cooked into a medium-thick paste with stock, crushed garlic, pepper and finely chopped onions.

Lumpia is another national favorite. This is a dish that combines shrimp, pork, vegetables and shredded coconut pith in a tissuelike wrapping, and it is served with a brown sauce. It is both a festive and an everyday item on the menu.

The Filipinos are not by any means a nation of drinkers, but on festive occasions they may sometimes be found sipping *tuba* or *basi* or *lambanog* . . . or San Miguel beer. *Tuba* is fermented coconut juice, *basi* is fermented sugar-cane juice, and *lambanog* is something to beware of. It is a powerful brew consisting of 98 per cent alcohol and is described by some of its admirers as being so potent that a car can run on it. For snacks, there are the little dried and salted *dilis*, tiny fish that are eaten head and all; *sitcharon*, a crispy snack made of the skin of a pig; and *kropek*, a nibble of crunchy dried shrimp.

The Filipinos are great fisheaters; fish is one of their staples. The *bangus*, or milkfish, is a great favorite; this is a herringlike fresh-water fish used in a number of dishes, but notably in *sinigang*. Then there is a dish called *pinakbet*, a standard among the Filipinos of northern Luzon. It features *talong* (eggplant), *ampalaya* (bitter melon) and the cook's choice of fish and ginger to flavor, steamed together under a tight lid in a small amount of water. The *talong* serves as a sort of cooking indicator: when the *talong* is cooked to the point where it's just short of mushy, the *pinakbet* is done.

Other favorites are the *alimango,* the big thick-crusted river crab, and the giant shrimp called *sugpo.* These are usually done *a la halabos,* that is, boiled with salt to taste and served with the shells on. The diner scoops out the flesh and dips it into a thin sauce of crushed garlic and vinegar in which tiny red-hot peppers have been marinated.

For spicy relishes, Filipinos enjoy the *dalok* and the *atchara. Dalok* is pickled green mango marinated in brine and pickling spice and *atchara* is pickled green papaya and *ampalaya* with sweet pepper, native onions, garlic and ginger, with a dressing of vinegar to which a little sugar has been added.

Cakes, candies, desserts and sweet snacks come in wonderful varieties under the collective name of *kakanin.* The basis for most of the *kakanin* is *galapong,* or rice dough, which is prepared by soaking the rice in water overnight and grinding it the next day in a small, hand-driven stone mill. (An ordinary grinder will do the job in a Western kitchen.) The rice becomes sour from the overnight soaking and thus the dough serves as its own leavening. *Bibingka* are special little rice cakes that are very popular. These require an extra rise in the dough, so a small amount of more than ordinarily well-fermented *galapong* is mixed with the standard rice dough. The rest of the ingredients that go into *bibingka* vary somewhat. Coconut milk and eggs are more or less standard; and for sweetening, granulated sugar is used sometimes, and sometimes *panocha,* which is cane sugar in lump form. Added touches may be salted duck's eggs, the native white cheese or grated fresh coconut meat. *Bibingka,* to be truly native, should be baked in a somewhat unusual way: the batter must be placed in clay pans, covered, and then baked *between* the coals of a charcoal fire so that there is fire both above and below it.

Other delicacies are *puto,* a sweet steamed rice cake; *makapuno,* a boiled coconut dessert; and various cakes and candies made, respectively, of *pili-nut,* yams or jackfruit. But probably the most native, or characteristic, Filipino sweet delicacy is the leaf-wrapped *suman,* a type of cake that looks rather like a large cigar or a slender candy bar. It is practically the first thing a housewife of the Philippines thinks of when she begins preparing for a fiesta. *Suman* is a mixture of *malagkit* (glutinous, or sticky, rice), sugar and coconut

142

milk, which is poured into a cast-iron saucepan and simmered until half done. At this stage it is removed from the flame, wrapped in banana or coconut leaves and boiled until thoroughly cooked. Sometimes, for variety, it may be fried and dipped in sugar. Either way, it is absolutely delicious, especially when eaten with mangoes in the Filipino way.

MAIN DISHES

CHICKEN-PORK ADOBO

1 chicken, about 3½ pounds
2 pounds pork
1 cup vinegar

1 clove garlic, minced
Salt and pepper to taste
2 tablespoons lard

Skin the chicken and cut the meat from the bones, then cut the chicken and pork into chunks. In a bowl mix the vinegar, garlic, salt and pepper and marinate the chicken and pork in this mixture. Place the meat and the marinade in a pan and simmer over low heat until tender. When all the liquid is gone, add the lard and brown the meat. Remove from heat. Serve hot.

CHICKEN ADOBO WITH COCONUT CREAM

1 medium-sized chicken
¼ cup vinegar
Ground black pepper
2 tablespoons salt

3 cloves garlic
2 cups coconut cream
  (see Glossary)

Skin, clean and cut the chicken into serving pieces. In a pot boil the chicken with the vinegar, pepper, salt and garlic until it is tender. Remove remaining sauce and add the coconut cream. Leave over low heat until the coconut cream thickens into sauce consistency. Remove from heat. Serve hot.

CHICKEN ADOBO

½ cup vinegar
1 clove garlic, or more to
  taste, minced
⅔ cup soy sauce

½ bay leaf
Black pepper to taste
1 1½ to 2 pound chicken, cut up

Place the vinegar, garlic, soy sauce, bay leaf and pepper in a pot and add the cut-up chicken. Cover and let simmer until the liquid has practically evaporated. Transfer the chicken pieces to a baking pan and broil about 25 minutes, or until brown. Serve hot.

ADOBO A LA MONJA

Chicken adobo
  (see recipe above)
1 cup pineapple cubes, fresh or
  canned

1 large ripe tomato, diced
¼ cup butter, melted

Prepare chicken adobo to the point when all the liquid has evaporated. Then add the pineapple cubes, diced tomato and butter. Cover tightly and simmer together in its own juice. Remove from heat. Serve hot.

PORK ADOBO

2 pounds pork, cut into pieces
    about 2 inches long and 1½
    inches thick
½ cup vinegar
1 head garlic, pounded

1 teaspoon ground black pepper
  Salt or soy sauce to taste
2 cups water
1 tablespoon lard

Place the pork in a saucepan. Add the vinegar, garlic, pepper, salt and water. Cover the saucepan and cook slowly until only ½ cup of the broth remains. Drain, reserving the broth, and separate the pieces of garlic from the pork and fry the garlic in the lard until brown. Add the pieces of pork and fry until brown. Then add the broth and simmer for 5 minutes. Remove from heat. Serve hot.

Note: If pressed for time, place the pieces of pork in a baking pan and broil until brown, basting occasionally with the pork fat.

CHICKEN FRITADA

1 tablespoon crushed garlic
2 tablespoons lard
1 medium onion, sliced
1 3½-pound chicken, cut up
2 medium ripe tomatoes, sliced
1 tablespoon salt

¼ teaspoon pepper
2 cups water
1 whole chicken liver
4 to 6 small potatoes
2 good-sized red-and-green
    peppers, cut into pieces

In a saucepan fry the garlic in the lard, then add the onion and fry for several minutes. Add the chicken, tomatoes, salt and pepper. Add the water and cook over medium heat until the chicken is tender. Add the liver, potatoes and peppers and continue cooking until the potatoes are done. Serve hot.

145

SINIGANG NA CARNE
Stewed Pork and Beef

½ pound lean pork, sliced
1½ pounds beef with bone
2 large ripe tomatoes, sliced
1 onion, sliced
  Salt to taste
  Juice of 4 lemons or limes

2 radishes, cut into large pieces
½ pound spinach
½ pound fresh green beans
  Soy sauce

Place the pork and beef in a kettle. Add just enough water to cover and simmer. Add the tomatoes, onion and salt. Add the juice from the lemons. Bring to a boil and if necessary add more water. Add the radishes and when soft add the spinach and green beans. Cook over medium heat until all is tender. Correct seasoning if necessary. Remove from heat. Serve hot with soy sauce.

EMBUTIDO

1 cup ground ham
2 pounds pork, ground
4 tablespoons flour
3 sweet pickles, sliced
3 tablespoons raisins
  Salt and pepper to taste
2 eggs

2 small cans tomato paste
3 hard-cooked eggs, sliced
2 chorizos, sliced thin
  (see Glossary)
  Beef broth
1 cup tomato sauce

Mix the ham, pork, flour, sweet pickles, raisins, salt and pepper in a bowl. Add the eggs and tomato paste and mix well. Form into a roll. Take a piece of clean muslin (18″ square) and place the roll on it. Arrange the hard-cooked eggs and chorizos on the roll. Wrap the muslin around it. Tie both ends and sew up the opening. Place in a deep pan and cover with the beef broth. Bring to a boil. Lower heat, cover pot and simmer until done (about 1 hour). Cool. To serve: Unwrap and cut into ½″-thick slices. Serve cold, with the tomato sauce.

LUMPIA WITH SWEET POTATOES

1 cup pork, cut into
    small cubes
6 tablespoons lard
3 cloves garlic, minced
1 medium onion, sliced
½ cup diced bean curd
1 cup raw shelled deveined
    shrimp

1 cup string beans, cut into
    1" pieces
1 cup cabbage, cut into
    1" squares
1 cup cubed sweet potatoes
  Salt to taste
1 stalk celery, finely chopped
20 lumpia wrappers
   Lumpia sauce

Boil the pork in a pot until tender and the fat comes out. Remove the pork from the pot and drain. Put the lard in a large skillet and sauté the pork, garlic, onion and bean curd. Add the shrimp, string beans, cabbage, sweet potatoes and a little water. Season with the salt and cook over medium heat until tender. Set aside on a platter to cool. When cool, add the celery on top.

Lumpia Wrappers
3 cups flour
1 tablespoon salt

5 cups water
  Pork fat

Sift the flour into a bowl. In another bowl mix the salt with the water. Add 1 cup of salted water to the flour to make a stiff dough. Beat the dough hard against the sides of the mixing bowl to soften and to make it elastic. Add more of the water to soften the dough. Continue beating and adding water until the mixture becomes very elastic and has a consistency of heavy cream. Use only enough water to achieve this consistency.

Heat a frying pan greased with pork fat and pour in about 2 tablespoons of the thin batter, tilting the pan to spread the batter as thin as possible. Turn the wrapper when it can be freed from the frying pan and fry quickly on the other side. Remove from pan. Do the same with the rest of the batter.

To serve, put 2 tablespoons of lumpia mixture in each wrapper and fold into a tight roll. Serve with lumpia sauce.

Sauce
6 tablespoons cornstarch
1 cup water

½ cup soy sauce
½ cup brown sugar

Mix the cornstarch with the water in a pan with the soy sauce and brown sugar. Cook over low heat until thick, stirring constantly. Remove from heat and let cool.

HUMBA—PIG'S LEG

Pig's leg (fresh ham)
1 bay leaf
½ teaspoon whole peppercorns
⅓ cup vinegar

6 cloves garlic, crushed
½ cup brown sugar
4 tablespoons soy sauce

Cut meat from bone, trim off fat, and cut into small pieces. Mix the remaining ingredients in a bowl and marinate the meat in this mixture for about 3 hours. Then transfer to a large pot with a cover and put the pot in a large pan of boiling water. Steam until the meat is tender. Remove from heat. Serve hot.

STUFFED SEA BASS

1 4- to 5-pound sea bass
  Salt and pepper to taste
2 medium tomatoes, diced fine
1 medium onion, diced fine
1 medium potato, diced fine

2 tablespoons raisins
3 tablespoons chopped sweet
  cucumber pickles
1 egg
  Fat for frying

Remove the scales from the fish, being careful not to destroy the skin. Rinse well. With the flat of a large kitchen knife beat the fish thoroughly on both sides from head to tail until the flesh is loosened from the skin. Slit the gills at the base of the neck and through the opening carefully remove all the flesh. Then remove all the bones from the flesh. Put the fish meat into a bowl and add a little salt and pepper. Then add the tomatoes, onion, potato, raisins, pickles and egg and mix well. Sprinkle the inside of the fish skin with salt and pepper. Stuff the fish skin with the above mixture until the fish looks whole again. Sew up the opening of the fish and fry in a pan in hot fat until brown. Drain on a paper towel. Serve hot.

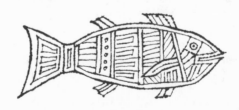

PANCIT MOLO

Dough
  3 cups flour
  ¼ teaspoon salt

  3 egg yolks
  ¼ cup water

Sift the flour and salt together into a bowl. Add the egg yolks and mix well. Gradually add the water and knead until a fine elastic dough is formed. Spread as thin as possible on a floured board and cut into small triangles, about 2½″ each side. Set aside and prepare the filling.

Filling
  1 cup chopped pork
  1 egg yolk

  ½ teaspoon salt
  ¼ teaspoon pepper

Combine all the ingredients in a bowl and mix thoroughly. Place 1 teaspoon of the mixture in the center of each of the triangle wrappers and fold over. Press the edges to seal. Set aside.

Broth
  2 cloves garlic, crushed
  ½ medium onion, chopped
1½ cups shrimp, shelled and
        deveined
     Lard
     Salt to taste

  3 cups shrimp juice (made by
        pounding the heads of the
        shrimp and squeezing out the
        juice with enough water to
        make 3 cups)
  1 chicken, cooked and cut into
        small pieces
  3 quarts chicken broth
     Salt and pepper to taste
  2 tablespoons chopped parsley

In a large pot sauté the garlic, onion and shrimp in a generous amount of lard and cook until brown. Add salt and the shrimp juice. Boil for a minute and add the chicken and broth. Boil for another minute. While broth is boiling, drop in the prepared triangles. Add salt and pepper to taste. Cook about 20 minutes. Sprinkle with the parsley and more pepper before serving. Serve hot.

SWEETS

PUTONG PUTI

2 cups rice soaked and ground
  with 1½ cups water
1½ cups white sugar

½ teaspoon salt
3 teaspoons baking powder
Grated coconut

The ground rice should have the consistency of thick batter. Add to this the sugar, salt and baking powder. Mix thoroughly. Pour into custard cups until each is two-thirds full. Arrange in a steamer and steam for half an hour or until done. Insert a toothpick in each and if it comes out dry, the puto is done. Sprinkle with grated coconut. May be served hot or cold.

MARUYANG CAMOTE

1 cup flour
2 teaspoons baking powder
1 tablespoon sugar
¼ teaspoon salt
  Camote, grated (4 medium
    sweet potatoes)

1 egg
¼ cup milk
  Lard for deep frying
  Sugar

Sift the flour and baking powder into a bowl; add sugar and salt. Add the sweet potato, egg and milk. Mix well and drop by tablespoonfuls into the hot lard. Deep fry until golden brown. Remove and drain on a paper towel. Sprinkle with sugar while still hot. Can be served either hot or cold.

Note: Sweet potato pieces may be fried without batter. After frying, drain well on a paper towel and serve dusted with sugar.

BIBINGKA ROYAL

3 *eggs*
¾ *cups sugar*
1½ *cups coconut milk*
    (*see Glossary*)
2 *cups flour*
4 *teaspoons baking powder*

2 *tablespoons melted margarine*
Butter
Grated cheese
Sugar
Grated coconut

Beat the eggs in a bowl until light and creamy. In a larger bowl dissolve the sugar in half of the coconut milk. Mix and sift the flour and baking powder in a bowl and add by spoonfuls to the sugar-and-coconut-milk mixture. Add the rest of the coconut milk alternately with the dry ingredients and beat well. Then add the eggs and the margarine. Grease a cake pan with butter and pour in mixture. Bake in a 350° F. oven for 50 minutes. When done, remove from pan, brush the top with butter and sprinkle with the cheese, sugar and grated coconut.

TURRON DE ALMENDRAS

1 *pound shelled almonds*
1 *cup sugar*

½ *cup honey*
Wafers

Blanch, peel, then roast and chop the almonds. If a mortar is available, pound the almonds and sugar together; if not, use a blender. Put in a saucepan or copper vat with the honey and cook the mixture over low heat, stirring, until the sugar melts and the mixture begins to brown. Pour into a shallow, 8″ buttered pan. Let cool. Cut into desired pieces and wrap in a wafer.

Wafers
½ *cup flour*

2 *cups water*

Mix the flour and water to make a smooth batter. Use a greased hot wafer iron or griddle to form round wafers of 3 to 4 inches diameter. While still warm and soft, wrap around filling.

LECHE FLAN

Caramelized sugar (see
    next recipe)
2 cups fresh milk
8 egg yolks

1 cup sugar
1 grated lemon rind or 1 teaspoon
    vanilla for flavoring

Make the caramelized sugar and while still hot use it to line a 12″ mold. Scald the milk in a double boiler for 15 minutes. Beat the egg yolks in a bowl with the milk, sugar and lemon rind. Pour the mixture into the mold and place this in a bigger pan half filled with water. Bake in a 300° F. oven until the mixture becomes firm. Cool before removing from the mold. Serve cold.

LECHE FLAN
Coconut

1 cup brown sugar
¼ cup water
2 cups coconut cream
    (see Glossary)

6 egg yolks
4 egg whites, slightly beaten
1 cup refined sugar
1 teaspoon grated lemon rind

Dissolve the brown sugar in ¼ cup water in a saucepan and cook over moderate heat until the sugar browns, or caramelizes. Line a suitable mold evenly with three-quarters of the caramelized sugar and set aside.

Stir the coconut cream into the remaining caramelized sugar. Place over low heat and stir constantly until all the caramel is dissolved. Combine the egg yolks and egg whites in a bowl and beat lightly to mix thoroughly. Add the sugar and lemon rind. Then add the coconut cream with the caramelized sugar and mix well. Strain through a cheesecloth and pour into the mold. Place the mold in a pan with hot water and cook slowly, without allowing the water to boil. After about 1½ hours, place a piece of plain metal sheet over the mold and on this place a few pieces of live charcoal to brown the top of the custard. Or place under the broiler just long enough to brown. Cool and unmold before serving. Serve cold.

BUDIN

1 egg white, unbeaten
1 cup milk
2 tablespoons butter
  Sugar to taste
  Assorted chopped candied
    peel, about ½ cup

¼ cup chopped nuts and raisins
5 egg yolks, beaten
  Maraschino cherries, cut into
    small pieces

Mix all the ingredients in a saucepan except the egg yolks and cherries and cook over low heat until dry. Remove from heat and cool. Then add the egg yolks. Blend well. Pour into small custard cups, garnish with small pieces of maraschino cherries and bake in a low oven until brown. Cool before serving.

BANANA CHIPS

1 cup sugar
⅓ teaspoon salt

20 unripe bananas,
    pared and sliced
  Fat for deep frying

Mix the sugar and salt together in a bowl. In another bowl add 3 tablespoons of the sugar-and-salt mixture to every 3 cups of the sliced bananas. Mix well and deep fry, a few at a time, in hot fat until golden brown. Remove, separate sticking pieces and cool.

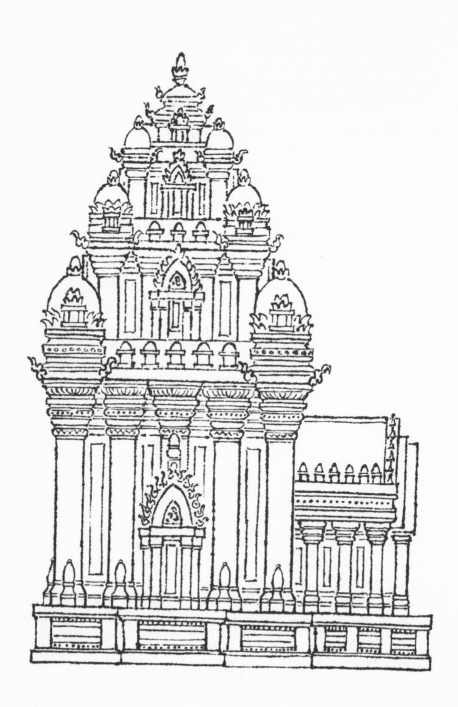

INDOCHINA

In the geopolitical sense there no longer is an Indochina, but the three countries—Cambodia, Vietnam and Laos—that formerly were the French Indochinese states can still be grouped together gastronomically. In their cuisines these countries are much alike. There are culinary differences but, since the three have been subjected to much the same cultural influences, the differences are outnumbered by the similarities. The cuisine of each is native Indochinese (if this word may still be used for want of a better), with overlays of French and Chinese cookery. The effect of these two outside cuisines is most noticeable—in fact, it is predominant—in the cities. The native foods are not dissimilar to the foods of Burma and Thailand, for ties with these countries predate those with the French if not with the Chinese. However, the Indian influence is less noticeable here than it is in Burma, and the subtleties of flavoring are neither so many nor so varied as in Thailand.

Outside the major cities, and the industrial area of North Vietnam, the people of all three countries live off the land and support themselves on its produce. The land is not superabundant in edible resources, and even though it is the source of life to its people, it is largely undeveloped; the modern farm is still a rarity. While cattle are raised in Cambodia and Vietnam, they are rare in Laos, and in none of these countries is there any apparent liking for beef. There's not much liking for lamb either, for that matter, and when meat *is* eaten, it is usually pork. Poultry is used as the main ingredient in quite a number of dishes; not only chickens and ducks, but many wild birds appear often on the dining table. Because of the lack of

155

enthusiasm for red meat (as well as its nonavailability), there is on the whole a protein deficiency in the Indochinese diet that is compensated for in part by the poultry and in part by green peas, corn and soy beans, often made into bean curd. Milk and milk products obviously are rare since there are few cows or goats.

Vegetables are the core of all country cooking. Rice is abundant and essential, a vital part of every meal; sweet potatoes and yams are widely eaten and are prepared in a number of ways. Leafy green vegetables are also popular. Fish, usually fresh-water fish, appears often on the menus of country and city folk alike. Desserts, when eaten, usually consist of fruit or little cakes made of rice or bean flour.

Even on city tables, foods are basically simple, though quite spicy. Omelets, usually with additions such as finely diced pork and shrimp, are often found on the menu, as are rice casseroles, steamed fish, pork stew and other dishes that sound and look like something less than gourmet specials. But it must be remembered that these are not rich countries, that they are not very well endowed with edible natural resources. They use what they've got, and they manage very well. It is the piquancy of the flavoring, the subtlety of the seasoning, that lifts these dishes beyond mediocrity; it is imaginative preparation that turns simple foods into mouth-watering delights. When cooked with verve and style, as they so often are by the Indochinese, the most plain-seeming dishes may be an epicurean experience.

This is probably somewhat less true of Cambodian foods than of the others, at least from a non-Cambodian point of view. Cambodian food is very, very hot; too heavily spiced for Westerners unless it is toned down. It does not lend itself too easily to American tastes. Most visitors to Cambodia, traveling chefs among them, seem to head for the many excellent French or Chinese restaurants and ignore the native variety. Those who do not will find themselves eating glutinous rice, spicy fish, currylike dishes, thick soups and stews. The soups are very good, more like meat-and-vegetable stews than soups. Most of them are rich and substantial, filled with a variety of small morsels. In fact, nearly all Cambodian food is served up in small morsels rather than in chunks or slices. Meat and poultry are seldom, if ever, served whole; almost invariably they are chopped up into bite-sized pieces . . . and then highly seasoned with curry spices. Stews are also popular among Cambodians. Like the soups, they contain a good many different ingredients, most of them quite spicy. Especially well liked are *mean timm,* a chicken stew, and *tea timm,* made with duck.

Authentic Vietnamese food is hard to come by, especially in the cities of South Vietnam. The cooking in Saigon is excellent, but most of it and the best of it is French. The rest of the best is Chinese. Only in normal times, if these are ever to come again, is it possible for an outsider to sample good Vietnamese cooking. Vietnam, particularly South Vietnam, is fairly well supplied with products of the soil and sea. There is seafood in plenty, and the land produces fresh vegetables, luscious strawberries and other fruits, cattle and wild game. Perhaps the best known of the native or near-native Vietnamese meals that are palatable and available to Westerners, and that can be easily prepared in American kitchens, are the shrimp fritters with *o-moi* sauce; the *cha-gio,* or spiced meat rolls; the *yam Vietnam,* a spicy salad of diced shrimp, pork and cucumbers with plenty of seasoning; and the braised chicken with five spices. Dessert is easy. It is nearly always fresh fruit, although by way of a change the Vietnamese may serve a very pleasant sweet dish consisting of lotus seeds cooked in sugar water.

It is the food of Laos that seems to tempt Westerners the most. The Laotian people are of Thai-Indonesian and Chinese origin, and their varied, colorful food (still basically simple) reflects their varied, colorful background. Much of the food is quite spicy, sometimes even rather sharp, but it is interesting food, imaginatively prepared and often extremely tasty.

There is, for example, a delectable semisweet dish called *khao tom* that consists of a mixture of sticky rice, coconut cream and banana slices wrapped in banana leaves and steamed. And surprisingly tasty is the *san ton pa,* a very fine mince of raw fish and seasonings that, eaten with a green salad, tastes very much better than it sounds. Anyone who has accustomed himself to Japanese or Polynesian food will take to it at once. The Laotian version of tartar steak is also most delicious. Then there is *kay phaneng,* stuffed chicken cooked in coconut milk; and *kay patkhin,* chicken with ginger, spicy but exquisite.

For a pleasant and unusual fish dish, the Western housewife might want to try *koy tioum,* or fish cornets. This—or rather, these —consist of fish that are broiled over a glowing fire, then pounded in a mortar, mixed with chopped herbs and vermicelli, served on a

157

large edible leaf (for instance, a cabbage leaf) and eaten with a briny, spicy sauce.

Khao poun is another epicurean experience. This is basically a dish of vermicelli served with raw vegetables and a special sauce; but the actual dish is much more delicate, and more exotic, than that simple description would indicate. The *khao poun* proper is a rice vermicelli that can be purchased ready for use at specialty food shops. The thick sauce with which it is served is made from finely chopped meat and fish cooked with coconut milk, ground peanuts and various seasonings to which a little tomato purée is sometimes added.

The *khao poun*—the rice vermicelli—is brought to the dining table in a soup tureen. Each guest has a soup plate, the bottom of which he covers with *khao poun*. Also on the table is a serving plate of the Laotians' favorite vegetables and greens: banana leaves, bean sprouts, various greens and mint, all cut up into very small pieces. Now the guest adds to his *khao poun* raw vegetables according to his own taste, and then covers both vermicelli and vegetables with a liberal helping of the creamy, tangy sauce.

Kow neo kwan is a very simple but most delicious Laotian coconut-rice cake that may be served as a coffeetime snack or as a dessert. It is nothing but glutinous rice, coconut milk and sugar, but it is delectable. Tea, by the way, is the favored beverage of Indochina.

Most of the Indochinese people serve only two meals a day as a general rule, one between nine and eleven in the morning and the other at around six in the evening or slightly earlier. The idea, of course, is to avoid the noonday heat—but the effect is to bring it back in the hot spiciness of the evening meal.

MAIN DISHES

SAN TON PA
Mincemeat of Raw Fish

2 *pounds fresh fish (sole,*
    halibut, flounder)
1 *teaspoon salt*
½ *cup water*
    Juice of 5 or 6 lemons
5 *medium onions*

5 *cloves garlic*
3 *or 4 fresh pimentos*
2 *tablespoons finely chopped*
    fennel, Chinese parsley,*
    shallots

Reduce the fish to mincemeat after removing all the bones. Place in a bowl. In another bowl mix the salt in the water, then add the lemon juice. Pour this mixture over the fish and let stand for 15 minutes. Chop the onions, garlic and pimentos very fine. Press out the water from the fish and boil this water. Set aside to cool. Mix this juice with the fish. Add the herbs and the onions, garlic and pimentos. The resulting dish is a pale-pink mincemeat of fish, with green speckles from the added condiments. Serve cold with a green salad.

KHAO TOM
Rice with Banana Stuffing

1. Soak in 2 cups cold water 1 cup glutinous rice (*see Glossary*) that has been well washed. Soak for 10 minutes.

2. Pour the milk of one or two coconuts into a square pan and let it boil until it has the consistency of thick oil. Add the drained rice to the coconut milk. Salt slightly and stir.

3. After 4 or 5 minutes remove the mixture from the heat.

4. Cut thin slices of banana lengthwise.

5. Take a piece of banana leaf, spread the prepared rice about half an inch thick on it, add a slice of banana on top of the rice, then another layer of rice. Cover carefully with the banana leaf. Close it well and tie both ends with white thread.

6. Put the little packets in boiling water for an hour and a half. Remove and drain on paper towel. Serve hot or cold.

* Chinese parsley, or coriander leaves, is often available in Oriental markets and in Mexican or Spanish markets.

KOY TIOUM
Fish Cornets

There are three elements:
   the fish itself,
   the sauce with which it is served,
   and the fresh leaves in which every mouthful is wrapped before eating.
   1. Fairly large fish are first skewered lengthwise with bamboo skewers and then grilled over hot embers. It is better to avoid fish with too many bones.

The grilled fish is pounded in a mortar after the bones have been removed.

Next a mixture of finely chopped aromatic herbs is prepared. About 3 tablespoons chopped herbs to 1 pound of fish. Mixture may consist of 1 tablespoon of chopped parsley, 1 tablespoon chopped scallions, 1 teaspoon chopped mint leaves, 1 teaspoon pepper and 1 teaspoon chopped fresh ginger.

An amount of rice vermicelli equal to about half the fish used in this recipe is cut up.

The pounded fish is lightly mixed with the chopped herbs and vermicelli.

2. The sauce is made by adding ½ teaspoon nam pla (*see Glossary*) to ½ cup boiling water. Add a very small amount of dried pimentos, well pounded, with roasted garlic and chervil. Allow sauce to cool.

3. Now the salad leaves are prepared, cabbage will do, and every variety of fresh herb that is available. Each person takes a large leaf, lays on it some of the fresh herbs and a good spoonful of fish; he then folds up his cornet and dips it into the little individual sauce dish that has been placed in front of him.

KAY PHANENG
Chicken with Coconut Milk

1 *medium onion, chopped*
1 *clove garlic, minced*
½ *pound ground pork*
¼ *or ⅓ package fried
     cured pork rinds*

Red or white pepper to taste
*Salt or nam pla (see
     Glossary)*
*Coconut milk (see
     Glossary)*
1 *2-pound chicken*

160

Mix together in a bowl the onion, garlic, pork, pork rinds, pepper, salt and just a little coconut milk. Stuff the well-cleaned chicken with this mixture and put the chicken in a deep pan half filled with coconut milk. Cook over low heat until the chicken is well done and the coconut milk is reduced to cream, then the sauce will be of the correct consistency. Remove from heat. Serve hot, with the coconut milk poured over the chicken.

KAY PATKHIN
Chicken with Ginger

1 1½-pound fryer, cut up	1 piece of fresh ginger
Salt to taste	1 clove garlic, minced
Oil	1 medium onion, sliced

Remove bones, then cut the chicken meat into small pieces and salt. Fry the chicken meat in a small amount of oil in a skillet until yellow, gradually adding hot water until well cooked. Wash and skin the ginger, then cut into very fine long slim pieces (quantity used according to taste). If too hot, squeeze salt into the ginger and wash again, removing all the water. Fry the ginger in a small amount of oil until it gives a good aroma (not too long), remove from the pan and set aside. Fry the garlic and onion until yellow and until they give a good aroma. Add to the ginger. Place the fried ginger, garlic and onion in the skillet with chicken, add a small amount of hot water and heat for 10 minutes before serving. Remove from heat. Serve hot.

LAOTIAN BEEF LAP

1 heaping tablespoon raw rice
3 small dried red chilies
2½ cups water
1 pound ground round or ground
    sirloin
1 teaspoon dried lemon grass
    or 1 teaspoon grated lemon
    rind
1 large yellow onion, chopped
    very fine

3 fresh green chilies, chopped
    fine
1 large green pepper, seeded and
    chopped
¼ cup mint leaves (about 30)
3 tablespoons lemon juice
    Nam pla or salt to taste

Roast the rice in a dry frying pan over a medium flame until it is a pale gold color. Transfer it to a mortar and pound it to the consistency of corn meal. Roast the dry chilies in the same way and pound them in the mortar.

Bring the water to a boil and add the lemon grass and the beef, stirring until the meat changes color. Drain the meat and place in a serving dish with the rice, dried chilies, onions, fresh chilies, green pepper, and the mint leaves (reserving some of the mint for garnish). Sprinkle the lemon juice over all and mix to blend well. Finally add salt or nam pla to taste and garnish with the remaining mint leaves. Serve with plain boiled rice.

SWEET

KOW NEO KWAN
Laotian Coconut-Rice Cake

2 cups glutinous rice
  (see Glossary)

Shredded coconut from
  1 or 2 coconuts
Sugar to taste

Soak the rice in 4 cups lukewarm water for 3 hours; steam in same pot. Thoroughly mash the shredded coconut in lukewarm water in a bowl to obtain coconut milk. Strain the coconut milk into a saucepan and boil over medium heat; simmer until there is a separation of oil on the top and cream on the bottom. Put aside half of this mixture for later use on finished cake. With a wooden spoon stir the cooked rice and sugar into the remaining mixture; continue stirring over low heat until of thick consistency. Lukewarm water may be added to prevent sticking. Remove from heat. Spread the other half of the oil thoroughly over the bottom and sides of a large aluminum dish to prevent sticking; use some to coat one side of a piece of wax paper. Flatten the coconut-rice mixture over the entire dish, as thick as desired. Press with the oiled wax paper. Remove the paper. Spread the other half of the coconut cream on top of the rice cake. Let stand until firm enough to cut. Serve cold.

KOREA

Most of Korea is on a mountainous peninsula jutting down between the Yellow Sea and the Sea of Japan. The rest of the country consists of 3,400 islands, more or less, scattered throughout the nearby seas. Occupied in the course of its history by invaders from neighboring Japan and China, Korea shares certain food habits with both of these countries—but adds an extra spice of its own.

Seafood is abundant in the Korean diet, but not so abundant as one might think in view of the vast stretches of fishing waters. The various invasions of the Japanese brought cattle to Korea, and now the most important—the favorite—meat is beef. Other meats that appear often on Korean tables are pork, chicken, rabbit, mutton, pheasant, deer and boar, but the most characteristic Korean meat dishes contain beef. Meats are usually roasted, broiled, steamed or simmered in water with spices to make soup. Frying is not a traditional method, although it has lately become popular. Most Korean dishes are, fundamentally, mixtures of meat and vegetables—with quite a bit of that extra spice already mentioned. Peppers, sesame seeds, ginger, pine nuts, hazelnuts and chestnuts are typical flavoring ingredients in Korean cookery. Soy sauce and bean paste are regarded as essential foods. Both are used as a base for soups and as flavoring for side dishes of many kinds. Garlic, too, turns up in a number of popular recipes, not infrequently in larger quantities than those to which Westerners are accustomed.

Vegetables, even more than beef, predominate in the diet of the Korean people. Culinary specialties of the various localities are mostly vegetable dishes, such as the *kongnamul* (bean sprouts) of Chongju, the *pibim-bap* (rice mixed with various vegetables and

165

meats) of Chonju and the *sinsollo* of Seoul. *Sinsollo* deserves special mention because it is more than a regional specialty; it is a distinctive dish that has been popular in Korea for centuries and is an instant favorite with nearly all foreign visitors. Some compare it with New England boiled dinners, although it is so distinctively Korean that the resemblance to the specialties of any other country is very slight indeed. It is a mixture of vegetables, meats, nuts and eggs that is slowly cooked in broth in a brass pot over a charcoal brazier on the dining table in front of the guests.

The vegetables used most abundantly in a variety of recipes are radishes and cabbages, while bean sprouts, spinach and lettuce are often cooked as separate dishes. Seasoning, even for vegetable dishes, often calls for liberal amounts of red pepper, black pepper, green onion, garlic, ginger and sesame, and if that sounds hot to you, it *is* hot. However, although Korean food is generally regarded as being on the hot and spicy side, most of it is more than palatable to Westerners who enjoy the flavor of the Orient.

Outside of *sinsollo*, the best known of the vegetable dishes is *kimchi*. *Kimchi* is peculiar to Korea; it is, if anything is, *the* national dish. It appears at virtually every Korean meal, not only at the beginning but at the end as well. This Korean specialty is actually a pickle or, perhaps more accurately, a sort of relish; a spicy combination of turnips, onions, cabbage, radishes and whatever other vegetables happen to be handy, seasoned with rather copious quantities of red and black peppers, garlic and pickled shellfish, all of which are fermented together in a pot of salt water for a number of days or weeks. When the weather is warm, fermentation takes place rapidly, and the *kimchi* is ready for serving within several days. Usually this summer *kimchi* is a little less salty than that prepared for winter and may be made primarily out of cucumbers, various greens and white radishes. Winter *kimchi*, called *kimjang* to distinguish it from its summer cousin, is made largely of cabbage and is distinctly pungent to the taste.

The time of year for making the predominant, the cabbage-based, *kimchi*, or *kimjang*, is late autumn or very early winter. At this season the market places are piled high with tons of cabbages and radishes. Each household buys them by the cartload, and all the womenfolk are kept busy for several days preparing the winter food; in each home, a large quantity of *kimjang* is prepared to ensure that the family has a full supply of this essential side dish throughout the winter, until springtime, when fresh vegetables will again be available. The *kimjang* is stored in giant pots buried in the earth and is removed bit by bit as needed for each meal. *Kimchi,* by any name and at any time of year, is very rich in dietary value. It smells strong and has quite a bite and doesn't sound too good to most non-Koreans, but actually a taste for it is quite readily acquired. Most people who like pickles will love *kimchi.*

Kim—only remotely related to *kimchi*—is artificially cultivated seaweed that is dried and pressed into thin strips looking rather like small pieces of flimsy green paper. *Kim* may be eaten just as it is, added to soups, or coated with sesame oil and broiled. In one form or another, it turns up in any number of dishes. Among the seafoods the Koreans favor are the fish caught in the surrounding waters, primarily pollack and bream. One favorite fish dish, not a spicy one, is *tomi-chun,* which is sea bream fried in batter and eaten with soy sauce. *See-ow chun,* again on the bland side by Korean standards, is fried shrimp that have been dipped into a delicately flavored egg batter. *Jokee-kook* is a chowderlike fish soup that is distinctly spicy and very popular. Other favorite soups feature pork, noodles and cabbage. *Koum-tang* is a rice soup embellished with thin slices of beef—rice being a Korean staple.

Chicken dishes there are in plenty. One that Westerners particularly enjoy is *tak mok am,* a stewed chicken of mild but subtly effective flavor. Not dissimilar is *tak-chim,* or steamed chicken and vegetables. A rather more daring taste experience is *tongtak juk,* traditionally served on holidays and special occasions. This is roast chicken, and it is a gourmet's delight, but only if the gourmet likes quite a lot of garlic. (Of course, the amount of garlic you use in your kitchen is *your* business . . . but the result may not be Korean cookery.)

The one dish that, more than others, seems to appeal to the Western palate just as much as to the Korean is *pulgogi.* Americans often describe this dish as "Korean barbecue," which is a fair enough description. *Pulgogi* ordinarily consists of marinated charcoal-broiled beef, although chicken and pork make fine substitutes. The meat is cut into thin slices, marinated in a spicy brew of soy sauce, chopped onions, ginger and other spices of the cook's choice, and then quickly broiled over a charcoal brazier at the dining table. This is one of the relatively few Korean dishes that is never served from the kitchen; it *must* be prepared in front of the diner, and for the best results, it must *not* be cooked for more than thirty seconds.

Other excellent beef dishes include *bok um pap*, simply beef with fried rice, and *jang-po*, thin slices of beef marinated in soy sauce with sesame seeds and then quickly broiled. Yet another is *sanki sanjok*, or *songi sahn-juhk*, which in one version consists of strips of steak with mushrooms and in another of alternate pieces of beef and vegetables cooked on skewers.

The Korean meal, as a rule, consists of one main dish and a number of side dishes. The main dish is usually steamed rice and the side dishes are soup, meat, fish and vegetables. Sometimes the main dish is rice mixed with other grain, such as barley, or with varieties of beans. Beef, pork, chicken and pheasant are popular meats for the so-called side dishes. Western taste, however, usually rearranges the Korean meal so that the rice is subsidiary to the rest. Such a meal usually starts with *kimchi* and soup and continues with a variety of main dishes, each with a principal component such as chicken, fish, vegetables or pork. Rice may be served on the side or held over for serving toward the end of the meal so that guests will not fill up on it at the expense of the main dishes. A typical meal consists of quite a lot of many things: the *kimchi* and the rice, radishes and seaweed, fried fish or shrimp, steamed or roast chicken, *pulgogi, sinsollo* and then more *kimchi*. Whatever else is served, the most important side dish is *kimchi;* this is an absolute must for the Korean table, if not for yours.

Ordinarily the meal is prepared in the kitchen and brought to the dining area on a small serving table. The typical traditional Korean house does not have a dining room as such; any central living room of the house may be used as a dining area. In well-to-do Korean homes, small braziers are used at the table to prepare food before the guests, in something like the Japanese style, but this is not the general practice except in the case of some few particular foods.

For a regular unceremonial meal, two persons sit on the floor face to face across a small dining table. Cooked rice is placed to the left and soup to the right of each place setting, *kimchi* within easy reach, and a spoon and a pair of chopsticks to the diner's right. Other dishes, which are usually shared by the two people, are placed in the middle of the table. When a meal is taken by more than two people, each couple is served at a separate table. The usual table for everyday meals (much less elaborate than that used for ceremonial occasions) measures about two feet long by one foot across by ten inches high, and is finished in black lacquer. Elegant! But perhaps uncomfortable for those unaccustomed to it; and exactly the same food can be served on your own dining room table, with greater convenience to you and more room for the guests.

Traditional food containers are, with a few exceptions, shaped in the form of the bowl rather than the dish. They are made of wood, brass or china. Today, wooden food containers are relatively rare and are used only on very special occasions. More typical food containers are made of shiny brass or inexpensive chinaware. In the "best families" not only the spoons but the chopsticks are made of sterling silver, but for most people the spoons are of brass or some other alloy and the chopsticks are of the same metal or perhaps of wood, plastic or ivory.

The drink most frequently used today after each meal is *sungnyung*, the warm water poured into the cooking pot of rice after the steamed rice has been taken out. The residue of the rice blends with the water to produce the beverage—which has, if you happen to care for it, the subtly delicious flavor of slightly scorched rice.

The traditional alcoholic beverages of Korea are *takju, yakju* and *soju. Takju* is a kind of wine made from inexpensive stock such as corn, barley or potatoes and is rather on the raw side. *Yakju* is a rice wine, slightly higher in alcoholic content than *takju*, slightly more expensive, somewhat smoother . . . but, like *takju*, inclined to sour quickly in warm weather. If you decide to try any in your home, keep it chilled. The strongest native liquor is *soju*. It is made from grain or potatoes, and though it looks as pure as water, its taste is something else and should be experienced to be described. Of far more delicate flavor are the traditional soft drinks of Korea . . . the teas of ginseng, of ginger and of cinnamon; *ssanghwan-tang* tea, which contains fruits, dates, chestnuts and other nuts; and honey water, bees' honey diluted with cool water. But perhaps you will be more comfortable with Korean beer, which goes well with any Korean meal and tastes as good as any Oriental beer.

BASICS

PREPARED SESAME SEED

1 *cup sesame seeds*   1 *teaspoon salt*

Place the sesame seeds in a heavy skillet over medium heat and brown slowly, stirring constantly. When the seeds are brown remove from heat and place in a bowl. Add the salt and mash or pound the seeds until crushed. Cool and place in a jar. Sesame seeds in this form are used in most recipes.

VINEGAR-SOY SAUCE

½ *cup soy sauce*   3 *tablespoons vinegar*
1 *tablespoon sugar*

Combine all the ingredients in a bowl and mix well. Sugar and vinegar may be added or reduced according to taste. Finely chopped pine nuts may be sprinkled over the top of the sauce, which is used in many recipes.

RICE

STEAMED RICE

2 *cups rice*   3 *cups cold water*

Place the rice in a pan, add the cold water and cover tightly. Bring to a fast boil. Lower heat and steam for 35 minutes. Keep heat as low as possible. Refrain from removing the lid and stirring while cooking. Remove from heat. Serve hot.

SOUPS

BEEF SOUP

½ cup sliced mushrooms
3 green onions, finely chopped
2 cloves garlic, minced
½ pound ground beef
1 tablespoon oil

6 cups water
4 tablespoons soy sauce
Salt to taste
1½ tablespoons prepared sesame
seed (see Basics, p. 170)

Combine the mushrooms, onions, garlic and beef in a bowl and mix well. Heat the oil in a deep pan, add the meat mixture to the hot oil and fry. Add the water and the soy sauce. Add salt to taste and the sesame seed. Bring to a boil. Lower heat and slowly cook until meat is tender. While the soup is cooking make the meatballs.

Meatballs
¼ cup bean curd (see Glossary)
or cottage cheese
1 tablespoon prepared sesame
seed
1 clove garlic, minced
1 green onion, finely cut
1 tablespoon oil

½ pound ground beef
2 tablespoons soy sauce
Salt to taste
Pinch of black pepper
¼ cup flour
2 eggs, slightly beaten
Oil

Press all the liquid from the bean curd or the cottage cheese. Combine the sesame seed, garlic, onion, oil and beef in a bowl and mix well. Stir in the bean curd, soy sauce, salt to taste and a pinch of pepper. Shape the mixture into very small balls, roll them in the flour and then in the eggs and fry in the hot oil in a frying pan. Set aside. In another hot, greased frying pan pour a layer of the remaining eggs and cook lightly, without stirring, on both sides. Remove and cut into small diamond-shaped pieces to be used for garnishing the top of the soup. Remove the tender meat from the soup and set it aside and bring the soup to a boil. Keep the liquid boiling and drop in the meatballs one at a time and continue to boil for 10 or 15 minutes. When serving, place several meatballs in each soup bowl. Return the meat that was removed from the pan and heat briefly. Pour the hot soup over the meatballs and garnish with the diamond egg shapes.

171

KORI KUK
Oxtail Soup

1 oxtail
10 cups water
1 tablespoon prepared sesame
    seed
1 tablespoon finely minced garlic

½ teaspoon fresh ground pepper
3 tablespoons minced onion
¼ cup light soy sauce

Have the oxtail cut into 8 pieces. Wash and place in a pot with the water. Bring to a boil, then simmer for 2 or 3 hours until the oxtail can be easily pierced with a fork. Keep removing the scum from the surface as it forms. Remove the oxtail and cut the meat from the bones into bite-sized pieces. Return the meat to the broth with the remaining ingredients. Bring to a boil again before serving. Remove from heat. Serve hot.

SHIKUMCHI KUK
Spinach Soup

¼ pound beef
1 teaspoon minced garlic
1 tablespoon prepared sesame
    seed (see Basics, p. 170)
2 green onions, cut into thin
    strips

1 teaspoon salt
¼ teaspoon pepper
4 tablespoons miso (see
    Glossary)
6 to 7 cups water
1 pound fresh spinach

Cut the beef into long narrow strips and put in a bowl. Add the garlic, sesame seed, onions, salt, pepper and miso, which has been diluted in a little water, and mix thoroughly. Place in a saucepan and cook over medium heat until the meat is well browned. Add the water and bring to a boil, then reduce heat and cook until the meat is tender. Add the spinach and cook about 5 minutes or until the spinach is tender. Remove from heat. Serve hot.

CHINESE CABBAGE SOUP

¼ *pound beef*
3 *tablespoons soy sauce*
1 *tablespoon prepared sesame*
 seed (see Basics, p. 170)
1 *clove garlic, minced*
 Dash pepper

2 *pounds Chinese cabbage, cut*
 into small pieces
3 *tablespoons minced green onion*
 About 6 or 7 cups water
 Salt to taste

Cut the beef into narrow, thin slices and place in a saucepan. Add 2 tablespoons of the soy sauce, the sesame seed, garlic and pepper. Mix thoroughly. Add the Chinese cabbage and the onion and, stirring constantly, cook over medium heat for several minutes. Add the remaining soy sauce and the water and cook until the ingredients are tender. Add salt to taste. Remove from heat. Serve hot.

KONG NAMUL KUK
Bean-Sprout Soup

3 *cups bean sprouts*
½ *pound lean beef*
1 *teaspoon minced garlic*
2 *teaspoons prepared sesame*
 seed (see Basics, p. 170)

¼ *teaspoon pepper*
1 *green onion, chopped*
4 *tablespoons soy sauce*
6 *cups water*
 Salt to taste

If using canned bean sprouts, drain well. If using fresh bean sprouts, remove the fine hair ends on each sprout and wash well. Cut the beef into thin, small pieces. Place in a saucepan and add the garlic, sesame seed, pepper and onion. Add one half of the soy sauce and mix well. Brown the meat, then add the bean sprouts, mix and cook over medium heat for several minutes. Add the water and the remaining soy sauce and cook, covered, about half an hour or until all the ingredients are tender. Season with salt. Remove from heat. Serve hot.

GREEN-ONION SOUP

¼ pound beef, round or chuck   Dash pepper
 1 clove garlic, minced   1 teaspoon sesame oil
 4 tablespoons soy sauce   6 cups water
 1 tablespoon prepared sesame   4 green onions
     seed (see Basics, p. 170)   Salt to taste

Cut the beef into thin square pieces and put into a saucepan. Add the
garlic, soy sauce, sesame seed, pepper and oil. Mix and cook over medium heat until the meat is thoroughly browned. Now add the water and
cook until the meat is tender. Cut the onions, including the tops, into
short lengths and add to the soup when it is almost done. Continue to
cook until the onions are tender. Season with salt. Remove from heat.
Serve hot.

CHICKEN SOUP

 1 medium-sized chicken   Dash pepper
 2 green onions, chopped   6 tablespoons soy sauce
 1 clove garlic, minced   1 teaspoon salt

Remove the chicken from the bones, cut into small cubes and place in a
bowl. Put the bones into a pot with 5 cups of water and simmer for an
hour. While the broth is cooking, add the onions, including the tops, garlic, pepper and soy sauce to the chicken and mix well. Then in a frying
pan brown the chicken thoroughly. Remove the chicken bones, measure
the broth and add enough water to make 2 quarts. Add the chicken and
salt and cook over medium heat until tender. Remove from heat. Serve
hot.

VEGETABLE DISHES

RICE AND BEAN SPROUTS

1 *cup prepared bean sprouts*
1 *clove garlic, minced*
2 *green onions, chopped*
2 *teaspoons prepared sesame seed*

1 *teaspoon sesame oil*
2 *cups rice*
3 *tablespoons soy sauce*
3 *cups cold water*

If using canned bean sprouts, drain well. If using fresh bean sprouts, remove the fine hair ends on each sprout and wash well. Mix the garlic, onions, sesame seed, bean sprouts and oil together in a saucepan. Cook over medium heat for several minutes, stirring constantly. Add the rice, soy sauce and water. Cover the pot tightly and bring to a quick boil. Turn heat very low and without removing the lid and stirring allow to steam for a half hour. Remove from heat. Serve hot.

RICE AND DATES

½ *cup pitted dates*
2 *cups rice*

3 *cups water*

Cut the dates into pieces and add to the rice in a saucepan. Add the cold water and bring to a quick boil. Lower heat and cover. Keep tightly covered and do not remove lid or stir while cooking. Cook on the lowest heat. Steam for 35 minutes. Remove from heat. Serve hot.

RICE AND GREEN PEAS

3 *cups cold water*
2 *cups rice*

½ *cup fresh green peas*

Add the water to the rice in a saucepan and bring to a quick boil. Boil for 10 minutes, then add the peas. Lower heat to the lowest setting, cover and steam for 20 minutes. Mix before serving. Remove from heat. Serve hot.

RICE WITH MUSHROOMS

1½ tablespoons oil
 ¼ pound ground beef
  1 cup thinly sliced mushrooms
  1 cup thinly sliced onions
     Dash pepper
  3 tablespoons soy sauce

2 teaspoons prepared sesame
    seed
2 cups rice
3 cups cold water
½ teaspoon salt

Measure the oil into a large skillet. Add the beef, mushrooms, onions, pepper, soy sauce and sesame seed. Mix together thoroughly, then cook over medium heat for a few minutes, mixing constantly. Add the rice, then the cold water and salt. Bring to a quick boil, cover, reduce to the lowest heat and steam for a half hour without removing the lid or stirring. Remove from heat. Serve hot.

RICE WITH BARLEY

2 cups boiling water
½ cup pearl barley

1½ cups rice
 2 cups cold water

Add the boiling water to the barley in a saucepan and let stand overnight. Cook the barley in the same water for a half hour over low heat. Add the rice to the barley with the cold water. Cover the pan tightly and bring to a quick boil. Lower heat to lowest setting and steam for a half hour. Do not remove cover or mix while cooking. Remove from heat. Serve hot.

RICE WITH POTATOES

1 cup peeled cubed potatoes
2 cups rice

1 teaspoon salt
3 cups cold water

Add the potatoes to the rice in a saucepan. Add the salt and water, cover tightly and bring to a boil. Lower heat and steam for a half hour without removing the lid or mixing. Remove from heat. Serve hot.

TURNIP-AND-CARROT SALAD

4 *carrots*	1 *teaspoon salt*
2 *turnips*	1 *tablespoon sugar*
3 *tablespoons vinegar*	*Dash of red pepper*

Wash and peel the carrots and turnips. Cut into short lengths and then shred the long way. Put the vegetables into a bowl and add the vinegar, salt, sugar and pepper and toss lightly.

GREEN BEANS

4 *cups green beans*	1½ *teaspoons sugar*
½ *pound beef, chopped fine*	2 *green onions, chopped*
3 *tablespoons soy sauce*	2 *teaspoons sesame oil*
2 *tablespoons sesame seeds*	

Clean the green beans and cut into 2-inch lengths. Parboil in a small amount of water for a few minutes. Drain and set aside. To the chopped meat in a skillet, add the soy sauce, sesame seeds, sugar, onions and oil and mix thoroughly. Cook meat over medium heat until done. Add the beans and continue cooking until the beans are tender but not over-cooked. Remove from heat. Serve hot.

FRIED SWEET POTATOES

4 *small sweet potatoes*	3 *tablespoons oil*
3 *tablespoons flour*	*Salt to taste*
1 *egg, beaten*	*Vinegar-Soy Sauce (see p. 170)*

Scrub, peel and cut the sweet potatoes into thin slices.

Partially cook in salted boiling water. Drain the potato slices and roll them in the flour and then dip them in the egg. Heat the oil in a frying pan and fry the potatoes until golden brown. Remove and drain on a paper towel. Season with salt and serve hot with Vinegar-Soy Sauce.

FRIED GREEN PEPPERS

½ pound finely ground beef
2½ tablespoons soy sauce
    Dash of pepper
 2 tablespoons prepared sesame
    seed
 1 clove garlic, minced

8 small green peppers
1 tablespoon flour
1 egg, beaten
3 tablespoons oil
   Vinegar-Soy Sauce (see p. 170)

Place the beef in a bowl and add the soy sauce, pepper, sesame seed and garlic; mix well. Wash the peppers, cut in half lengthwise and remove the seeds. Fill the peppers with the meat mixture. Dip each pepper in the flour and then roll it in the egg. Gently fry in the oil until the peppers are almost soft. Cover the pan and steam until the meat is cooked through. Remove from heat. Serve hot with Vinegar-Soy Sauce.

KONGNAMUL
Bean Sprouts

4 cups fresh bean sprouts
2 tablespoons sesame seed
3 green onions, chopped
3 tablespoons soy sauce

2 teaspoons oil
   Dash of red pepper
1 teaspoon salt

Wash the bean sprouts and remove the fine hair ends from each sprout. Cover with boiling water and cook over medium heat until soft. Drain well. Add the sesame seed, onions, soy sauce, oil and pepper. Mix well and reheat until the seasonings are well blended. Add the salt. Remove from heat. Serve hot.

CARROT, CELERY AND CHINESE CABBAGE SALAD

1 *Chinese cabbage*
1 *small bunch carrots*
3 *stalks celery*
2 *teaspoons salt*

1 *teaspoon oil*
2 *tablespoons vinegar*
3 *tablespoons sugar*

Cut the Chinese cabbage into very narrow short strips. Do the same with the carrots. Shred the cabbage very fine and cook with the carrots in a small amount of salted water for 3 or 4 minutes. Drain and set aside to cool. Shred the celery very fine, sprinkle with 1 teaspoon of salt and set aside for 10 minutes. Then rinse well and drain. Heat the oil in a frying pan and fry the celery for a few minutes, stirring constantly. Set aside to cool. Now mix all the vegetables together in a bowl and add the remaining teaspoon of salt, the vinegar and sugar. Mix thoroughly and serve.

FRIED EGGPLANT

1 *medium eggplant*
1 *egg*
  Salt to taste

¼ *cup flour*
  Oil
  Vinegar-Soy Sauce (see p. 170)

Wash and peel the eggplant, then cut into small pieces about ¼-inch thick. Beat the egg and salt together in a bowl. Dip the pieces of eggplant into the flour, then into the egg. Slowly fry in a small amount of oil until golden brown on both sides. Remove from heat. Serve hot with Vinegar-Soy Sauce.

MAIN DISHES

SPINACH WITH BEEF

2 *pounds spinach*
¼ *pound ground beef round*
2 *green onions, chopped*
  Dash of red pepper
1½ *tablespoons prepared sesame seed*

1 *clove garlic, minced*
2 *tablespoons soy sauce*
1 *teaspoon oil*
1 *tablespoon sugar*
  Salt to taste

Pick over the spinach and wash well. Cook in a small amount of water until tender. Do not overcook. Drain well, cut into small strips and place in a bowl. To the beef in a skillet add the onions, red pepper, sesame seed, garlic, soy sauce, oil and sugar. Mix thoroughly. Brown the meat, then mix it with the spinach and salt to taste. Remove from heat. Can be served hot or cold.

TURNIPS WITH BEEF

6 *small turnips*
3 *tablespoons salt*
½ *pound ground beef round*
¼ *teaspoon red chili powder*
3 *green onions, chopped*
3 *tablespoons prepared sesame seed*
1 *clove garlic, minced*

3 *tablespoons soy sauce*
  Dash of black pepper
2 *teaspoons oil*
5 *tablespoons water*
3 *tablespoons sugar*
  Salt to taste
1 *teaspoon chopped candied ginger*

Clean, peel and cut the turnips into small cubes. Sprinkle with the salt and let stand for 15 minutes. To the beef in a skillet add the chili powder, onions, sesame seed, garlic, soy sauce, pepper and oil and mix thoroughly. Brown well. Wash the turnips, removing all the salt, and add to the meat mixture. Add the water, sugar, salt to taste and ginger. Cook over medium heat until tender. Remove from heat. Serve hot.

FRIED BEEF PATTIES

1 *pound ground beef round*
2 *tablespoons prepared sesame*
  seed
¼ *cup soy sauce*
  Dash of pepper
½ *teaspoon salt*

3 *green onions, chopped*
1 *clove garlic, minced*
¼ *cup flour*
2 *eggs, beaten*
  Oil
  Vinegar-Soy Sauce (see p. 170)

Place the beef in a bowl and add the sesame seed, soy sauce, pepper, salt, onions and garlic. Mix thoroughly and shape into patties. Coat the patties with the flour, then dip into the egg. Fry in a small amount of oil until done. Serve hot with Vinegar-Soy Sauce.

CHARCOAL-BROILED BEEF

1 *pound beef sirloin*
¼ *cup sugar*
2 *tablespoons oil*
2 *green onions, chopped*
1 *clove garlic, chopped*

½ *cup soy sauce*
  Dash pepper
¼ *cup prepared sesame seed (see*
  Basics, p. 170)
1 *tablespoon flour*

Cut the beef into thin squares and place in a bowl. Add the sugar and oil and mix thoroughly. In another bowl mix together the remaining ingredients. Add to the meat and again mix well. Allow to marinate for a half hour. Place on skewers and broil over a charcoal fire.

FRIED BEEF

Use the same ingredients and prepare as for Charcoal-Broiled Beef (*see above recipe*). After marinating the meat, fry in a small amount of oil. When the meat is well browned, add a little water, cover tightly and steam until tender. Remove from heat. Serve hot.

BROILED OR FRIED CHICKEN

2 1½-pound fryers
¼ cup sesame seed
3 green onions, chopped
2 tablespoons sugar

½ cup soy sauce
   Pepper to taste
2 cloves garlic, minced

Clean the chickens, remove the meat from the bones, cut into thin slices and place in a bowl. Combine all the other ingredients, mix and add to the chicken. Allow to stand for a half hour. Broil until browned and done. If desired, chicken meat may be slowly fried in a small amount of oil. If frying, add a little water after the chicken is well browned, cover tightly and steam until tender. Remove from heat. Serve hot.

CHICKEN POK-KUM

1 3-pound fryer
3 scallions, chopped
2 cloves garlic, chopped
   Dash pepper
3 tablespoons sesame seed

2 tablespoons sugar
¼ cup soy sauce
½ cup sliced mushrooms
   Salt to taste

Remove the chicken from the bones and cut into small pieces about 1½ inches square. Place in a pot with enough boiling water to cover and simmer until partially cooked. Combine the scallions, garlic, pepper, sesame seeds, sugar and soy sauce in a bowl and mix well. Drain the broth from the chicken and reserve. Add the seasonings to the chicken with the mushrooms and just enough of the broth to partially cover the chicken and mushrooms. Simmer until the chicken is very tender. Season with salt to taste. Remove from heat. Serve hot.

BROILED PHEASANT

1 pheasant
2 green onions, chopped
   Pepper to taste
1 clove garlic, minced
2 tablespoons prepared sesame
   seed (see Basics, p. 170)

¼ cup soy sauce
1 teaspoon salt
1 tablespoon sugar
1 teaspoon oil

182

Clean the pheasant, remove the meat from the bones and cut into thin slices. In a bowl mix together the remaining ingredients. Place the meat in the combined seasonings and let stand for 15 minutes. Broil until tender. Serve hot.

BROILED OR FRIED PORK

1 *pound pork*	3 *green onions, chopped*
3 *tablespoons sugar*	2 *tablespoons prepared sesame*
1 *clove garlic, minced*	*seed (see Basics, p. 170)*
Pepper to taste	1 *teaspoon candied ginger*
½ *cup soy sauce*	2 *teaspoons oil for frying*

Cut the pork into thin squares and place in a bowl. Combine all the other ingredients except the oil, add to the pork and mix well. Allow to stand for a half hour. Broil or fry in the oil. If frying, add a little water after the meat has been well browned, cover tightly and cook until tender. Remove from heat. Serve hot.

BOILED PORK

2 *pounds pork*	¼ *cup soy sauce*
3½ *cups boiling water*	*Vinegar-Soy Sauce (see Basics,*
2 *teaspoons salt*	*p. 170)*

Cover the pork in a pot with the boiling water. Add the salt and simmer until almost tender. Add the soy sauce and simmer for another 20 minutes. Remove from the broth and allow to cool thoroughly. Cut into very thin slices and serve with Vinegar-Soy Sauce.

BOILED BEEF

Same as the above recipe for Boiled Pork, but substitute beef brisket.

SINSOLLO

This recipe is prepared in a sinsollo, which is a brazier similar to a chafing dish. It is a metal bowl with a tube in the center for the burning charcoal. Meat and vegetables are arranged around the tube, the cover is put on, burning charcoal is placed in the tube and the food is cooked at the table. A large chafing dish makes a good substitute.

½ pound beef (¼ pound ground and ¼ pound cut into small square pieces, about 1 inch)
6 tablespoons soy sauce
1 tablespoon sugar
2 cloves garlic
  Pepper
2 tablespoons prepared sesame seed (see Basics, p. 170)
¼ cup oil
2 tablespoons pine nuts
¼ cup flour

3 eggs
4 small turnips
2 cups salted water
¼ pound beef liver, cut into small pieces
1 teaspoon salt
4–6 mushrooms
1 egg, separated
½ teaspoon flour
1 hard-cooked egg
10 pistachio nuts
3 walnuts

Divide the beef squares in half and marinate half in a mixture of 1 tablespoon soy sauce, 1 teaspoon sugar, ½ clove garlic, minced, dash of pepper, 2 teaspoons prepared sesame seed and 1 teaspoon oil. Set aside for 15 to 20 minutes. Sauté in a small amount of oil until tender. Set aside.

To the rest of the beef squares, add 3 tablespoons soy sauce, 2 teaspoons sugar, 1 clove garlic, minced, dash of pepper, 1 teaspoon prepared sesame seed and ½ tablespoon oil. Mix thoroughly. Set aside.

To the ground meat add 2 tablespoons soy sauce, ½ clove garlic, minced, dash of pepper, 1 tablespoon prepared sesame seed and 1 teaspoon oil. Mix thoroughly, then make tiny meatballs. Shell and remove the skin from the pine nuts, placing 1 pine nut in the center of each ball. Roll in flour and dip in the beaten egg. Sauté in a small amount of oil until done. Set aside.

Peel the turnips and boil them, whole, in 2 cups salted water until done. Remove the turnips and save the water. Cut the turnips into 2-inch squares about ¼ inch thick. Set aside.

Place the liver in boiling water and cook for 3 minutes. Remove all skin and cut into small pieces. Sprinkle with the salt, dredge in the flour, dip in the egg and sauté in a small amount of oil until tender. Set aside.

Slice the mushrooms and lightly sauté in oil. Set aside.

Add a dash of salt and ¼ teaspoon flour to the white of the egg and also to the yolk and beat each slightly. Cook separately by swirling small amounts of each over the bottom of a heated greased frying pan. When firm turn and cook slightly on the other side. Cut the egg into small pieces. Set aside.

Slice the hard-cooked egg for decoration. Set aside.

Shell and blanch the pistachio nuts. Shell the walnuts and carefully separate in half, then blanch. Set aside.

When all the food is prepared, place in the bottom of the sinsollo a layer of turnips, then a layer of uncooked beef, pieces of the fried egg, mushrooms, liver and cooked beef until the sinsollo is filled. Put the tiny meatballs around the center stem of the sinsollo. Decorate with all the nuts and the slices of the hard-cooked egg. Add the water from the turnips, cover the sinsollo, fill the center with burning charcoal and cook at the table.

LIVER

2 cloves garlic, minced	2 teaspoons oil
¼ cup soy sauce	1 pound beef liver
Pepper to taste	2 medium onions
2 tablespoons sesame seed	1 cup water
3 tablespoons sugar	Salt to taste

In a skillet mix together the garlic, soy sauce, pepper, sesame seed, sugar and oil. Cut the liver into very thin short strips and place in the seasoning mixture. Cut the onions into small slices and add to the liver. Cook over medium heat about 5 minutes, add the water and continue to cook until tender. Salt to taste before serving. Remove from heat. Serve hot.

FRIED LIVER

1 pound beef liver	1 egg, beaten
2½ cups boiling water	2 or 3 tablespoons oil
2 teaspoons salt	Vinegar-Soy Sauce (see p. 170)
3 tablespoons flour	

Cook the liver in boiling water about 4 or 5 minutes, then drain. Remove all skin and cut into very thin slices. Salt, dredge in flour and dip in the egg. Sauté in the oil. Remove from heat. Serve hot with Vinegar-Soy Sauce.

BOILED TONGUE

1 small tongue, about 1 pound	2 tablespoons soy sauce
2½ cups boiling water	1 teaspoon salt

Wash the tongue. Place in a pot with the boiling water and simmer until almost tender. Remove the skin, return to the pot, add the soy sauce and salt and continue to cook for another 20 minutes. Remove and thoroughly cool. Before serving cut into very thin slices. Good served with Vinegar-Soy Sauce (*see Index*).

FRIED FISH

1 pound boned fish	2 eggs, beaten
1 teaspoon salt	¼ cup oil
4 tablespoons flour	Vinegar-Soy Sauce (*see p. 170*)

Cut the fish into thin 2-inch squares. Salt, then dredge in the flour and dip in the egg. Sauté in the oil until golden brown and tender. Remove from heat. Serve hot with Vinegar-Soy Sauce.

FRIED SHRIMP

½ cup flour	¼ cup oil
1 teaspoon salt	Salt to taste
1 pound raw deveined shrimp	Vinegar-Soy Sauce (*see p. 170*)
2 eggs, beaten	

Combine the flour and salt. Roll the shrimp in the flour and dip in the egg. Fry in the oil until tender. Season with salt. Remove from heat. Serve hot with Vinegar-Soy Sauce.

FRIED OYSTERS

1 pound oysters	¼ cup oil
½ cup flour	1 teaspoon salt
2 eggs, beaten	Vinegar-Soy Sauce (*see p. 170*)

Check over oysters and remove shells. Dredge each oyster in the flour, dip in the egg and fry in the oil. Season with the salt. Remove from heat. Serve hot with Vinegar-Soy Sauce.

SALTED FISH

1 pound perch or mackerel	¼ teaspoon pepper
¼ cup water	1 scallion, chopped with top
1 tablespoon sugar	1 clove garlic, minced
4 tablespoons soy sauce	½ teaspoon candied ginger

Have the fish skinned and boned. Cut into small squares and place in a skillet. Add the remaining ingredients and mix thoroughly. Cook over medium heat until the fish is tender. Remove from heat. Serve hot, in small portions, with rice.

CONDIMENTS

CUCUMBER KIMCHI

5 medium-sized cucumbers	¾ teaspoon chopped red chili
1 tablespoon salt	peppers
2 green onions, very finely	1 teaspoon salt
chopped	½ cup water
1 clove garlic, minced	

Wash the cucumbers, cut unpeeled into quarters lengthwise and re-move the seeds. Cut each piece into 2-inch strips and place in a bowl. Add the salt, mix thoroughly and allow to stand for 20 minutes. In an-other bowl mix the onions, garlic and red chili peppers. Wash the salt from the cucumbers and drain. Combine with the onion mixture and the salt and water. Mix well, put in a jar, cover and set aside for 2 days to a week.

187

SOY-SAUCE KIMCHI

3 Chinese cabbages	1 tablespoon chili peppers
1½ cups soy sauce	Pepper
1 cup sliced turnip	¼ cup water cress
1 medium cucumber	1 or 2 medium firm pears
1 tablespoon salt	6 dates
3 cloves garlic, minced	4 chestnuts
3 green onions, minced	¼ cup pine nuts
1 teaspoon candied ginger, chopped	⅓ cup sugar, if desired

Discard the outer leaves from the cabbages. Wash the cabbages, then cut into 1½-inch pieces. Place in an earthen jar. Add ¼ cup soy sauce and mix well. Allow to stand for several hours or until the cabbage is soft. Mix several times to let the soy sauce flavor the cabbage. Clean and peel the turnip and cut into very thin slices. Wash the cucumber (don't peel it), cut in half lengthwise and remove the seeds, then cut into thin slices. Mix the turnip and cucumber and ½ cup soy sauce thoroughly. Set aside until soft, about 3 hours. Mix a few times.

Drain the soy sauce from the turnips and cucumbers and the cabbage and save it. Combine the vegetables, add the salt and mix. Add the garlic, onions, ginger, chili peppers and pepper. Shred the water cress and add to the vegetables. Peel and slice the pear into thin small pieces. Pit the dates and cut into small pieces. Peel and thinly slice the chestnuts. Add the pear, dates, chestnuts and pine nuts to the vegetables and mix thoroughly. Add the sugar to the mixture and add the saved soy sauce plus any more necessary to make ½ cup soy sauce to each 2 cups of water needed to cover the vegetables. Let stand in the earthen jar, covered, for 3 weeks.

TURNIP KIMCHI

8 *medium turnips*
2 *tablespoons salt*
1 *red chili pepper, chopped*

1 *teaspoon chopped candied*
  ginger
Water

Wash, peel and cut the turnips into quarters. Place in a bowl, add 1 tablespoon salt and 1 cup water and set aside for 48 hours. Remove the turnips and save the salt water. Cut the turnips into ¼-inch pieces. Place the turnips in a jar and add the chili pepper, ginger and the remaining tablespoon of salt. Add enough water to the salt water saved from the turnips to make 2 cups and add to the turnips. Mix thoroughly, cover, and place in the refrigerator for 2 weeks.

SPRING KIMCHI

3 *cups Chinese cabbage, cut in*
  1-inch squares
¼ *cup salt*
4 *green onions, with tops*
1 *tablespoon chopped candied*
  ginger

1 *tablespoon chopped red chili*
  peppers
1 *clove garlic, minced*
1 *tablespoon salt*
1½ *cups water, or more*

Wash the cabbage and place in a bowl. Sprinkle with the salt and set aside for 20 to 30 minutes. Cut all of the onions into short strips and shred. In another bowl combine the onions, candied ginger, chili peppers and garlic. Wash the salt from the cabbage three times. Thoroughly mix the cabbage with the onion mixture, add 1 tablespoon salt and place in a crock or jar. Add enough water to cover the cabbage. Let stand, covered, for 1 week. Will keep for several weeks in the refrigerator.

SWEETS

CHESTNUT BALLS

5 cups chestnuts, in the shell
¼ cup sugar
4 tablespoons honey

2 teaspoons cinnamon
4 tablespoons minced pine nuts

Boil the chestnuts until tender. Remove the shells and the skins and mash or put through a sieve. In a bowl mix the sugar, honey and cinnamon with the chestnuts and shape into small balls. Roll in the minced pine nuts.

DATE CANDY

1 cup pitted dates
3 tablespoons honey

½ teaspoon cinnamon
½ cup minced pine nuts

Mince the dates in a bowl until very sticky. Add the honey and cinnamon to the dates and mix well. Roll the mixture into small shapes, place a pine nut in each and roll in the minced pine nuts.

FRIED CAKES

1 cup flour
1 teaspoon baking powder
½ teaspoon salt
3 tablespoons sugar

Water
6 dates, shredded
Small amount oil for frying

Mix the flour, baking powder, salt and sugar in a bowl and add just enough water to make a firm dough. Roll out to about ⅛ inch thick. Cut into 2-inch circles. Press bits of the dates into the dough. Fry on both sides in the oil until browned. Serve hot.

SWEET DRINKS

SWEET FRUIT DRINK

1 grapefruit
1 cup sugar
5 cups water

¼ cup whole pine nuts
Fresh or candied cherries and/
or citron

Remove all the pulp from the grapefruit and place in a bowl with ¼ cup sugar and set aside for a half hour. Boil the remaining sugar with the water, then set aside to cool. Place a spoonful of grapefruit pulp in small individual glass bowls. Add about 1 cup of the sugar-and-water mixture to each bowl. Place some pine nuts on top and add cherries and/or thinly sliced citron. Serve with a spoon.

STRAWBERRY DRINK

2 cups strawberries
1½ cups sugar

1 quart water
3 tablespoons whole pine nuts

Wash the strawberries, remove the stems and slice. Add 1 cup of sugar and set aside. Boil the water and the remaining ½ cup of sugar for several minutes and set aside to cool. Place the berries in dessert bowls and add the sugar sirup and some pine nuts to each bowl. Serve with a spoon.

MALAYSIA

Strictly speaking, there is no "Malaysian" cooking, for Malaysia is more than one country or one race; but this is a minor technicality for the gourmet and one that is easily overcome. What he is looking for is the food style that is most characteristic of the area, and one that represents it best.

The traveler to Malaysia finds, first, a fascinating plural society with a great many multicolored threads of national tradition and culinary custom. External influences are many, but mostly so old and well established that they no longer seem external. In fact, Malaysia, more than any other nation, can rightly be called *the* melting pot of Southeast Asia. The cultures that rub shoulders with one another on the streets and in businesses and in the marketplaces are Malayan, Indian, Chinese, European and Eurasian, and the foods that may be found are some of each and sometimes something like a mixture of all. Among the nations that had influence in this area, only the British have not left their mark upon the national cuisine.

Malaysia, because of all these influences, is a paradise for the visiting gourmet. With the slightest effort he will find the simplest of Indian foods (fried noodles, sold and eaten at the wayside) and the most complex of French; he can sample the many courses of an elaborate Chinese meal or the hot curries and *satays* that appear in so many different forms on the true Malayan menu.

What concerns us here is the latter—Malay food, the native food of the majority of the peoples of Malaysia. "Malaysia" is, after all, a political term; "Malay" and "Malayan" are terms descriptive of a particular people, a particular culture and a particular cuisine. Truly indigenous and at the same time distinctive dishes are not found among the Chinese or Indians of these parts nor, indeed, among the natives of Sabah or Sarawak. They are found among the Malays of the eleven Malay states that comprised the Federation on the Malay Peninsula.

Even among the Malays themselves, however, fine dishes are slightly disguised by the intermingling of cultures, and meals served in a Malayan household may not be Malayan at all—just as meals served in an American household may be of French, Italian or Oriental origin. The Malayan housewife is capable of serving almost every type of Chinese food—with the Malayan touch—and every type of Indian food. The rich *biryani,* or *biriani,* rice dishes so well known in India are often to be seen on the Malayan menu, accompanied by spicy chicken or mutton curries similar to those of India. Since the Malayans are largely a Moslem, or Islamic, people, it is not surprising that some of their foods have an affinity with those of India-Pakistan. Nor is it surprising that the Malayan diet is not totally dissimilar to that of neighboring Indonesia, whose culture and customs are closely allied. The Malayan *satay,* for instance, can easily be recognized as a close cousin to the Indonesian *saté.*

Yet with all the intermingling, there are differences between the Malayan and the other cuisines of the area, and it is in these differences that Malayan food finds its true excellence. It begins with an abundance of fresh foods. The sight-seer, or the gourmet who goes in search of native-style restaurants, is almost bound to pass a market square, and if he does he will surely note a profusion of fresh and prepared foods. Not far away is the lush greenery of an abundant countryside; here in town are stalls laden with exotic fruits of unfamiliar name, brilliant flowers and little tasty cakes, and vegetables and yams of all descriptions. Here is the produce that he will find: fruit of the palm, jackfruit, passion fruit, hog plum and Chinese pear, bananas in a variety of colors; rice and tapioca; pineapples, coconuts, edible roots and tubers; coffee, tea, sugar and pepper—and, with the pepper, a multitude of other spices. These are all everyday foods, the most essential of which is rice, the bread of the Malayan diet and its least dispensable element. There is also protein in plenty: beef, mutton, poultry and fish. With these re-

194

sources there is little wonder that Malayan food is so very good.

The climate in Malaysia is hot and moist, and the style of eating is easygoing and unhurried. Meals are leisurely family affairs. The traveler, wondering what he dare eat for his first meal in this spice-loving land, is likely to try the *satays* first. The *satay*, probably even more popular among the Malays than the hamburger or hot dog is among Americans, can be found at the best of restaurants and the lowliest of sidewalk *satay* stands. A walk down almost any street will turn up a view of a vendor with his charcoal brazier and an irresistible aroma of *satays* slowly turning crisp and brown on the glowing coals.

The *satay* consists of small chunks of beef or chicken threaded onto a skewer (preferably bamboo) and broiled with a sort of barbecue sauce. Simple enough—but the sauce is like no barbecue sauce of the Western world. Spices for marinating and sauces for garnishing; these are what make the *satay*. And what makes the *satay* so surprisingly hot is the superbly tangy sauce, based on hot chilies and roasted peanuts pounded fine. It is a marvelous dish for an evening in Malaysia or a Saturday afternoon in an American back yard.

The spices appear in almost every Malayan main dish, fresh spices usually pounded into curry and used to flavor meat, fish and vegetable dishes of all kinds. Even a potentially mild dish such as shrimp and vermicelli is braced with garlic and chili peppers, and a beef or mutton curry usually contains an admixture of chili pepper, black pepper, coriander, cardamom, dill, anise, mustard seed, cumin and turmeric, with all the spices carefully ground and mixed by the mother of the house or by the restaurant chef.

Favorites on the Malayan menu, with Malayans and visitors alike, are the chicken soups, fish curries, fish in papers and the spiced meats served with rice. Easy to prepare and delicious to taste are *rendan santan,* or coconut chicken with onions and spices; lobster coconut curry; the spicy chicken fricassee, or *opor;* and *rendang kering,* beef and coconut curry. The coconut does much to counteract and yet enhance the sharp tang of the curry. Malayans, in common with many Oriental peoples, prefer fruit to practically anything else for dessert, although once in a while they will choose little cakes instead or a delectable coconut concoction such as *sarikauja,* or coconut custard.

The American housewife will have no difficulty in finding suitable ingredients for a Malayan meal. All are easily obtainable from Chinese, Indian or Mexican food stores or specialty food departments. Even if no such stores are accessible, there is no harm in using one's imagination or ingenuity once in a while and making a substitution —resulting in a Malayan dish with the personal stamp of the American cook. That, after all, is the way the Malayan housewife does it herself.

MAIN DISHES

FISH WITH SWEET-AND-SOUR SAUCE

1 *teaspoon ginger root, finely*
  chopped
  Salt and pepper to taste
1 *1½-pound bass*
2 *teaspoons cornstarch*
  Fat for deep frying

2 *tablespoons tomato ketchup*
1 *cup water*
1 *teaspoon sugar*
  Salt and pepper
1 *small cucumber, minced*

Mix the ginger root with the salt and pepper to taste. Cover the cleaned fish with this mixture and marinate for 15 minutes. Cover the fish lightly with 1 teaspoon cornstarch and let stand for about 15 to 20 minutes. Deep fry the fish in the hot fat until golden brown. Remove and drain on a paper towel. Place on a serving plate.

Combine the remaining teaspoon of cornstarch, the ketchup, water, sugar and salt and pepper to taste in a saucepan. Cook over medium heat until the sauce is thick. Pour over the prepared fish and serve hot, garnished with the cucumber.

RICE AND FISH

2 *medium onions, chopped*
¼ *cup butter*
1 *pound cooked cod or scrod*
1 *teaspoon salt*
¼ *teaspoon pepper*

4 *tablespoons finely chopped*
  toasted almonds
2 *hard-cooked eggs, chopped*
½ *cup water*
2 *cups hot cooked rice*

Fry the onions in a pan in the melted butter. Flake the fish in rather large pieces, add to the onions and continue to fry until the onions are soft. Add the salt, pepper, almonds and eggs. Then add the water and the hot rice and mix well. Remove from heat. Serve hot.

SHRIMP CURRY

1 small onion, chopped
2 tablespoons butter
2 tablespoons finely chopped
    ginger
2 tablespoons curry powder
    Salt to taste
⅓ cup beef broth

1 pound cleaned shrimp
    Juice of 1 lemon
1 small cucumber, unpeeled,
    seeded and diced
    Dash of hot pepper
1 cup milk

Sauté the onion in the butter in a skillet until a golden color. Mix the ginger, curry powder and salt to taste and add to the beef broth. Mix well. Add to the onion and simmer for 20 minutes. Add the shrimp, lemon juice, cucumber and a dash of hot pepper. Add the milk and simmer until tender. Remove from heat. Spoon over hot rice.

LOBSTER CURRY

2 1¼-pound live lobsters
2 cups chopped onions
2 cloves garlic, minced
½ cup butter
3 tablespoons curry powder
2 teaspoons ground ginger
1½ teaspoons salt

2 teaspoons sugar
    Dash of cayenne pepper
3 cups coconut milk (see
    Glossary)
2 medium cucumbers, peeled,
    seeded and diced
2 tablespoons lemon juice

Boil the lobster for 10 minutes and save the liquid. In a large frying pan fry the onions and garlic in the butter until a golden color. Add the curry powder, ginger, salt, sugar, cayenne pepper and coconut milk. Mix thoroughly and simmer for 15 minutes. Remove lobster meat from shell. Add lobster meat, cucumbers, and the water in which the lobster was boiled. Cover the pan and simmer slowly for 20 minutes. Add the lemon juice to taste and bring to a boil. Remove from heat and serve hot with light fluffy cooked rice.

198

LAMB CURRY

2 *teaspoons curry powder*
3 *teaspoons salt*
1 *pound lamb, cut into tiny cubes*
  About 1 pint boiling water

1 *pound fresh grated coconut*
¼ *cup minced onions*
  Fat for frying
  Lemon juice

In a bowl sprinkle the curry powder and salt over the lamb and mix well. In another bowl pour the boiling water on the coconut and soak for 5 minutes. Strain the coconut through cheesecloth and squeeze out the milk. Set aside. Sauté the onions in fat in a frying pan until a golden color. Add the lamb and continue frying over low heat for 15 minutes. Add the coconut milk and simmer for a half hour with the pan covered. When the lamb is tender add lemon juice to taste and bring to a boil. Gravy should be thick. Remove from heat. Serve hot with rice.

CHICKEN CURRY

2 *1½-pound chickens*
¾ *cup fresh grated coconut*
¼ *cup butter*
2 *cups sliced onions*
¾ *teaspoon ground saffron*
½ *teaspoon ground dried chili peppers*
1 *tablespoon ground coriander*
2 *teaspoons salt*

2 *cloves garlic, minced*
2 *teaspoons ground ginger*
1 *tablespoon lemon or lime juice*
1½ *teaspoons sugar*
1 *tablespoon cornstarch*
2 *cups coconut milk (see Glossary)*

Clean the chickens and remove the bones. Cut the meat into small pieces. In a deep frying pan lightly brown the coconut in 2 tablespoons of butter. Remove from the pan and reserve. Add the remaining 2 tablespoons of butter to the pan and brown the onions. Combine the chicken with the onions and add the saffron, chili peppers, coriander, salt, garlic, ginger, lemon juice and sugar. Simmer over low heat for 5 minutes, stirring often. Mix the cornstarch with the coconut milk. Add to the pan and stir in. Simmer over low heat until the chicken is tender. Remove from heat. Serve with rice.

BIRYANI

3 cups water
8 ounces grated coconut
1 tablespoon minced fresh ginger
1 teaspoon paprika
½ teaspoon chili powder
½ teaspoon ground turmeric
1 1½-pound frying chicken, cut
    up
3 medium onions, sliced
3 tablespoons fat
5 cloves
1 head garlic, crushed
1- inch stick cinnamon
½ cup whole cashew nuts
1 cup raisins
3 cardamom seeds
4 cups raw rice
    Salt to taste
2 medium tomatoes, quartered
2 green peppers, cut in 1-inch
    pieces

Pour 1 cup water over the coconut in a bowl. Press out firmly with your fingers and pour through a strainer. Follow the same procedure with the remaining 2 cups of water. Reserve the coconut milk. Mix the ginger, paprika, chili powder and turmeric and sprinkle over the chicken. Brown the onions in the hot fat in a large deep pan. Add the cloves, garlic and cinnamon and fry. Add the nuts, raisins and cardamom seeds and continue cooking. Add the chicken and mix thoroughly with the mixture in the pan. Brown lightly. Add the rice and salt to taste, mix and add the coconut milk. Cover the pot and bring to a quick boil. Arrange the tomatoes and peppers on top without mixing them in the chicken-and-rice mixture. Cover tightly and continue cooking over low heat until liquid is absorbed. Mix occasionally. Remove from heat. Serve hot.

CHICKEN FRICASSEE

1 3- to 3½-pound frying chicken
½ teaspoon ground cumin
½ teaspoon ground anise
2 teaspoons cinnamon
2 tablespoons ground coriander
⅛ teaspoon ground cloves
⅛ teaspoon ground cardamom
1 teaspoon freshly ground black
    pepper
2 teaspoons salt
½ teaspoon ground nutmeg
¼ cup butter
¼ cup fresh grated coconut
½ cup chopped onions
2 cloves garlic, minced
4 medium onions, sliced
1 teaspoon lemon juice
½ cup coconut cream (see
    Glossary)

Remove the chicken from the bones and cut into small pieces. In a bowl mix together thoroughly the cumin, anise, cinnamon, coriander, cloves, cardamom, pepper, salt and nutmeg. Pierce the chicken pieces with a fork, mix with the seasonings in the bowl and marinate for about an hour. Melt the butter in a skillet and brown the coconut, chopped onions, garlic and chicken. When browned add the sliced onions, lemon juice and coconut cream. Cook over low heat, covered, until the chicken is tender and the gravy has cooked down. Remove from heat. Serve hot.

BEEF SATAY
Barbecued Skewered Beef

1 *pound boneless beef*	*Pinch of caraway seeds*
1 *tablespoon sugar*	3 *cloves*
5 *shallots, minced*	1 *tablespoon peanut butter*
2 *tablespoons curry powder*	*Skewers*
Dash of garlic powder	

Cut the beef into small strips or cubes. Combine the remaining ingredients in a bowl and add enough water to make a paste. Mix thoroughly. Cover the meat completely with the mixture and set aside for an hour and a half. Then barbecue over glowing coals after threading pieces of beef onto skewers. Serve with a bowl of the following sauce.

Sauce

Ground red pepper to taste	½ *cup oil*
2 *teaspoons peanut butter*	2 *teaspoons sugar*
1 *teaspoon shrimp paste*	1 *tablespoon lemon juice*

Fry the red pepper, peanut butter and shrimp paste in the oil until well blended. Add the sugar and lemon. Simmer over low heat about 1 hour. Remove from heat. Serve hot.

RENDANG KERING
Malaya's Beef Curry

2 cloves garlic
½ teaspoon dried ground chili
  peppers
1 cup chopped onions
1 tablespoon ground ginger
½ teaspoon ground coriander
2 teaspoons salt
3 tablespoons oil

¼ cup shredded fresh coconut
2 pounds beef, cut into small
  cubes
2 cups coconut milk (see
  Glossary)
2 tablespoons lemon juice
1 teaspoon brown sugar

Pound the garlic, chili peppers, onions, ginger, coriander and salt to make a thick paste. In a heavy saucepan heat the oil, add the coconut and brown. Mix in the paste mixture; then add the meat cubes, mixing thoroughly. Cook over medium heat for 10 minutes. Add the coconut milk, lemon juice and brown sugar. Cover and simmer over low heat until the meat is tender, 45 minutes to an hour. Remove from heat. Serve hot.

SALAD

1 medium head lettuce
2 medium cucumbers
1 small can pineapple chunks,
  drained

½ pound boiled bean sprouts
6 pieces fried bean curd (see
  Glossary)

Shred the lettuce, cut up the unpeeled cucumbers and place in a bowl with the pineapple. Add the bean sprouts and fried bean curd. Stir in the following dressing.

Dressing
½ pound ground peanuts, roasted
1 tablespoon vinegar
1 teaspoon lime juice

1 tablespoon ground chili peppers
2 tablespoons sugar
1 teaspoon soy sauce

Mix the peanuts in a bowl with the vinegar, lime juice, hot peppers and sugar. Add the soy sauce and mix.

SWEETS

COCONUT CANDY

4 *cups fresh grated coconut*   1 *cup evaporated milk*
3 *cups sugar*   1 *pinch salt*
2 *teaspoons butter*   1 *teaspoon vanilla*

Place all the ingredients except the vanilla in a saucepan. Cook over low heat, mixing well, until the mixture is boiling and all the sugar has melted. Keep mixing constantly to prevent burning. Reduce heat when the mixture starts to thicken. Continue cooking until the mixture is thick and leaves the side of the pan to form a lump. Add the vanilla, mix well and turn the mixture out onto a buttered plate. Without pressing down spread the mixture out to cool. Cut into pieces while still slightly warm, but do not separate until the candy is hard.

SARIKAUJA
Coconut Custard

6 *eggs*   2 *cups coconut cream* (*see*
¼ *teaspoon salt*   *Glossary*)
2 *cups sugar*   ½ *cup fresh grated coconut*

Preheat oven to 350° F. Combine the eggs, salt and sugar in a bowl and beat until thick and light. Add the coconut cream and continue beating. Stir in the coconut. Pour into buttered individual custard cups or a long buttered casserole. Place in a shallow pan with cold water. Bake about 25 minutes or until a knife inserted in the custard comes out clean. Prevent water from boiling in the pan by adding a small amount of cold water as needed. Serve cold.

JAPAN

The simple word "cooking" does little justice to the Japanese manner of preparing and serving food. "Culinary art" is by far the better term, for each step in the presentation of a meal is like a movement in a symphony. A Japanese meal reflects the very essence of the Japanese people, with their love for disciplined beauty and their appreciation of all forms of artistry.

The food customs of the Japanese are rooted deeply in their history and in their soil and seas. Fish, rice and green tea have been staple foods throughout the centuries. The narrow Japanese islands are encircled by rich fishing waters, and the changing of the seasons provides a changing scene of fish, shellfish, kelp and seaweed. But only a small portion of the land area is suitable for farming, so the products of the soil have always—with one or two exceptions—taken second place to the products of the seas. The major exception is rice, mainstay of the Japanese diet since ancient times and still on the menu for breakfast, lunch and dinner.

Yet the cultivable land is more than one large rice paddy. For more than a thousand years, vegetables, fruits and nuts have been plentiful in Japan. A generally mild climate permits lavish growth of berries, wild fungi and cultivated strains of the same fruits, nuts and vegetables that flourished throughout the centuries. Pears, apples, mandarin oranges, persimmons, peaches and grapes grow in controlled profusion, as do tea, wheat, barley and potatoes.

The people of former days were confined to these products of their land and waters; they taught themselves to eat whatever was edible and to prepare it in many different, imaginative ways. While the idle rich were toying with chrysanthemum petals, the farmers and peasants ate such earthy foods as oats and millet, sweet potatoes and *daikon,* the large carrot-shaped Japanese radish that appears today on the most elegant of Japanese menus. As early as the sixth century, the upper classes were beginning to appreciate the finer things of life, particularly well-prepared food, and by the fourteenth century, they had developed the everyday business of cooking and eating into a fine art. Making skillful use of the materials at hand, from octopus through rice to lotus roots, they evolved a native cuisine of superb quality, possessing unique flavors and an extra something found in few other countries either then or now—beauty, a beauty that made food not only a pleasure to eat but a delight to feast the eyes upon. It was at this time, too, that the famous tea ceremony was born, and many other ceremonial observances relating to the preparation and service of food. An unwritten set of rules came into being, a code prescribing virtually every act connected with food from the correct manner of slicing a lily bulb to the appropriate way for an aristocrat to wipe his fingers. Many of these food ceremonials still exist in the same form today, and the education of a cultivated Japanese lady of the twentieth century necessarily includes a thorough grounding in every phase of culinary custom.

In some cases the people of today's Japan have made certain changes in traditional practice in order to meet their own modern needs and to include new items in their diet, but even in these cases it is possible to see traces of old custom lingering under various disguises. Since time immemorial, for instance, it had been the informal custom to partake of foods in a particular and proper order: first the products of the mountains, then of the seas, then of the fields and finally of the towns. The leisured folk of the fourteenth century formalized the custom and elaborated upon it, and the busy people of the twentieth century have changed the practice but kept the spirit of it. In the raw fish delicacy called *sashimi* the ingredients are often arranged in a design representing a landscape of hill, field and water, and the dish *kuchigawara* usually consists of the seasonal offerings of sea, fields and hills attractively arranged in a single container. Thus custom remains, transmuted by time though it may be.

Japanese meals are light and they are easy on the waistline. This, too, has much to do with custom: the aristocrats of old did no work at all and thus had no need for calories. The food they preferred (in fact, most of the food that was available) was free of animal fat, light in starch except for the inevitable rice and mild in taste. Spices were not required because the main ingredients were of such high quality that spices could only spoil the natural taste, and of course the palate of the true aristocrat was so delicate that he could appreciate only the most subtle of flavors. Curries and other spicy-hot flavorings were definitely *out*. Their harshness drowned true taste. Quick-cooking, too, it was discovered, preserved the fleeting natural flavors, and certain subtle condiments enhanced them.

"Enhancement" became, and remained, the key word. The essential principle of Japanese culinary art is to preserve the fresh, true flavor of all ingredients while retaining and enhancing the natural beauty of the foods. By expert use of such natural seasoning products as *katsuobushi* (dried bonito), *kombu* (sea kelp), *shiitake* (dried mushroom), *shoyu* (soy sauce) and *miso* (soybean paste), the practiced cook can transform the simplest dish into a taste treat without disguising its true character.

Ajinomoto is another name you will encounter frequently as you explore the byways of Japanese cookery, for it is used in almost every dish to accent the essential flavor. The chances are that you use it in your kitchen right now; it is monosodium glutamate, a crystalline salt that improves the natural taste of food without changing it.

Fish, rice, green tea, vegetables (pickled or fresh) and soup. . . . These were, and are, the essentials of a Japanese meal. But the two dishes best known outside Japan appeared relatively late on the scene. These are *tempura* and *sukiyaki,* and even though they don't date back to the sixth or even the fourteenth century they are nonetheless authentically Japanese. They are tremendously popular in Japan among the Japanese themselves and they have a high rate of acceptability to guests from other lands. Therefore, they are doubly qualified to serve as an introduction to Japanese food.

Tempura is an assortment of small pieces of seafood and crisp fresh vegetables, all thinly coated with a feather-light batter— "light as silk gauze," as the Japanese describe it—and fried in vegetable oil until golden brown at a constant temperature of exactly 380° F. If the oil is too hot, the Japanese cook warns, the crust will be tough or the batter will be burned before the meat is done; if it is not hot enough, the *tempura* will have too oily a taste. And too much flour in the batter makes the *tempura* doughy, instead of filmy and

207

crisp. Sounds difficult? Not at all; it can be done in any American kitchen by any reasonably patient cook.

You might enjoy tasting *tempura* at a Japanese restaurant or *tempura* bar before trying the cooking experience for yourself. In the more traditional Japanese restaurants the cook sits on the floor facing the guests across the low dining table and, in that position, both cooks for the guests and serves them, keeping pace with their appetites. One after the other the bite-sized morsels pass from the chef's platter of ingredients into the sizzling oil and then onto the diner's plate. The moment the plate is empty the chef replenishes it with whatever the diner likes best. You have only to indicate your favorite and it will be there before you, crisp and still sizzling from the oil. Now you dip it into a sauce of grated white radish, *shoyu* and fish broth, pop it into your mouth—and find fresh offerings already on your plate.

A great variety of ingredients may be used in *tempura*, but *ebi*, or shrimp, are practically indispensable. Other favorites are the little whitebait and other very small fish, fried whole; tiny scallops, bits of eel, clams and cuttlefish; strips of salmon or sole and occasionally chicken; vegetables of many sorts, ranging from mushrooms through mildly spiced herbs, green onions, garden beans and peppers to the lowly sweet potato. It is possible to find all these items served together at one *tempura* feast, while on other occasions you might find yourself being offered a very delicate combination of prawns, chrysanthemum leaves and seaweed. A more typical happy-medium *tempura* is likely to include samplings of shrimp, flounder, eel, clams, octopus, fragments of ginger root and root of lotus and five or six vegetables.

A *sukiyaki* dinner, even more than *tempura*, should be taken in company with several other diners, for its very nature demands that it be prepared in the midst of a group so that the guests may help themselves at will. *Sukiyaki* is a kind of meaty equivalent to *tempura*, though without the batter. It is a meal of fresh meat, sautéed with vegetables in a sauce of *shoyu* and sugar—and at the same time it is very much more than that. The combination of ingredients, and the subtlety with which they are combined, is what makes *sukiyaki* something more than merely meat sauté and sauce.

No one really knows the origin of *sukiyaki*, but it may have been inspired by the favorite fare of the hunting Mongolians. They, it is said, would cut the freshly killed game into small pieces, place the meat on the end of a *suki* (or spade) and grill it over an open charcoal fire that they called *yaki*. Today the meal is cooked indoors, and the materials vary according to the ingenuity and imagination of the chef. The master chefs of Tokyo usually insist upon using Kobe beef as the main ingredient; chicken, pork and duck are also considered suitable. But whatever else may be used, certain items are vital: a charcoal brazier and pan; the best of all available meat, sliced as thin as the sharpest of knives will cut it; strips of *konnyaku* (a jellied paste of devil's-tongue, which is related to the taro of the South Sea Islands); slices of onion or leek; *shoyu;* and sugar or *mirin*, a sweet spirit distilled from rice, and for which *sake* may be substituted. Less vital but nevertheless highly desirable are bamboo shoots and fresh mushrooms; *shirataki*, a kind of vermicelli made from *konnyaku;* strips of carrot, string beans and spinach or Chinese celery and *tofu*, or bean cake. Rice and raw egg must be provided on the side for the diner to do his share.

If you were to serve *sukiyaki* Japanese style, you would dip the ingredients into the sauce of *shoyu* and *mirin* and sizzle them quickly in hot fat in a heavy iron saucepan over the *hibachi*. Your guests would help themselves from the pan with their chopsticks, each taking/whatever strikes his fancy and transferring it to his bowl of beaten egg. Here it cools for a moment, before he dips it into the rice and eats it. Provide forks, if you like, for your Western guests, but not for your Japanese friends, for the Japanese feel that cold metal against one's lips detracts from the taste of the food.

Other Japanese foods may not have the instant appeal of *tempura* and *sukiyaki* because they seem rather strange at first encounter. But even the fabled raw fish turns out to be less exotic and far more palatable than the words "raw fish" would suggest. The secret is in the preparation.

A great Japanese favorite is *sushi*, served as a snack or hors d'oeuvre. *Sushi* bars and sidewalk carts and stands are probably even more common in Japan than hot dog stands or ice cream counters are in America. There are many kinds of *sushi*, but in nearly all of them the basic ingredients are raw fish, vinegared rice and a little grated *wasabi* root, which is much like horseradish. Some *sushi* lovers like their *sushi* in the form of *chirashi-sushi*, a mixture of the rice, vegetable and fish; but the choice of most *sushi* devotees is *nigiri-sushi*, which comes in the form of small balls of rice with a tracing of *wasabi* along the top and the delicately flavored thin slice of fish molded over it.

Yet another favorite is *sashimi*. This is raw fish without rice, although rice is certain to turn up later on the menu. It is a simple dish, nothing more than small, thin slices of fresh mackerel, tuna, eel, prawn, bream, lobster or other seafood served with garnishes of green seaweed and *daikon,* dipped into a mildly vinegary sauce and eaten as an appetizer.

Kabayaki, or broiled eel, is also very popular. The eel must be absolutely fresh; it comes directly from the sea or the eel pond to the chef, who splits it in one deft motion, skewers it on bamboo sticks and broils it over a charcoal fire. At just the right moment, known only to the chef himself, the chef removes it from the fire and steams it until tender. Then he dips it into *waricho* sauce, which is based on *shoyu* and *mirin* but always contains, in addition, the chef's own special ingredients, and broils it again. The dipping and broiling process is repeated until all sides are done and the eel is juicy with the basting liquid.

Then there are the soups, the thick and the clear. *Suimono,* the clear soup, is basically a broth made from dried bonito flakes. To this base many things may be added, so long as they do not muddy the liquid and prevent the diner from seeing the clear shapes of the extra ingredients. The contents vary according to the occasion and the season. Sometimes the soup bowl may reveal a design representing tiny shells on the bottom of a pond; sometimes the impression of small fish swimming under floating petals or the leaves of a water plant; sometimes a view of clouds drifting over a field. The designs are all edible, for they are produced by artistic placement of small pieces of fish and vegetables in the lucid soup of the bowl. The heartier *miso-shiru* soup is made of essentially the same broth with *miso* stirred in and vegetables added in large quantities without regard to design. Often, at formal meals, *suimono* is served early and *miso-shiru* toward the end of the meal with rice.

Other Japanese favorites are *chawan-mushi,* an interesting and tasty concoction that is part custard and part soup. . . . *Yakitori,* skewered broiled chicken. . . . *Tonkatsu,* pork cutlets in the Japanese style. . . . *Soba,* buckwheat noodles cooked in soup. . . . *Norimaki,* a kind of *sushi* with a seaweed wrapping. . . . *Teriyaki,* beef, fish or chicken marinated and broiled. . . . *Yosenabe,* a chicken, shrimp and cabbage casserole. . . . And the many kinds of *tsukemono,* the Japanese pickle dishes.

The people of today's Japan, unlike the people of most other Oriental countries, usually eat three regular meals a day with occasional snacks in between. Breakfast may at first appear unusual to Western eyes and palates: the Japanese believe that a bowl of bean-paste soup is the best way to start the day. Some Japanese have learned to prefer oatmeal and fried eggs, but a more typical morning meal still consists of *miso-shiru,* the bean-paste soup, served with *tofu* (bean-curd cake) and *negi* (green onion); a bowl of rice to which is added a beaten raw egg seasoned with *shoyu;* two or three thin sheets of *yaki-nori* (dried seaweed) and a small dish of *tsukemono,* or pickles.

Lunch may be as simple as a bowl of noodles in hot soup, with perhaps a trace of meat and a few vegetables added for variety, or it may be a full-course meal of rice, fish, vegetables, a thick or clear soup, salad, pickles and a portion of meat. Dinner depends on the occasion. A formal dinner for honored guests usually consists of two soups and five side dishes. At such a meal one might be served a clear *suimono* soup; *sashimi,* the vinegared raw fish; *tsukemono;* a steamed dish of either meat or fish; then the thick potagelike *miso* soup followed by a boiled dish; then a marinated dish; and then a serving of broiled fish. If the dinner is even *more* formal you might be expected to work your way through three soups and eleven side dishes, not to mention the pickles and the repeated servings of warm *sake,* or rice wine, and quantities of green tea. It sounds formidable, but the portions are manageable and there are no rich sauces or overpowering spices to dull the appetite.

Even more manageable is the dinner served in the average middle-class home when there are no guests present. It consists of a clear soup with a little design of fish and vegetables resting in the bottom of the bowl, a small serving of *sashimi,* a larger serving of a broiled fish or meat dish and the inevitable bowl of fluffy boiled rice. Salad or pickles may be served, and sometimes a light dessert such as fruit-juice jelly or iced bean curd. Or the dinner may be a full meal of *sukiyaki* or *tempura.*

Unless the meal is particularly formal and elaborate, the several courses of a Japanese dinner do not come one after the other but are all served at once. Each guest is given a square lacquer tray on which there are several plates or lacquered bowls containing the various courses, one of which is always rice and another is soup. There is also a pair of chopsticks on a pottery rest and a *sake* cup. Dishes for a Japanese meal are quite unlike our own, for they are designed to match the food being served rather than each other.

There are dozens of designs to go with every food in the Japanese cuisine. Color is of first importance and after that the shape. Plain white is very rarely used. Most Japanese ware is covered with designs of fish and fruits and vegetables in a variety of colors. The underlying theme is that of harmony of color and shape between the dishes and the foods that they contain. Thus the container is always selected to complement the contents, not only the main food item but the garnishes as well. The food itself, whatever it may be, must look beautiful both on the precooking platter and on the dining plates or bowls. Slices must be even, garnishes must create interesting color effects, and all must always be delightful to the eye.

The American housewife probably has no desire to immerse herself in the details of color harmony or the intricacies of aristocratic custom. But there is every reason why she should want to try the nourishing low-calorie Japanese diet on her family and friends. They will be surprised that something so "exotic" can be so very palatable!

BASICS

DASHI
Soup Stock

Dashi is a light, clear fish stock, indispensable in Japanese cooking. It is used as a soup base and as the liquid ingredient in many recipes. Dashi one is used chiefly for soups. Dashi two is used in such dishes as tempura and chawan-mushi. Either one may be stored in the refrigerator.

Dashi one
- 1 inch nori (*see Glossary*)
- 5 cups water
- 1 cup flaked dry bonito
- 2 teaspoons salt
- 1 teaspoon soy sauce

Rinse the nori well and place in the water in a saucepan. Bring the water to the boil quickly and remove the nori. Reserve it for dashi two. Add the bonito to the still-boiling broth, then remove from heat immediately and let stand for 2 minutes. Pour the broth into another pan, straining through clean cloth, and season with salt and soy sauce. Save the bonito for dashi two.

Dashi two
- ⅓ cup flaked dry bonito
  Flaked bonito saved from dashi one or 1⅓ cup dry bonito
  Nori saved from dashi one, or 1 inch nori (*see Glossary*)
- 3 cups water
- ½ teaspoon monosodium glutamate

Put the flaked dry bonito and the bonito and nori saved from dashi one in the water in a saucepan. Bring to a boil and remove from heat at once. Strain through cloth and add the monosodium glutamate.

STEAMED RICE

The Japanese prefer their rice plain and unflavored, with the grains firm but slightly sticky. Its blandness permits other flavors to be accented.

1 cup rice   *1½ cups water*

Place the rice in a heavy 1-quart saucepan. Add the water and place over high heat. Bring to a rolling boil, cover, reduce to medium heat and cook for 10 minutes. Reduce heat to very low and steam for another 10 minutes. Do not lift the lid at any time during the cooking process. Turn heat off altogether and let the pot stand for a final 10 minutes. Keep covered until ready to serve and do not stir.

SOUPS

EBI NO SUIMONO
Shrimp Soup

The suimonos are the clear soups with a dashi base decorated with a small, edible design. In making most Japanese clear soups, stock and solid ingredients must be prepared separately and then combined for serving. In this way each of the ingredients retains its own flavor.

4 strips of fresh spinach, 1 inch wide
Lightly salted water
8 small shrimp, shelled and deveined

4 pieces Chinese mushrooms (see Glossary), or whole button mushrooms, or sliced fresh mushrooms
3 cups dashi one

Rinse the spinach in the lightly salted water. Drain, squeeze out the water and set aside. Boil the shrimp for about 5 minutes in lightly salted water. Drain and set aside. Boil the mushrooms for a minute or two in the shrimp water and then drain. Heat the dashi to a low simmer. Place 2 shrimp, one strip of spinach and one piece of mushroom in each of 4 small bowls. Pour the hot dashi into the bowls. Serve hot.

CHICKEN SOUP

1 *whole chicken breast*
½ *cup soy sauce*
6 *scallions, finely chopped*

4 *pieces Chinese mushrooms (see*
   Glossary), or whole button
   mushrooms, or sliced fresh
   mushrooms
3 *cups dashi one*
1 *piece ginger root*

Remove the chicken from the bones and cut into bite-sized pieces and combine with the soy sauce in a saucepan. Boil the chicken in the soy sauce until tender, then remove. Divide the chicken, scallions and mushrooms among 4 small soup bowls. Heat the dashi to simmering point. Press the juice from the ginger root and put 2 drops in each bowl. (The juice may be extracted from the ginger root with a garlic press.) Pour steaming-hot dashi into each bowl and serve.

EGG SOUP

3 *teaspoons cornstarch*
2 *tablespoons water*
4 *cups dashi one or other clear*
   soup stock
1 *teaspoon salt*
3 *tablespoons soy sauce*

½ *teaspoon monosodium*
   glutamate
2 *eggs*
1 *ginger root*
½ *ounce mitsuba (see Glossary)*
   or 2 tablespoons chopped
   scallions

Mix the cornstarch with the water, then add it to the soup stock in a saucepan. Add the salt, soy sauce and monosodium glutamate. Bring to a boil, stirring. Beat the eggs thoroughly and pour slowly into the hot soup in a thin stream using a circular motion. Cook until the eggs float to the surface in strips. Pour into soup bowls. Extract the juice from the ginger root with a garlic press and add 2 drops to each bowl. Add the mitsuba if available, or sprinkle with the scallions. Serve at once.

215

EGG CUSTARD SOUP

½ cup cooked chicken, finely cut
4 ⅛-inch slices bamboo shoots
4 ⅛-inch slices kamaboko (see
    Glossary)
½ cup cooked green peas

4 Chinese mushrooms (see
    Glossary), cubed and soaked
    in water 6 hours
4 eggs
4 cups cold dashi one
    Salt to taste

In 4 individual chawan-mushi bowls (see Glossary) put an equal amount of chicken, bamboo shoots, kamaboko, peas and mushrooms. Beat the eggs and blend into the cold dashi. Add salt to taste. Pour the egg-and-dashi mixture over the chicken and vegetables in the bowls in sufficient amount to cover them. Place the bowls in a pan that has about 2 or 3 inches of boiling water in it. Cover and allow to steam for 25 minutes over low heat. A green leafy vegetable may be used instead of the peas and cooked cut-up shrimp may be substituted for the chicken. Serve hot.

Note: Do not use soy sauce for seasoning because it will discolor the eggs.

EGG AND SCALLION SOUP

6 cups dashi one
1 tablespoon soy sauce

4 eggs
4 scallions, chopped fine

Bring dashi to a boil. Add soy sauce. In a small bowl beat the eggs well. Turn off the heat under the dashi. Gradually add the beaten eggs to the hot soup, beating constantly. Garnish each portion with some of the chopped scallion.

USHIO-JIRU
Clam Soup

1 dozen large fresh clams
5 cups water
1 teaspoon salt

1 teaspoon soy sauce
1 tablespoon sake
8 sticks ginger

Wash the clams thoroughly and scrub with a stiff brush to remove all sand. Bring the water to a boil in a large saucepan. Drop in the clams and continue to boil until the shells have opened. Remove from heat, discard the shells and flavor the broth with the salt, soy sauce and sake. Serve 3 clams to a bowl filled with the broth. Float 2 ginger sticks on top of each serving.

MISO-SHIRU
Bean-Paste Soup

¼ pound raw shrimp
5 cups beef broth (dashi one may be used if preferred)
1 cup miso (see Glossary)

½ teaspoon monosodium glutamate
1 square bean curd (see Glossary)
4 scallions

Shell, devein and chop the shrimp. Bring the broth to a boil in a saucepan and stir in the chopped shrimp. Reduce heat and cook for 5 minutes. Stir in the miso and add the monosodium glutamate. Cook for another 5 minutes. Dice the bean curd and chop the scallions. Add the bean curd and scallions to the soup and immediately remove the soup from the heat. Serve hot.

UWO DANGO NO SHIRU
Soup with Fish Balls

1 pound filet of flounder, fresh or frozen
2 tablespoons miso (see Glossary)
1 small piece ginger, grated
3 scallions, finely chopped
¼ teaspoon salt
⅛ teaspoon pepper

3 tablespoons cornstarch
6 cups dashi one or 3 cups clam juice and 3 cups beef bouillon
⅓ pound fresh spinach, shredded
1½ tablespoons soy sauce
1 tablespoon vinegar

Chop the fish fine and place in a bowl. Add the miso, ginger and scallions and grind or mash together. Blend in the salt and pepper. Add the cornstarch and mix well. Bring the dashi to a boil in a saucepan. Using a spoon and rubber spatula, form the fish mixture into small balls and slide them into the boiling liquid. Cook over low heat for 5 minutes. Increase the heat slightly and add the spinach. Cook for another 3 minutes, then add the soy sauce and vinegar. Remove from heat and skim if necessary. Serve hot.

SATSUMA-JIRU
Miso Soup with Chicken and Vegetables

6 cups dashi one
½ teaspoon monosodium
    glutamate
¼ pound chicken breast
½ cup finely chopped carrots

1 cup finely diced potatoes
2 scallions, chopped fine
½ cup miso (see Glossary)
   Sansho (see Glossary), minced
   (optional)

In a saucepan bring the dashi to a boil and add the monosodium gluta-mate. Remove the chicken from the bones and cut into small pieces. Add the vegetables and the chicken to the soup stock and cook over low heat until tender. Add the miso and cook gently for another 5 minutes. Re-move from heat. Pour into soup bowls and serve. Sansho may be added when serving.

HORS D'OEUVRE

SASHIMI
Raw Fish Appetizer

½ pound filet of fresh tuna,
   boneless swordfish, salmon or
   sea bass
   Parsley

Small quantities of soy sauce, hot
   mustard, grated fresh horseradish and finely sliced ginger
   root

Select a block of absolutely fresh tuna about 1½ inches thick. Remove skin, if any. Chill thoroughly in the refrigerator so that the flesh is firm and icy-cold, though not frozen. Place the fish flat on a board and cut against the grain with a very sharp knife, slicing the fish into neat, thin sections no more than one-tenth of an inch thick. Arrange the slices on a fish-shaped dish, letting each slice overlap another, and garnish with the parsley. Serve with the fish platter surrounded by small condiment dishes of the soy sauce, mustard, horseradish and ginger root. Each guest dips his own fish slices into the condiment of his choice.

LOBSTER SASHIMI

1 *lobster tail removed from freshly killed lobster*	1 *teaspoon monosodium glutamate*
Lettuce, cabbage and radishes	2 *teaspoons lemon juice*
½ *cup soy sauce*	*Horseradish*

Cut off the soft undershell of the lobster tail—without damaging the upper shell. Remove the meat from the tail, taking care not to damage the shell. Devein and rinse the meat in very cold water. Cut it into 10 or 12 small pieces, then place the pieces in ice water and chill for about 15 minutes. Remove from the water and dry thoroughly with clean absorbent cloth or a paper towel.

Boil the meatless shell until it turns red. Rinse the shell and chill it. Line the inside of the cooled shell with equal amounts of shredded lettuce and cabbage and finely shredded radishes. Place the lobster meat on the vegetable lining in the shell.

Combine the soy sauce, monosodium glutamate and lemon juice and serve it in small individual bowls. Provide each guest with a tiny condiment dish containing grated fresh horseradish. Each diner then prepares his own mixture of horseradish and sauce and dips the lobster meat into it before eating.

SASHIMI TO KYURI
Cucumber-and-Raw-Fish Appetizer

4 *small cucumbers*	1 *tablespoon sugar*
4 *teaspoons salt*	1 *teaspoon grated ginger root or*
1 *pound filet of sole*	½ *teaspoon ground ginger*
⅓ *cup soy sauce*	1 *tablespoon sake or white wine*
⅓ *cup vinegar*	

Peel the cucumbers, cut in half lengthwise and remove the seeds. Slice into thin strips. Spread the strips out on a platter and sprinkle with 2 teaspoons of salt. Allow to stand. Rinse the fish in icy water and dry. Cut into paper-thin slices, slightly smaller than the cucumber strips. Sprinkle with the remaining 2 teaspoons of salt and allow to stand for half an hour. Prepare the dressing by combining the remaining ingredients in a bowl. After the fish has stood for half an hour, place a fish slice on each of the cucumber strips. Roll each cucumber-fish strip into a tight roll and secure with a toothpick. Place the rolls in a bowl and pour the dressing over them. Refrigerate for 1 hour, then serve as an appetizer.

NIGIRI-SUSHI
Rice-and-Raw-Fish Appetizer

2 *cups rice*
3 *cups water*
3 *tablespoons vinegar*
1 *teaspoon salt*
1 *tablespoon soy sauce*
1 *tablespoon mirin (see Glossary)*
   or sherry

¼ *teaspoon monosodium*
   glutamate
1 *ounce wasabi (see Glossary),*
   grated fine, or fine horse-
   radish
6 *ounces fresh tuna, chilled*
6 *ounces fresh cuttlefish*

Place the rice in a heavy saucepan, add the water, set over high heat and bring to a rolling boil. Cover, lower heat and cook for 20 minutes. Let stand in covered pan while preparing the sauce.

Combine in a small pan the vinegar, salt, soy sauce, mirin and monosodium glutamate. Heat to simmering point. Remove from heat and stir into the rice, blending thoroughly. Transfer the rice to a large platter and let cool. When cool enough to work with, mold into small rectangular shapes, then place a pinch of wasabi or horseradish on top of each patty.

Slice the chilled raw tuna into thin rectangular pieces of a size to match the rice patties. Arrange over the rice. Slice the cuttlefish into small, thin sections and place over the tuna slices. (If cuttlefish is used raw it must be very fresh. Otherwise it may first be sliced and then cooked for a minute or two in rapidly boiling water. Or, if preferred, cuttlefish may be dispensed with altogether and the amount of tuna fish doubled.) Refrigerate until completely cooled. Serve on a large platter with garnishes of your choice.

220

GOMOKU-SUSHI
Vegetable Sushi

2 cups rice
3 cups water
¼ cup vinegar
3 teaspoons salt
3 tablespoons sugar
½ ounce Chinese mushrooms (see Glossary)
½ cup water
½ carrot
2 tablespoons soy sauce
1 tablespoon sugar

½ teaspoon monosodium glutamate
2 eggs
6 ounces white-meat fish
1 tablespoon sugar
Red food coloring
2 ounces fresh tender green beans
½ teaspoon pickled ginger
1 sheet nori (see Glossary), crumbled

Cook the rice in the water in a heavy saucepan and place in a bowl. Season with the vinegar, 2 teaspoons salt and sugar. Soak the dried mushrooms in ½ cup water until soft. Cut into narrow strips and save the water. Cut the carrot into narrow strips. Place the carrot and mushrooms in a small saucepan. Add the ½ cup of liquid in which the mushrooms were soaked. Add the soy sauce, sugar and monosodium glutamate. Cook over medium heat until the juice is absorbed. Cool and mix with the cooked rice.

Beat the eggs well in a bowl with ¼ teaspoon salt. Fry in a little oil to a thin sheet, then cut into narrow strips.

Boil the fish in water to cover. When flaky, break into small pieces and drain. Return to the pan, add a small amount of water, the sugar, the remaining ¾ teaspoon of salt and the red food coloring and stir together until the fish is uniformly colored.

Clean and remove the strings from the green beans. Boil until tender and cut into narrow strips. Cut the pickled ginger into small pieces. Spread the rice mixture over a platter. Top with the cooked fish. Decorate with the crumbled nori, egg strips, beans and pickled ginger. Serve as an appetizer.

CHAWAN-MUSHI

3 ounces Chinese mushrooms
  (see Glossary)
3 eggs
2 cups dashi two (see p. 213)
1 teaspoon salt
1 tablespoon soy sauce

½ cup cooked chicken, finely
  diced
6 small shrimp, cooked and diced
6 water chestnuts, finely diced
1 tablespoon mirin (see Glossary)
  or sweet sherry
4 spinach leaves

Wash the mushrooms and soak in water for about an hour or until soft. In a bowl thoroughly beat together the eggs, dashi, salt and half the soy sauce. Drain the mushrooms and dice. In another bowl mix the mushrooms, chicken, shrimp, chestnuts and mirin. Add the remaining soy sauce and stir together until well mixed. Divide the mixture between 4 chawan-mushi bowls (see Glossary), or use custard cups.

Add the egg mixture to the bowls. Wash the spinach and place one spinach leaf over the contents of each bowl. Bring water to a boil in a steamer or a deep saucepan and place the bowls in it. The water should reach to about half the height of the bowls. Cover the steamer and let the custard steam for 13 to 15 minutes over medium heat. If chawan-mushi bowls are used, the lids should be on during the cooking process. If custard cups are used, cover the cups with aluminum foil and leave the steamer slightly uncovered.

To test whether the chawan-mushi is done, pierce it with a toothpick. It is done when the custard is set. Do not permit to overcook or the custard will separate.

Serve hot in the same bowls as one main course or as a side dish to a meat course.

ODAMAKI-MUSHI
Chicken Custard with Noodles

1 cup udon (see Glossary) or
  fine egg noodles
¼ pound white chicken meat,
  chilled for fine slicing
1 tablespoon soy sauce
4 Chinese mushrooms (see
  Glossary)
⅓ cup shredded spinach
2 eggs

1½ cups dashi two
1 teaspoon salt
1 tablespoon mirin (see
  Glossary) or sweet sherry
½ teaspoon monosodium
  glutamate
8 small slices kamaboko (see
  Glossary)

222

Cook the udon in boiling water until tender. Rinse in cold water, drain and place in a large rice bowl with a lid or other heatproof lidded bowl. Cut the chicken into small, very thin slices, place in a bowl and add the soy sauce. Soak the mushrooms in water until soft and discard the stems. Cut each mushroom into 4 pieces and stir into the soy-soaked chicken. Wash and drain the spinach; set aside. Beat the eggs and add the dashi, salt, mirin and monosodium glutamate and beat again. Pour the egg mixture over the udon. Arrange the chicken, mushrooms, kamaboko and spinach on top, cover, place in a steamer or a deep saucepan and steam for 15 to 20 minutes. Serve hot.

KAMABOKO
Fish Cakes

Kamaboko may be made at home, fried in deep fat or oil and served hot as an hors d'oeuvre or an appetizer.

1 pound filet of sole or flounder
2 tablespoons cornstarch
1 teaspoon salt
1 teaspoon soy sauce
¼ teaspoon monosodium glutamate

1 teaspoon sugar
⅓ cup cold water
Fat or vegetable oil for deep frying

Make sure that the fish is free from bones and grind it to a fine consistency. Add the cornstarch, salt, soy sauce, monosodium glutamate and sugar and blend thoroughly. Add as much of the water as the mixture can take and still hold its shape. Form the fish mixture into bite-sized balls and deep fry in the fat at 380° F. until crisp and golden brown. Remove and drain on a paper towel. Serve hot.

MAIN DISHES

TEMPURA
Seafood Fried in Batter

There is no hard-and-fast rule dictating the ingredients for tempura, nor is it possible to say with certainty how many portions any particular recipe will make. Ingredients depend on personal preference and quantities depend on appetites. But, as a general rule, it can be said that tempura is stimulating to the appetite and is usually eaten in large quantities as a one-course meal. It is served with tentsuya soup as sauce and white radish, horseradish and ginger as condiments. A light batter is very important; the secret is to avoid overmixing. Any good vegetable oil may be used for frying. Tempura fried in animal fat tends to be less crisp than desired.

To Prepare Tempura
1½ pounds shrimp
 1 ¾-pound filet of flounder
 1 lobster tail

2 medium carrots
½ medium eggplant
½ pound string beans

Wash, drain and peel the shrimp, leaving the tail intact. Slit down the middle and remove the vein. Cut across the underside of the shrimp near the tail to prevent excessive curling. Wash the flounder and cut into 2½-inch squares. Remove the lobster meat from the shell and cut into small pieces. Dry all the seafood carefully. Wash and dry the vegetables. Scrape the carrots and cut into thin 3-inch-long strips. Peel the eggplant and cut into ¼-inch slices, then cut each slice into quarters. Remove the ends and strings from the beans, then cut into 3-inch lengths.

To Prepare Batter
1½ cups all-purpose flour
 1 egg

1 cup water

Sift the flour. Beat the egg and water together in a bowl. Add the flour gradually to the egg and water, mixing very lightly with a fork or whisk. An electric beater must not be used; care must be taken not to overstir the flour.

To Prepare Tentsuya Soup (Tempura Sauce)
1 cup dashi two
⅓ cup mirin (see Glossary) or
   sherry
1 teaspoon sugar
⅓ cup soy sauce
⅓ teaspoon monosodium
   glutamate

Combine all the ingredients in a saucepan. Bring to a boil, stirring, then remove from heat and cover until needed.

To Serve Tempura
Vegetable oil for deep frying
Daikon (see Glossary) or white
   radish, freshly grated
Horseradish, freshly grated
Ginger root, freshly grated
Lemon juice

Pour the vegetable oil into a heavy pan to a depth of 2 to 3 inches and heat to 350° F. (Japanese chefs may prefer 380° F., but at 350° F. there is less chance of overheating during the course of cooking. Whatever the temperature, it must be kept constant.) While the oil is heating, pour the hot tempura sauce into bowls and set one bowl at each guest's place. Serve each person condiment dishes of daikon or radish, horseradish and ginger root. Place a small pitcher of lemon juice where all may reach it.

Take the shrimp by the tail, dip into the batter, then drop into the bubbling oil. Fry on both sides until lightly browned. Remove, drain quickly and serve at once. Dip the other items into the batter with a spoon, drop into the oil and fry in the same way. Serve each batch as soon as cooked. Repeat the cycle until all ingredients are fried and served. Each person helps himself to sauce and condiments.

FRIED CRAB

4 ounces canned crab meat
2 tablespoons chopped parsley
   Mayonnaise to taste
2 sheets nori (see Glossary)
1 egg, beaten
¼ cup water
⅓ cup flour
   Vegetable oil for frying

Drain the crab meat and crumble it in a bowl. Add the parsley and mayonnaise (more or less according to your taste) and divide the mixture into 8 portions. Cut the nori into 8 pieces and use each to wrap a portion of crab meat. Prepare the batter by lightly mixing the egg, water and flour. Dip the nori-wrapped crab in the batter and fry in the heated oil in a pan. Remove and drain on a paper towel. Serve hot as an appetizer or a side dish.

TENDON
Prawns and Rice

Tendon is prawn or shrimp tempura served over rice in a *domburi,* or large rice bowl.

3 cups cooked rice
8 whole fresh prawns, or 8 whole
    fresh shrimp
1 egg, beaten
¼ cup water
⅓ cup flour
    Vegetable oil for deep frying

½ cup dashi one or other clear
    stock
3 tablespoons soy sauce
1 teaspoon sugar
3 tablespoons mirin (see
    Glossary) or sherry
⅓ teaspoon monosodium
    glutamate

Prepare plain boiled rice and place the hot rice in a *domburi* or other covered serving bowl. Remove the head and shell of the prawns, leaving the tail section intact. Devein and clean. Make several small cuts along the length of the underside to prevent the prawns from shrinking when fried.

Make a batter with the egg, water and flour, taking care not to over-mix. Hold the prawns by the tail, dip in the batter and deep fry in the oil at a temperature of 350° F. When golden brown, remove and drain on a paper towel.

Prepare the tentsuya (tempura sauce) by combining the dashi, soy sauce, sugar, mirin and monosodium glutamate in a saucepan and bringing to a rapid boil. Remove from heat. Stir the fried prawns into this sauce and soak for several minutes. Transfer the prawns, and as much sauce as desired, to the rice bowl. Stir the rice lightly to distribute the sauce and cook over low heat for 1 minute. Serve covered.

HAMAGURI YAKI
Broiled Clams

½ cup soy sauce
2 tablespoons miso (see
    Glossary)
½ cup sake or dry sherry
1 teaspoon salt

1 teaspoon sugar
½ teaspoon monosodium
    glutamate
1 pound shucked clams

Mix all the ingredients except the clams in a saucepan and bring to boil. Lower heat and dip the clams into the mixture. Remove the clams, leaving the sauce over low heat. Thread the clams onto skewers and broil over a charcoal fire, either hibachi or barbecue. Serve hot sauce on the side as a dip.

Clams may be oven-broiled if a charcoal fire is not available. Lightly oil a shallow pan, arrange the clams in a single layer and broil for 1 to 2 minutes on each side. Serve with the hot sauce.

SAKANA NITSUKE
Scallops in Soy Sauce

1 cup soy sauce
2 tablespoons sugar
1 tablespoon mirin (see Glossary)
    or sherry

2 teaspoons finely grated ginger
    root
½ teaspoon monosodium
    glutamate
1 pound small scallops

Combine all the ingredients except the scallops in a saucepan and bring to a boil. Stir in the scallops and cook over medium heat. Scallops are done when they have absorbed all the liquid. Remove from heat. Serve either as an appetizer or as one of several main dishes.

UNI-YAKI
Fish Broiled with Uni Paste

1 ¾-pound see bass or other
    firm white-meat fish,
    cleaned, scaled and boned
2 tablespoons mirin (see
    Glossary) or sweet sherry

¾ teaspoon salt
2 tablespoons uni paste (see
    Glossary)
1 egg yolk, beaten

Slice the fish into 4 sections and thread onto 2 parallel skewers. Broil briefly over heat, first on one side, then the other. Mix the remaining ingredients in a bowl, stirring well. Brush over the surface of the half-broiled fish and continue broiling. Repeat brushing 2 or 3 times until the fish is well coated and completely cooked. (If uni paste is hard to come by, it may be dispensed with. The result is not uni-yaki, but nevertheless a good broiled fish dish.) Remove skewers and serve.

SALMON TERIYAKI
Broiled Marinated Salmon

½ cup soy sauce
⅓ cup mirin (see Glossary) or
    sherry
¼ cup sugar

½ teaspoon monosodium
    glutamate
4 small salmon steaks (about
    1 pound total weight)

Prepare the sauce by mixing all the ingredients except the salmon steaks. Marinate the salmon steaks in the sauce for about half an hour. Remove from the sauce and place in preheated broiler. Warm the sauce and use it to baste the fish as it broils. Broil the steaks on one side for about 10 minutes, basting twice. When well browned, remove from the broiler, sprinkle lightly with the sauce and serve.

If preferred, the fish may be skewered and broiled over a charcoal fire. Brush with the sauce and broil about 7 inches above the hot coals. Broil each side for about 5 minutes, brushing the mixture on once or twice during cooking. Serve with the warm sauce.

BAKED FISH WITH MUSHROOMS

4 large fresh mushrooms
4 sheets of wax paper, approx.
    6 × 10 inches
    Salad oil
¾- to 1-pound flounder filet, cut
    into 8 pieces
    Salt

Pepper
¼ teaspoon monosodium
    glutamate
4 teaspoons sake or dry sherry
12 pieces ginkgo nuts (optional)
4 sheets of aluminum foil,
    approx. 6 × 10 inches

Remove the ends of the mushroom stems, rinse the mushrooms, drain and slice lengthwise. Brush the wax paper with salad oil. Arrange 2 pieces of fish on each sheet of wax paper, sprinkle with salt, pepper, salad oil, monosodium glutamate and sake, top with the sliced mushrooms and the ginkgo nuts and wrap carefully. Then encase each wax-paper package in aluminum foil and twist the ends of the foil wrappers. Preheat oven to 325° F., place the fish packages on a baking sheet and bake for 15 to 20 minutes. Serve in the wrappers, with lemon wedges and sliced tomatoes on the side.

SHRIMP ONIGARA
Saucy Broiled Shrimp

12 *prawns or jumbo shrimp*
½ *cup soy sauce*

½ *cup mirin (see Glossary) or*
sherry
Ground sansho (see Glossary)

If the prawns are not already trimmed, remove the head and legs. Rinse. Slit the underside open from head to tail. Skewer the prawns and broil at high heat, starting with the shell side. When nearly broiled, combine the soy sauce and mirin and pour over the open end and underside of the prawns. Broil again until the sauce dries. Sprinkle with sansho (Japanese pepper) and serve at once.

YAKITORI
Broiled Chicken

Yakitori is best prepared over an outdoor charcoal fire or a hibachi, though an oiled heavy frying pan may be substituted with good results. Skewers may be either wood or metal and should be about 6 inches long. Ingredients, which should be tightly sandwiched together, may be varied according to taste and appetite; pork or veal may be used in place of chicken, and green pepper may take the place of scallions or onions.

½ *pound boned chicken meat*
¼ *pound chicken livers*
8 *scallions or more*
½ *cup soy sauce*
3 *tablespoons sugar*
½ *cup sake*

½ *teaspoon finely grated ginger*
¼ *teaspoon monosodium*
glutamate
Ground sansho (see Glossary)
or cayenne pepper

Cut the chicken meat and livers into bite-sized pieces. Cut the scallions into 2-inch lengths. Prepare the sauce by combining the soy sauce, sugar, sake, ginger and monosodium glutamate in a saucepan and heating over low heat. Alternate pieces of chicken, scallion and liver on each skewer. Baste with the sauce and put to broil, keeping about 4 inches above the hot coals if a charcoal fire is used. Turn frequently so that the ingredients cook evenly on all sides. Remove from the fire several times to baste with the sauce. Broil until well done, but do not allow to overcook or the chicken will be dry. Sprinkle with the sansho and serve immediately.

CHICKEN TERIYAKI
Marinated Broiled Chicken

1 pound boned breast of chicken
3 tablespoons soy sauce
½ teaspoon finely grated ginger

2 tablespoons mirin (see
Glossary) or sherry
2 tablespoons cornstarch
2 tablespoons cooking oil

Cut the chicken into 4 to 6 sections. Combine the soy sauce, ginger and mirin. Pour over the chicken and marinate for half an hour. Remove the chicken from the sauce, dry with a cloth and then rub in the cornstarch. Preheat oven broiler; heat the oil in the broiling pan. Or, preferably, pan-broil in a heavy skillet on top of stove or brazier. In either case the procedure is the same. Place the chicken in the sizzling oil. Fry on one side for 3 minutes. Turn the chicken over, add sauce and fry for 3 minutes. Turn again, baste with the sauce and fry for another 2 minutes. Remove the chicken, drain quickly on a paper towel and slice into thin slivers. Serve at once with tomato slices and celery strips.

YOSENABE
Chicken, Shrimp and Vegetables

This dish is best prepared at the table, sukiyaki style, for it should be eaten the moment it is done. Either hibachi pot, chafing dish or electric skillet may be used.

2 small frying chickens, boned
and chopped into 2-inch
pieces
½ pound medium shrimp, shelled
and cleaned
4 large pieces shiitake (see
Glossary) or 8 ounces
canned mushrooms

1 cup young green sugar peas in
pods
1 Chinese cabbage
1 large carrot
1 cup canned bamboo shoots
2½ cups dashi two
1 tablespoon soy sauce
2 teaspoons mirin (see
Glossary) or sherry
Salt

Wash the chicken pieces and dry thoroughly. Boil the shrimp in lightly salted water just until they turn pink. Drain and set aside. Soak the shiitake in cold water until soft. Scald the peas in pods, remove from

230

heat and allow to stand. Discard all but the heart of the Chinese cabbage and cut the heart into 2-inch pieces. Scrape the carrot and slice into thin strips. Drain the bamboo shoots. Put the pieces of cabbage heart, carrot strips and bamboo shoots into very lightly salted boiling water and boil for 3 minutes. Remove from heat and drain. Drain the peas. Drain and dry the shiitake and cut into narrow strips.

Arrange all the ingredients on a platter and take to the table. Pour the dashi into a pan or skillet placed over heat and bring to a vigorous boil. Add the chicken, mushrooms, cabbage, carrots and bamboo shoots. Stir these ingredients well into the boiling dashi. Add the soy sauce and mirin. Cook for about 5 minutes. Add the shrimp and cook 2 minutes more. The dashi must be kept boiling all the time. Add the peas and cook for 1 to 2 minutes or until the chicken is just done. It is important not to overcook or the ingredients will lose their fresh flavor. Serve with rice or a side dish of chawan-mushi.

MIZU-TAKI OF CHICKEN
Chicken in Casserole

5 pieces of shiitake (see Glossary), soaked and ready for use
3 cups of water
1 piece of kombu (see Glossary)
2 whole boned chicken breasts (1 to 1½ pounds)
2 scallions
5 leaves of Chinese cabbage

½ cup canned bamboo shoots, sliced
½ cup shredded spinach
¼ teaspoon monosodium glutamate
Salt or soy sauce to taste
4 ounces bean curd (see Glossary)

Soak the shiitake well ahead of time and save the water. The shiitake liquid should be included in the 3 cups of water to be used for cooking. Pour the 3 cups of liquid into a fairly deep flameproof casserole. Bring to a boil over high heat and drop in the kombu. Reduce heat and simmer for 10 to 12 minutes.

While the kombu stock is simmering, cut the chicken into bite-sized pieces. Chop the green onions. Trim the cabbage leaves and rinse. Drain the sliced bamboo shoots. Wash and drain the spinach.

Discard the kombu and add the monosodium glutamate and a pinch of salt to the water. To this stock add the chicken and green onions and simmer briskly for 15 minutes. Then add the rest of the vegetables and cook over medium heat for another 15 minutes. Season to taste with salt or soy sauce. Cut the tofu into small pieces and add when all the other ingredients are cooked. Remove from heat and serve, with stock, in the same dish.

231

OYAKO-DOMBURI
Rice Dish with Chicken and Egg

Oyako means "parent and child" and refers to the chicken and the egg. *Domburi* is the large rice bowl in which the meal is served. If the amount of rice seems excessive, that is because this is essentially a rice dish trimmed with chicken and egg, rather than a chicken dish served with rice.

6 *ounces chicken meat*	4 *tablespoons mirin (see*
3 *medium onions*	*Glossary) or sherry*
½ *pound fresh mushrooms*	1 *sheet nori (see Glossary)*
1½ *cups dashi one or chicken*	*(optional)*
stock	6 *eggs*
6 *tablespoons soy sauce*	10 *cups cooked rice*

Cut the chicken into thin slices. Slice the onions. Trim the mushrooms, wash and slice. Combine the dashi, soy sauce and mirin in a saucepan and bring to a boil. Add the chicken, onions and mushrooms and let simmer gently.

If nori is to be used, toast lightly in a pan and crumble into fine pieces. In the crumbled state it is called momi-nori. Set aside until needed.

Beat the eggs lightly. When the chicken is cooked, transfer all the solid ingredients to a large, deep frying pan with enough of the stock to cover the bottom. Reserve the remaining stock. Pour the beaten eggs over all the ingredients. Cover the pan and turn off heat, but leave the pan in place.

Place the hot cooked rice in a *domburi* or other large serving bowl. Pour the remaining stock over the rice.

When the eggs are half done, transfer all the ingredients to the rice bowl and arrange on top of the rice. Sprinkle with momi-nori and serve.

The Japanese require that the eggs for this dish be no more than half cooked. However, if the preference is for well-done eggs, then the eggs should be well done.

KAMO NO KOMA-GIRI
Duck Cakes

1½ cups raw duck meat, chopped
    very fine
½ teaspoon monosodium
    glutamate
2 teaspoons soy sauce
2 teaspoons sake

1 teaspoon cornstarch, or more as
    needed
1 tablespoon water, or more as
    needed
Fat for frying, if desired

Blend all the ingredients thoroughly in a bowl. The mixture should form easily into balls; if necessary, add a bit more cornstarch or water. Shape into balls about 1 to 1½ inches in diameter. Grill over low heat or fry in deep fat in a skillet. Cook until well done. Serve hot as one main course.

PORK AND SOY SAUCE WITH ONIONS

1 pound pork
3 medium onions
4 tablespoons vegetable oil
4 teaspoons sugar
1 teaspoon salt
3 tablespoons soy sauce
2 cups chicken stock

2 teaspoons sake
⅓ teaspoon monosodium
    glutamate
Pepper to taste
2 tablespoons cornstarch
2 tablespoons cold water
4 tablespoons cooked green peas

Slice the pork and onions into thin pieces. Heat the oil in a pan and fry the pork, add the onions and continue cooking over medium heat until tender. Add the sugar, salt, soy sauce, soup stock, sake and monosodium glutamate and boil for 10 or 15 minutes. Add pepper to taste. Mix the cornstarch in the cold water and add to the soup to thicken. Add the green peas and serve piping-hot.

PORK WITH BAMBOO SPROUTS

½ *pound pork*
1 *pound canned bamboo sprouts*
¼ *cup green peas*
3 *tablespoons oil*
4 *tablespoons soy sauce*

2 *tablespoons sugar*
3 *tablespoons sake*
   Scant teaspoon monosodium
   glutamate

Cut the pork into ½-inch cubes. Cut the bamboo sprouts into narrow slices. Cook the peas rapidly in boiling salted water. Fry the pork and bamboo sprouts in the hot oil in a frying pan. Add the soy sauce, sugar, sake and monosodium glutamate and simmer. When the meat is cooked, add the peas, mix thoroughly and remove from heat. Serve hot.

SUKIYAKI
Gyunabe

Cook this dish in an electric skillet, chafing dish or skillet right before your guests. It has a natural crispness and fragrance and the cooking time is brief.

½ *cup soy sauce*
3 *tablespoons sugar*
¾ *cup chicken broth*
½ *head Chinese cabbage*
½ *pound fresh spinach*
12 *scallions*
1 *large onion, peeled*
2 *large mushrooms*

10 *½-inch cubes bean curd (see*
    Glossary) (optional)
2 *bamboo shoots (canned)*
1 *cup canned shirataki (see*
   Glossary) (optional)
1 *pound beef tenderloin or*
   sirloin, very thinly sliced
   Suet or oil for frying

One Hour Before Guests Arrive
Combine the soy sauce, sugar and broth in a pitcher and set aside. Prepare 3 cups of Chinese cabbage in diagonal slices, ½ inch wide. Snip 3 cups of spinach and slice scallions into 2-inch lengths. Cut the onion in half lengthwise, then into ¼-inch slices. Slice the mushrooms and bamboo shoots thin. Arrange the vegetables, shirataki and meat on a platter or tray. Transfer the suet or oil and the pitcher of soy sauce to the table, which has been set with a chafing dish, skillet or an electric skillet.

When Your Guests Are Seated
Heat the suet or oil in the skillet and with a long fork, transfer all but

the meat and spinach from the tray to the skillet. Pour on sauce and let cook over high heat for 8 minutes. Then add the spinach and meat to the vegetables and let it all simmer for 2 minutes. Now press the meat and spinach down into the sauce and cook for 3 minutes more. Serve with hot fluffy rice and hot green tea.

SUKIYAKI MONGOLIAN STYLE

For sukiyaki Mongolian, the meat and vegetables are not cooked in flavored stock but are lightly fried in butter or oil. To flavor the meat, place the thinly sliced filets of beef in a marinade of 1 cup soy sauce, 2 tablespoons sherry and one teaspoon sugar. Turn frequently to allow the meat to be permeated with the marinade. Heat oil or butter and fry the marinated meat slices. Then fry for a short time assorted vegetables such as onion rings, slices of fresh ginger, green peppers, slices of eggplant, Chinese cabbage, mushrooms. Keep the pan well greased and hot all the time.

BEEF TERIYAKI

3 *tablespoons soy sauce*   ½ *teaspoon finely grated ginger*
3 *tablespoons mirin (see Glossary)*   1 *pound beef tenderloin or sirloin*
   or sherry   2 *tablespoons oil*

Prepare a marinade of soy sauce, mirin and ginger. Place the beef in this and allow to marinate for 1 hour. Heat a pan, add the oil and fry the beef on both sides. Pour the sauce over this and fry until a brown sheen appears over it. Remove from heat. Cut the beef into thin slices and serve hot with fried or boiled vegetables.

VEGETABLE DISHES

SPINACH WITH SESAME AND BEAN PASTE

1 *pound young spinach*
3 *tablespoons sesame seeds*
1 *tablespoon sugar*
2 *tablespoons soy sauce*

3 *tablespoons miso (see*
  Glossary)
⅓ *teaspoon monosodium*
  glutamate

Wash the spinach and cook without adding any water to the pot. When the liquid from the spinach is boiling, remove the spinach and place in a bowl of cold water to cool. Drain thoroughly, cut into 2½-inch strips and place in a bowl. Roast the sesame seeds until they are about triple in size. Grind or crush them thoroughly and then mix very well with the sugar, soy sauce, miso and monosodium glutamate. Combine with the prepared spinach leaves and serve. This salad should be prepared just before serving, not in advance.

PICKLED CAULIFLOWER

1 *medium head cauliflower*
1 *medium green pepper*
1 *teaspoon salt*
1 *large stalk celery*
½ *cup vinegar*

2½ *tablespoons sugar*
⅓ *cup water*
¼ *teaspoon monosodium*
  glutamate

Separate the cauliflower flowerets and rinse. Dip the flowerets quickly into boiling water and set aside to drain. Slice the green pepper into thin pieces and also dip into boiling water, then add to the cauliflower. Add ⅓ teaspoon salt and mix. Wash, trim and slice the celery into ⅛-inch slices. Place the celery in a bowl, add ⅔ teaspoon salt, then drain off the liquid. Combine the vinegar, sugar, water and monosodium glutamate in a saucepan and heat. Allow to cool. Place the vegetables in a large bowl (not metal). Pour the vinegar mixture over the vegetables. Place a heavy weight on top of the vegetables and let stand for about 5 hours before serving. Chill before serving.

BROCCOLI MUSTARD RELISH

1 *pound broccoli, coarsely*
chopped
½ *teaspoon salt*
1 *cup vinegar*

¼ *teaspoon monosodium*
glutamate
2 *tablespoons + ½ teaspoon*
prepared mustard
4 *teaspoons sugar*

Wash and clean the broccoli and bring to a boil in salted water to cover. Remove from heat, pour off the hot water and add cold water to cool rapidly. Drain and place in a bowl. Mix the rest of the ingredients together, then mix with the broccoli. Put the mixture in a jar, cover and let stand for two days before serving. Chill before serving.

EGGPLANT SHIGIYAKI
Broiled Eggplant with Bean Paste

5 *small eggplants*
¼ *teaspoon salt*
½ *teaspoon monosodium*
glutamate
2 *tablespoons vegetable oil*

2 *tablespoons dashi one or other*
clear soup stock
3 *tablespoons miso (see Glossary)*
3 *tablespoons sugar*
2 *tablespoons mirin (see*
Glossary) or sweet sherry

Remove the stems from the eggplants and discard. Wash the eggplants, dry and cut into round slices about ¼ inch thick. Sprinkle the slices lightly with salt and monosodium glutamate and brush both sides with vegetable oil. Preheat the broiler. Mix the remaining ingredients in a saucepan, making a thin paste. Heat the paste to a low simmer. Broil the eggplant on both sides until golden brown. When done, coat with the paste and allow to broil for 1 minute more. Serve hot.

FRIED EGGPLANT WITH SAUCE

4 *small eggplants*
4 *tablespoons vegetable oil*
3 *tablespoons dashi one*
3 *tablespoons sugar*

1 *tablespoon sake*
4 *ounces ground chicken meat*
4 *tablespoons miso (see Glossary)*

Remove the stems from the eggplants and discard. Wash the eggplants, dry and slice in half lengthwise. Make shallow crisscross gashes in the skin. Sauté slowly in the vegetable oil until tender, turning frequently. Mix together in a saucepan the dashi, sugar and sake and heat to a simmer. Cook the chicken in this mixture until well done. Add the miso and stir until blended. Arrange the eggplant ovals on plates, skin side down, and pour the chicken-and-bean-paste sauce over them. Serve hot.

CUCUMBER-TOMATO SALAD WITH SESAME SEEDS

½ *teaspoon ground toasted*
   sesame seeds
2 *tablespoons vinegar*
1 *teaspoon soy sauce*
½ *teaspoon salt*
2 *teaspoons very fine sugar*

1 *medium cucumber, peeled and*
   sliced thin and salted
1 *medium tomato, cut into small*
   pieces
¼ *cake fried bean curd (see*
   Glossary), cut into thin long
   slices

Mix the sesame seeds with the vinegar, soy sauce, salt and sugar. Drain the cucumber and combine with the drained tomato and the bean curd. Mix well with the vinegar dressing. Chill before serving.

CHINESE-CABBAGE PICKLES
Quick Method

2 *pounds Chinese cabbage*
2 *scallions*
1 *red pepper*
½ *lemon*

3 *tablespoons vinegar*
4 *teaspoons soy sauce*
¼ *teaspoon monosodium*
   glutamate

Cut the Chinese cabbage into 1½-inch widths, pour boiling water over the cabbage and drain. Chop the scallions. Cut the red pepper into thin slices. Cut the lemon into thin strips. Mix these ingredients in a bowl and add the vinegar, soy sauce and monosodium glutamate. Place a heavy weight (about 1 pound) on top of the salad and let stand for 1 hour before serving.

SWEETS

JAPANESE CAKES

Filling

   2 *cups azuki* (*see Glossary*)   1 *cup chestnuts*
   2 *cups sugar*

Cover the azuki with water and soak for at least 8 hours. Boil the azuki until tender, then drain and press through a sieve. Place over heat again for several seconds, stirring constantly to prevent burning, until all the liquid is gone. Add the sugar to the hot azuki paste and mix until dissolved. Boil the chestnuts until soft, remove the shells and chop very fine. Add the chestnuts to the azuki mixture, mix and allow to cool.

Dough

   2 *cups flour*   1 *teaspoon baking powder*
   1 *cup sugar*   1 *egg*
   ½ *teaspoon salt*   2 *tablespoons oil*

Sift the dry ingredients together into a bowl. Slightly beat the egg and add it to the dry ingredients. Add the oil and enough water to make a rather stiff dough. Place on a floured board and knead well. Roll out to about ¼ inch thick or slightly thinner, then cut into different shapes.

Place a heaping tablespoon of the filling on each piece and press the edges together to seal the filling in. Steam on a rack in a covered pan over boiling water for about 45 minutes, then quickly brown in a hot oven.

MAIL ORDER SOURCES
FOR FOREIGN FOODS

CHINESE

Wing Fat Co., 33–35 Mott Street, New York, N.Y. 10013
New China Supply Co., 709 H Street, N.W., Washington, D.C. 20001
Yee Sing Chang Co., 966 N. Hill Street, Los Angeles, Calif. 90012
Kwong Hang Co., 918 Grant Avenue, San Francisco, Calif. 94108
Sun Wah Hing Trading Co., 2246 Wentworth Avenue, Chicago, Ill.
  60616

JAPANESE

Japan Food Corp., 900 Marin Street, San Francisco, Calif. 94124
Katagiri & Co., 224 E. 59 Street, New York, N.Y. 10022
K. Tanaka Co., 326 Amsterdam Avenue, New York, N.Y. 10023
Ginza Market 2600 W. Jefferson Boulevard, Los Angeles, Calif. 90018
Japan Food Corp., 920 Mateo Street, Los Angeles, Calif. 90021

INDIAN

Java-India Co., 442 Hudson Street, New York, N.Y. 10014
A. M. Gurjar, 438 Hudson Street, New York, N.Y. 10014

INDONESIAN AND MALAYSIAN

Mrs. De Wildt, RFD 1, Bangor, Pa. 18013

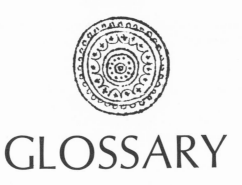

GLOSSARY

Ajinomoto—Monosodium glutamate.

Arrowroot—A tropical American plant. May be bought at Spanish markets.

Azuki—A small Asian bean, varying in color from dark red to cream. Important in Asian cuisine. Red kidney beans may be substituted.

Bean curd—A soft white cake made from soy beans that is similar in texture to cheese. Dried bean curd usually comes in twists or flat sheets. Fresh, dried and canned varieties can be purchased in Oriental food shops. Bean curd squares are usually 3 inches square.

Bean curd leaves—Slices of bean curd.

Bird's nest—The nest of a particular type of swallow that makes its home along the high cliffs of the China Sea. The swallow ingests certain kinds of marine life and plants that are transformed into a glutinous substance used in building the nest. Pre-prepared nests may be bought in Chinese food stores.

Brown bean sauce—A sauce with the consistency of ketchup, made of crushed soy beans, chilies, garlic and salt. It is available in bottles or 8-ounce cans. The Cantonese word for it is DOW-BARN-JEUNG. May be purchased in Oriental food stores.

Cassava flour—Flour made from the cassava, a starchy root vegetable. Buy at Chinese markets.

Chawan-mushi bowls—Lidded deep bowls about the size of large coffee mugs. Available in Japanese stores.

Chinese mushrooms—Dried whole mushrooms with a very dark skin, they are stronger in flavor than the white mushrooms and give a distinctive taste to the dishes in which they are used. Before cooking they must be soaked in warm water until soft. Available in Oriental food shops.

Chorizos—Highly spiced Spanish pork sausages. May be obtained in Spanish markets.

Cloud ears—A tree fungus (mushroom) that resembles clouds and ears. May be purchased in Chinese food stores.

Coconut cream—Add 1 cup hot water to 2 cups grated coconut (use a blender to grate coconut) and let stand half an hour. Squeeze through cheesecloth to extract the cream.

Coconut milk—Scrape the meat from a fresh coconut. A blender is very useful for grating coconut. Add 2 cups hot water to each cup of coconut meat. Let stand for half an hour, then squeeze through cheesecloth to extract the milk.

Congee—A thick rice soup or porridge.

Daikon—Japanese large white radish. May be purchased in Japanese food shops.

Dried shrimp—Small sun-dried shrimp. Soak in hot water 15 minutes before using. Buy in Oriental markets.

Duk sauce—A sweet sauce similar in taste to peach jam. Available in specialty food shops.

Eggfruits—Brown, egg-shaped fruit resembling a potato. About 1½–3 inches in diameter. They are sweet and have a fudge-like texture. May be purchased in Spanish or Chinese markets.

Fermented black beans—Whole, dried black beans cured in salt. They come in a plastic bag and may be stored indefinitely in a covered jar in the refrigerator. May be purchased in Chinese food shops.

Ghee—Clarified butter. To make, melt butter in small saucepan, strain, and pour clear liquid into container to store.

Glutinous (sticky) rice—A special variety of rice used in Oriental recipes. May be obtained at Chinese markets.

Horapa leaves—An herb that is widely used in Southeast Asian cooking. Sweet basil may be substituted.

Kamaboko—Japanese fish cake (*see Index*).

Kapi—Available at Chinese markets, but half the amount of anchovy paste or shrimp paste may be substituted.

Katsuobushi—Japanese dried bonito.

Kimchi—Korean condiment which is a combination of spiced, pickled cucumbers, onions, cabbage, turnips and many more ingredients. It is available in jars and cans in Oriental markets.

Kombu—Japanese seaweed.

Laos powder—Laos or java root looks like ginger but tastes more medicinal. May be purchased in Oriental food shops.

Lemon grass—May be purchased in powder form in Oriental specialty food shops. One teaspoon equals one stalk of fresh lemon grass. If neither fresh nor powder is available, substitute a thin slice of lemon peel, grated.

Lumpia—Indonesian and Filipino version of Chinese egg roll.

Makrut leaves—Dried leaves of a wild lime tree; used as a seasoning. Lime rind may be substituted.

Mirin—Sweet sake.

Miso—Soybean paste. May be purchased in Japanese food shops.

Mitsuba—Trefoil, a spicy herb.

Monosodium glutamate—a white powdered flavor enhancer sold in U.S. under trade name Aćcent.

Mortar and pestle—Use electric blender. Follow instructions on grinding vegetables.

Mung beans—Green or yellow edible seeds of an Asian plant or the plant itself. May be purchased in Oriental food shops.

Nam pla—A fish sauce used in Thai and Indonesian cooking. Available in Chinese and specialty shops as fish sauce. Or substitute soy sauce with a touch of anchovy paste.

Nori—Japanese seaweed. May be purchased in Oriental food shops.

Oyster sauce—Extract of oyster, soy sauce and cornstarch. Available in Chinese and specialty food shops.

Padak—Salted fish. May be bought in Chinese markets.

Palm sugar—Buy at Spanish markets or use light-brown sugar.

Rose water—May be made by floating rose petals in water overnight.

Saku—Tapioca.

Sansho—Japanese pepper.

Sashimi—Japanese raw fish appetizer.

Scented water—May be made by floating jasmine flower in water overnight.

Shiitake—Japanese dried mushrooms.

Shirataki—Japanese noodles resembling vermicelli. Made of gelatinous starch. Often cooked with sukiyaki.

Shrimp paste—May be purchased in Oriental food shops.

Slant-cut—Cut diagonally.

Soy sauce—Japanese soy sauce is always dark in color. Chinese soy sauce comes in light and dark varieties and the type used depends upon the other ingredients in the recipe. The dark is more bitter.

Split-pea flour—May be made by pounding split peas with mortar and pestle or an electric blender.

Stir-fry—Sauté.

Tamarind pods—May be bought in Spanish markets.

Tapioca—You may use instant. But cook in whatever stock is called for.

Taro—Edible, starchy root from the plant known in temperate regions

243

as elephant's ear. It can be boiled, baked or made into a pudding or bread. Its stalks are cooked in the same manner as asparagus and its leaves are cooked like spinach.

Tofu—Japanese bean curd. Served with sukiyaki, after being cooked in the stock for a few minutes.

Trassi—an orange-red fermented shrimp paste.

Udon—Japanese vermicelli. Available in Japanese stores.

Uni—Sea urchin.

Vermicelli—Transparent noodles. Buy at Chinese markets.

Vindaloo mixture—A blend of spices similar to curry powder used in Indian cooking. Available at specialty food stores.

Wasabi—Japanese horseradish that is usually grated and served in a small bowl as a condiment, especially with sashimi.

Wok—A bowl-shaped metal pan for stir-frying foods. May be purchased at American-Chinese stores.

Wun sen—A transparent vermicelli made from mung beans.

INDEX

252